CACHED

CRITICAL CULTURAL COMMUNICATION

General Editors: Sarah Banet-Weiser and Kent A. Ono

Cached

Decoding the Internet in Global Popular Culture

Stephanie Ricker Schulte

NEW YORK UNIVERSITY PRESS
New York and London

NEWYORK UNIVERSITY PRESS
New York and London
www.nyupress.org

References to Internet Websites (URLs) were accurate at the time of writing.
Neither the author nor New York University Press is responsible for URLs that
may have expired or changed since the manuscript was prepared.

LIBRARY OF CONGRESS CATALOGING-IN-PUBLICATION DATA

Schulte, Stephanie Ricker.
Cached : decoding the Internet in global popular culture / Stephanie Ricker Schulte.
p. cm. — (Critical cultural communication)
Includes bibliographical references and index.
ISBN 978-0-8147-0866-8 (cl : alk. paper)
ISBN 978-0-8147-0867-5 (pb : alk. paper)
ISBN 978-0-8147-0868-2 (e-book)
ISBN 978-0-8147-8868-4 (e-book)
1. Internet—Social aspects. 2. Popular culture. I. Title.
HM851.S34 2013
302.23'1—dc23
2012038382

New York University Press books are printed on acid-free paper,
and their binding materials are chosen for strength and durability.
We strive to use environmentally responsible suppliers and materials
to the greatest extent possible in publishing our books.

Manufactured in the United States of America
c 10 9 8 7 6 5 4 3 2 1
p 10 9 8 7 6 5 4 3 2 1

For Bret Schulte

And for Judith Ricker, Mark Cory, and Charles Ricker

CONTENTS

ACKNOWLEDGMENTS

I owe a great deal to the many people who have helped me along this path. Just one class with Melani McAlister inspired me to pursue a Ph.D. in American Studies. She's that good. I was lucky enough to have her as my adviser. She offered professional mentorship, personal guidance, tough love (when I needed it), and somehow always understood my poorly stated ideas. Sean Aday's mentorship and candor taught me to be a better writer and thinker. I thank him, above all, for humoring me. I am indebted to Chad Heap for lending his intellectual precision and historical rigor to this project through his close readings. I extend my gratitude to Kerric Harvey for sparking my interest in technology, for teaching me how to think about it, and for years of warm collegiality. Thanks to Robert Entman and Phyllis Palmer for their productive skepticism. The librarians at the Motion Picture, Broadcasting, and Recorded Sound Division at the Library of Congress contributed to both this work and my research process. The George Washington University American Studies Department provided me with instruction and funding while I was writing. The University of Arkansas Communication Department provided institutional support, mentorship, and grants as I edited. I am particularly grateful for the opportunity to join the Critical Cultural Communication series and the NYU Press family. First and foremost I want to thank Eric Zinner, for his persistent and enthusiastic support of this work. I am indebted to Ciara McLaughlin, to Despina Papazoglou Gimbel and her team, to series editors Sarah Banet-Weiser and Kent Ono, as well as to Thomas Streeter and two anonymous reviewers for their thoughtful comments. Thank you all for your many meaningful contributions.

I worked through the concepts in this book at many conferences, including American Studies Association, Collected Stories, Cultural Studies, International Communication Association, Popular Culture/American Culture, and Society for Cinema and Media Studies. I thank the audiences, respondents, fellow panelists, and selection committees for helping me hone these ideas. I also presented part of the final chapter in the Colloquium Speaker Series hosted by the Culture and Communication Department at Drexel University. Thank you to Devon Powers for that visit and for her friendship. Finally, a portion of chapter 1 of this book was first published in "'The WarGames Scenario': Regulating Teenagers and Teenaged Technology (1980–1984)," in Television and New Media 9:6 (2008): 487–513; a portion of chapter 4 was first published in "Self-Colonizing eEurope: The Information Society Merges onto the Information Superhighway," in Journal of Transnational American Studies 1:1 (2009), http://repositories.cdlib.org/acgcc/jtas/vol1/iss1/art13.

I was stunned and grateful when an early iteration of this study received several awards, including the 2009 Ralph Henry Gabriel Prize from the American Studies Association, the 2010 Dissertation Award from the Society for Cinema and Media Studies, and Honorable Mention for the 2009 Margaret Blanchard Doctoral Dissertation Prize from the American Journalism Historians Association. Without such recognition, this book might never have found a publisher. I am indebted to the organizations and the award selection committees, including Catherine Stock, Roberta Pearson, and David Abrahamson.

It was my privilege to learn from a great number of talented and dedicated teachers and researchers over the years. In particular, I want to thank the late Janice Rushing, who first introduced me to cultural studies. I also owe a debt to Hector Amaya, Jim Deutsch, Joel Dinerstein, Kim Gross, Tom Guglielmo, Kimberly Hamlin, Jim Horton, Nicholas Jankowski, Steve Jones, Maureen Kentoff, Kip Kosek, Marwan Kraidy, Steve Livingston, Vicki Mayer, Suzanne McCray, Charles McGovern, Robert McRuer, Jim Miller, Terry Murphy, David Park, Carolyn de la Peña, Benjamin Peters, Jennifer Petersen, Damien Pfister, Patricia Phalen, Rick Popp, Andrew Ross, Peter Schaefer, Bill and Judy Schwab, Travers Scott, Lynn Spigel, and, especially, Siva Vaidhyanathan for his invaluable advice.

My writing group provided continual intellectual and emotional support. This book is as much theirs as it is mine (except for any mistakes, which are entirely mine). I thank Julie Passanante Elman for buttressing my theory, directing my readings, clarifying and polishing my prose and, most of all, talking me off the ledge; Laura Cook Kenna for her theoretical rigor and mind-reading skills, and for so generously sharing her brilliance; Kyle Riismandel for keeping me historically grounded, sharpening my mind and dulling my stress; and Laurel Clark Shire for mapping the big picture, boosting my confidence, and for sharing her baking. Thank you also to Allison Perlman for late-night brainstorms, and to Kevin Strait for many "useful" distractions. Long live the Trust.

Thank you to friends and colleagues in D.C. and Arkansas for advice and mentorship, for animated discussions, happy hour debriefings, embarrassingly amateur sports, and for supporting me during the course of this project. These friends and colleagues include Myria Allen, Trish Amason, Becky Bailey, Matt and Allison Balus, Emily Bliss, Bob and Laurie Brady, Erin Brasell, Geoff Brock, Sunshine Broder, Matt Burch, Jon Cavallero, Kurtis Cooper, Nicholas M. Copeland, Sarah Denison, Ramzi Fawaz, Joshua Fisher, Tom Frentz, Jesse Gelwicks, Marti Harris, Hershel Hartford, Andrew Hartman, Sandra Heard, Erin Helf, Jeremy Hill, Lisa Hinrichsen, Jen Hoyer, Laura and Kyle Kellams, David Kieran, Keith Kincaid, Todd Kluss as Head of the Farragut Family, Christine Labuski, Lars Lierow, Cameron Logan, Chad and Liza Lorenz, Joseph Malherek, Ann Marchand, Lisa Margulis, Brenda McCrory, Irene McMullin, Lynn Meade, Simone Meyer, Karen and Justin Minkel, Megan Moores, Shauna Morimoto, Aimée Papazian, Alexandra Pappas, Janine Parry, Aaron Potenza, Sara Sanders, James Savage, Frank Scheide, Bill Schreckhise, Steve Smith, Scott and Leslie Stephens, Jason Thompson, Yusuke Torii, Joan Troyano, Padma Viswanathan, Lauren Van Damme, Lynne Webb, Rob and Jan Wicks, and Griff Witte. In particular, thank you to Lisa Corrigan, Angie Maxwell, Tom Rosteck, Kasey Walker, Ron Warren, and Laura Wexler for their advice on parts of this work.

For their understanding and support, I thank my family: Götti Abderhalden, Debbie and Tom Deere, Robin and Genevieve Cory, Joachim Rumpf, Mark Schulte, Patty and Joe Schulte, Amanda and Tommy Visty, Trudy and Morry Wexler. In particular, thank you to my parents—Judith Ricker, Mark Cory, and Charles Ricker—for passing on their passion for knowledge, for sage advice, for being great role models, and, most importantly, for their love. To Bret, thank you for letting me bore you, for supporting and loving me, for reminding me to laugh, eat, and breathe, and for raising Ava and Leo with me. I owe a debt to you I can't begin to repay.

Humorist Dave Barry's burlesque *Dave Barry in Cyberspace* provided mid-1990s Americans with a how-to manual for participating in what was rapidly becoming *the* new and necessary—if intimidatingly foreign—technological experience: getting online. In it, he described the internet as global public and private network run by Jason, a hormonal thirteen-year-old. After signing up for a "user-friendly interface" with a company like America Online, you could do a variety of things, like "waste time in ways that you never before dreamed possible" and communicate with "millions of people all over the entire globe...many of whom are boring and stupid." Should you accidentally type an incorrect character, Barry warned, "You will launch U.S. nuclear missiles against Norway."[1] Dave Barry's comic vision of the internet worked because it played on the different yet overlapping ways the internet was understood in the United States in the last two decades of the twentieth century. The internet was conceptualized simultaneously (and often paradoxically) as a state-sponsored war project, a toy for teenagers, an information superhighway, a virtual reality, a technology for sale and for selling, a major player in global capitalism, as well as a leading framework for comprehending both globalization and the nation's future in it. Comprised of so many competing dreams and investments, the internet was, and continues to be, a major transforming component of life for much of the United States and, increasingly, the world.

As internet use began to skyrocket between the 1980s and 2000s, news media, popular culture, and policymakers tried to make sense of the technology. In this period it was not obvious what the internet would be or what it would mean. A number of cultural sites and entities offered different visions of the technology. These representations were by no means univocal, but instead overlapped, contradicted, competed, and dovetailed with one another, sometimes simultaneously. Ultimately, these numerous imaginings of the internet not only reflected the technology, but also shaped it in often complicated and indirect ways as the internet emerged as a site of transnational commerce, identity, and regulation.

This book delves into the political and cultural meanings—primarily in the United States but also in Europe and elsewhere—that helped make the internet a technology able to revise economic, political, and religious life, a place where life itself happened. Interrogating the narratives that circulated about the internet is a way of examining the larger cultural history of the last thirty years, of exploring who we are as users, humans, consumers, and national and global citizens, as well as a way of understanding and comparing the policy and regulatory practices that governed the internet and its users in the United States and elsewhere.

Networking the Computer

This story begins in the 1980s, when internet technology was "new" to the public. In these early years, understandings of the internet and its potential avenues for development hinged largely on understandings of the still relatively new phenomenon of computing. Hence, a brief history of computer use can illuminate what the internet would later become.[2] Investigating what media scholar Lisa Gitelman has called a medium's "novelty years, transitional states, and identity crises," is especially useful in determining how the technology took shape.[3]

The release of the first successfully marketed personal computer (the Altair 8800) in 1975 meant that some Americans could have computers at home, but these computers were primarily for enthusiasts. The popularity of home computing really took off in the early 1980s, when computers became easier to use and had more applications. Computing quickly became an important element of American life, as demonstrated powerfully by the January 3, 1983, issue of *Time* magazine, which declared the computer "Man of the Year."[4] Although computing became a relatively common domestic activity in the 1980s, sending data between connected computers ("computer networking") was not widespread in homes until the 1990s and early 2000s. In 1983, there were only 500 host computers—that is, computers with unique Internet Protocol (IP) addresses that could receive material via computer networks.[5] By 2000, however, there were over 200 million host computers.[6] Charting this rapid adoption rate, the U.S. Census Bureau report on computer use found that whereas 0 percent of Americans had the internet at home in 1984, by 2010, 80 percent of Americans had home internet access and almost all (96 percent) were internet users.[7] As both the computer and internet use gained popularity, two initially separate practices, "computing" and "the internet," began to merge. This terminological melding signaled a conceptual collapse, as computing was increasingly imagined as networking and the computer apparatus was imagined primarily as a gateway to the internet. As the internet lost its body, in a sense, it became easier to imagine the internet as a deterritorialized space or experience rather than a product of hardware.

In addition to the conceptual blurring between computing and networking, the cultural history of the internet has been characterized by terminological slippage of the words "internet" and "web." These terms, which actually indicate different entities, blurred in 1990s news media and popular culture. The World Wide Web ("Web" or "WWW"), a site-linking hypertext system that operates on but is not equivalent to the internet, was developed in 1991 and has become virtually synonymous with the term "internet."[8] But the term "internet" first appeared in 1974 in reference to a technology that connected numerous networks. The root of the term, "Internet Protocol," (IP) is a phrase used in combination with "Transmission Control Protocol" (TCP) to describe packet-switching, or the process through which computers transfer bits of information over networked wires.[9] Beginning in the late 1980s and early 1990s, the technologically derived term "internet" became shorthand for all packet-switching or computer networking activities. This term coexisted with a variety of culturally derived terms like science fiction's "cyberspace," and more academic terms for studying cultural formation online such as cyberia, digital-, techno-, cyborg-, and cyberpunk-culture.[10] These terms reflect the variety of visions existing in disparate cultural locations that competed and mixed as they flowed through media representations and academic studies of the internet.

For the purposes of this book I use terms as they were used in the period discussed. This is an attempt to curb presentism in favor of a historical specificity that reflects the particularities of thinking about the internet within each time period. That means, for instance, that what I refer to as "computer networking" in the first chapter, I call "the internet" in the remaining chapters. In addition, when shifts in terminology play important roles in conceptual shifts, I highlight those. For example, in 1990s news media reports and policy debates about the internet stopped using the term "computer-networks" and started using terms such as "virtual reality," "cyberspace," "new frontier," and "information superhighway." Understanding these terminological fluctuations is vital to understanding how and why spatial metaphors dominated 1990s cultural and political visions of the internet because these meanings were not self-evident, as they may seem today.

The military used variously networked computer systems during the 1970s and 1980s—including computers networked via satellites, radio waves, telephone lines, timesharing lines, and private intranets. These systems laid the groundwork for what we now understand as "the internet," a term popularized when computer networking became a mass phenomenon in the 1990s. In 1991, the National Science Foundation (NSF) created NSFNET, a networking system that linked the military's packet-switching system (which originated as ARPANET) with computers located at several universities including Princeton, the University of California at San Diego, and Cornell. These university links benefited the military because computer science departments (primarily their graduate students) helped maintain the finicky computer systems.[11] The departments benefited by being able to use the network, train their students, and attain (university or military) resources. The NSF and ARPA provided the initial technological backbone onto which commercial computer networking technologies were built.[12]

Computer networking in the early years was no easy practice since it required not only expensive equipment, but also a highly technical knowledge base. Technological developments in the mid-1990s, however, made networking easier and thereby promoted public use of what was increasingly called the "internet." In 1993, the internet's user interface became graphic, not merely textual. Mosaic, a groundbreaking program, allowed users to attach hyperlinks to images and to post images on websites. Because Mosaic was so much more visually appealing and easy to use, "for most people, for business, and for society at large, the internet was born in 1995."[13] One of the first "product-oriented" programs designed as a commercial enterprise, Mosaic became Netscape Navigator, the first commercial browser developed explicitly to make money and not simply to develop or extend the networked world. Thus, Mosaic not only changed the functionality and cultural understanding of computer networking, but also sparked one of the first commercial technology wars—namely, the one between Netscape and Microsoft, which was also developing its own commercial browser, Internet Explorer.[14] Corporate technological developments such as Mosaic also helped shape internet technologies as well as American visions of their potentials. Extending the capacities of the initially military and university systems, commercial innovators helped make the internet a virtual reality as well as a marketplace, in large part by advancing the technology's graphical capabilities, which, in turn, made it easier for users, news media, and popular culture producers to imagine the internet as an experiential "space" different from previous computing activities.

As computing became networking and as the public began doing both, actors ranging from corporations, the military, journalists, popular culture producers to computer users themselves became involved in defining what the internet was, what it meant for users, the nation, and the economy, and what it could and should be in the future. As historian Paul Edwards argues, the 1980s and 1990s were in many ways the most critical decades in the shaping of public understandings of the internet because representations of the internet began appearing in mainstream films, newspapers, magazines, and advertisements and transforming the ways that people thought about the internet. These representations and transformations, he argues, were tied to larger political shifts at the end of the Cold War, newly globalized trade patterns, and social shifts as Americans struggled with the rapid restructuring of communication and entertainment.[15]

This book begins in that same rich period, charting the trajectory of narratives that were laid out in news media, popular culture, and public policy, as well as by users themselves, that increasingly imagined the internet as less a technological medium and more a cultural experience. As this book's title suggests, through this process I seek to recover the underlying assumptions involved in the adoption and development of this technology some of which have been erased or at least diminished by our present uses and the accepted memories of the internet. Only by interrogating the "intersection of authority and amnesia," can we understand, for example, how "hello" became the protocol answer for telephone calls instead of something else, like "ahoy!"[16] Recovering the origins of today's prevailing understanding of the internet from among the oft-forgotten false starts and competing models that also shaped the technology, its uses, and meanings requires an investigation into the discourses that surrounded and supported internet technology and into the complicated and intertwined powers that produced it culturally, politically, socially, and historically. This inquiry necessitates interdisciplinary engagement with a diverse set of models and literatures, spanning history, policy studies, economics, as well as internet and science studies, cultural and media studies, communication, and studies of globalization and nationalism.

The Internet as Discursive Object

Although the last three decades brought many innovations in internet technology, its core function has not changed much. Bits of information travel faster, more accurately, and over fiber optics or wireless connections instead of cable wires, yet the internet's goal is still to transfer bits from one computing device to another. But the internet is not merely technology, and neither can a careful history of the internet be merely technological. As Manuel Castells argues, the "internet is, above all else, a cultural creation."[17] Indeed, the internet's cultural meaning has been as complicated as its technological functions, if not more so. The internet was (and continues to be) a culturally-constituted, historical object and a "subject of history," meaning that qualities essential in the technology itself did not alone determine the ways it was, and is, understood.[18] Cultural representations, popular practices, and public policies produced often competing narratives about the internet and shaped its development. Film makers, software designers, marketers, journalists, and others all have different intentions when creating visions of the internet. In light of these and other forces shaping the ways that people engage the internet and ways that the internet itself took shape, this book argues that technology (and not just the language used to describe it) is culturally flexible and not fixed by its material parameters. For television scholar Anna McCarthy, the variety of meanings that emerge about communication technologies reveal a technology's ability to serve as an "apparatus capable of linking everyday locations and their subjects to wider, abstract realms of commerce, culture, and control."[19] Likewise, the number of shifting and conflicting conceptualizations of the internet I have already noted in the brief history sketched above reinforces that this notion of flexibility is similarly relevant to historicizing and theorizing the internet.

In its attention to historical specificity and discursive construction, this book differs from many studies, which treat the internet as a static medium, alternately without a history or with a history that was determined or driven by technological development itself.[20] These problematic studies replace broad and multimodal historical scope with limited and progressive narratives of "heroic" individuals who forged the early networks—"prophets" who predicted the direction of the internet. In this way, technological histories of innovators becomes less a history of culturally-shaped technologies and more a "history of prognostication."[21] The effect is to "naturalize or essentialize media," or to "cede to them a history that is more powerfully theirs than ours."[22] Making history teleological masks structures of power in that it strips agency from cultural and social forces and makes technology seem as if it developed on its own.[23] Constance Penley and Andrew Ross, who were two early critics of technological determinism in framing internet research, write, "Technologies are not repressively foisted upon passive populations, any more than the power to realize their repressive potential is in the hands of a conspiring few. They are developed at any one time and place in accord with a complex set of existing rules or rational procedures, institutional histories, technical possibilities, and, last, but not least, popular desires."[24] At the same time, some have noted this as a problem of youth, arguing that the field of internet studies is "under construction—with boundaries not yet set, with borders not yet fully erected, and with a canon not yet established."[25]

This book develops the field by building on the work done in science studies to dismantle technological determinism and by writing in direct opposition to technological determinist impulses that have characterized internet studies in past decades.[26] In studying the internet as a culturally constituted, historical object this book puts "intention" back into the study of technology.[27] Throughout, I attend to the internet's culture (on- and offline), its history (national, international, technical, and economic), and its many spheres of contest (in popular representations and policy formulations). For example, instead of simply rehearsing the tired utopian-dystopian binary that focuses on whether the internet will liberate or oppress us—what Jeffrey Sconce calls an "irrational bifurcation" and Erik Davis pithily terms a "Manichean" battle between the "doomsdays of the neo-Luddites" and the "gleaming Tomorrowlands of the techno-utopians"—this book focuses on how, why, and where this binary emerged, on how it functioned culturally, and on those whose interests it served.[28] Telling the story of these and other conflicting visions of the internet builds on the work of technology scholars by tackling the history of internet technology as the history of power struggles between and among corporate giants, Congress members, journalists, academics, hackers, and others.[29] Since technology is embedded in history and culture and not outside of either, the following chapters investigate the internet within cultural and historical tensions, including tensions in academic debates, as histories of the internet are themselves invested in and investing competing knowledge about the internet.[30]

Discourse and Power

The following chapters trace productive historical and cultural tensions, those struggles for power among a range of actors which functioned to discursively construct the internet. While the term "discourse" is also used in the field of rhetoric, I mean "discourse" here in the broader cultural sense associated with the work of Michel Foucault. Here, discourse includes whole ways of conceiving the world and of framing problems and solutions. It incorporates a panoply of popular representations including policies, "expert" knowledge, and personal narratives used to navigate the world. Discourse is also a modality through which power is exercised and contested. Hence, discourse is itself constitutive and revelatory of power relations rather than deployed by already-existing power blocs. Discourse, then, is "not a conspiracy, nor a functionalist set of representations in the service of power, but a process of convergence, in which historical events, overlapping representations, and diverse vested interests come together in a powerful and productive, if historically contingent, accord."[31] Therefore, the guiding questions for this book are: How did overlapping and conflicting voices in advertising, news media, use practices, technological developments, and policy debates and decisions establish common sense notions about internet technology? How did common sense, or what French theorist Pierre Bourdieu calls "habitus," about the internet form and to what consequence?[32]

To answer these questions means studying how representations of the internet—including those in news media, popular culture, and policy— and practices of using the technology converge in what Bourdieu calls "fields." Society is made up of multiple fields, which are not static structures, but are characterized by the relationships among agents within fields. These relationships are continually contested, and the contestations help form particular visions of what the technology is—visions that people internalize and that become part of their "doxa," or their unthought beliefs that form the boundaries of what is thinkable. Doxa ultimately form habitus, or a conscious set of dispositions or "common sense" assumptions. The power to set doxa is not only the power to determine what a population assumes without thinking. It is also the power to define the boundaries of opposition, for, in order to be understood, the voice of the opposition must speak in language understood by or "legible" to the dominant voice.[33] In thinking about discourse in this way, this book "'explains the coincidence' that brings specific cultural products into conversation with specific political discourses."[34] While a textual or ideological analysis of the popular film *WarGames* (1983) may help determine and explain the purpose or statement made by the film, a discursive analysis—such as the one presented in chapter 1—may help explain why the film caused a media panic and why U.S. Senators thought it both useful and appropriate to watch the film while debating the first internet policy.

Therefore, this is book is about how parties—sometimes strange bedfellows—aligned with one another even in disagreements to define problems or possibilities in similar terms. It tells stories of how conflicts produced winners and losers, but does not tell *only* those stories. The process by which some won and some lost was itself a place where options were eliminated or elevated. As options were contested, certain types of logic gained sway, certain terms became popular, certain actors curried legitimacy. So telling the story of a win/lose scenario lends insight into why something won out, what actors, ideas, and logics converged to make a new common sense. Telling this story also exposes what was at stake, what was lost, who was excluded, what was forgotten.

Thinking about the internet's technological capacity and use as being in a reflexive relationship with surrounding popular, economic, and political culture provides insight into how the internet assumed its current shape and cultural status. In addition, the history of the internet becomes a potent example of how discourse operates as a modality of power to constitute and contest the boundaries of both our material realities and the meanings we use to mold and makes sense of them. By taking this approach, this book contributes to a rising tide of research epitomized by Thomas Streeter's book, *The Net Effect*, which understands the internet "not as a thing that has an effect but itself as a process of social construction. The net effect is in the making of it."[35] Like Streeter, I am mainly concerned with the ways in which narratives constitute knowledge, policy, and technology. Therefore, when I examine a wide variety of cultural images and policy accounts about the internet, I am less interested in evaluating them for representational "accuracy" of some underlying material truth and more interested in what those narratives can tell us about power and resistance within and through cultural production. Instead of neatly sorting and cataloguing a history of internet representations, I strive to illuminate the messy processes of culture and history as they occur, or as ideas, policies, cultural actors, agents, and artifacts operate in tandem, in opposition, and by indirection.

In their engagement with discourse, the chapters in this book answer the often lobbied (and often undeserved) critique that to study discourse is to ignore materiality, or to render everything "sign and sign system."[36] I hope that media scholar Jeffrey Sconce was correct in hypothesizing new media's potential to be the "discipline where this problem with discursive analysis is first corrected."[37] In this effort, the chapters that follow focus on the internet as a physical object with productive power, on social relations and the means through which they privilege particular voices, and on discourse as an element in the production of both objects and society. My methodology stitches together what Bruno Latour calls the "three great resources of the modern critique—nature, society, and discourse," taking the internet, then, as a "quasi-object," or one that is "simultaneously real, discursive, and social."[38] Such objects are neither self-evident, "natural" entities nor the "arbitrary receptacles" of society, but instead are simultaneously discursively produced and participants in their own discursive construction.[39] "Cloud computing" or "the global village" are discourses—ways of organizing thinking, representations, and practices that affect the internet's development—but the legacies of code and the architecture of the internet, simultaneously constitute the development of those discourses ("global village," "cloud computing") and the positions of their users and advocates.[40]

However, engaging the internet's discursive production requires attending to cultural and historical process of erasure—or what Foucault calls "silences." That is, media and policy representations of the internet may redirect attention *away* from particular aspects or possibilities of the technology. For example, the internet's technological structure and the ways that structure was imagined in U.S. news media and popular culture contributed to the cultural erasure of its infrastructure and origins as a state technology wedded to the Department of Defense. Internet hardware and software development, institutions of government finance, state regulation, and corporate prerogatives actively re-imagined the internet as a space to explore or inhabit or as a state of being rather than a product of digital code and programs contained within computer infrastructures and networking wires. In short, internet technology became "invisible"—a transformation continued by the wireless revolution—or as Marshall McLuhan wrote, the focus shifted from the medium itself to the content being mediated.[41]

To give another example—although the U.S. Department of Defense built the first internet technology in 1969 through its creation of ARPANET, by 1974 the technology was already being used and further refined internationally.[42] Despite this, U.S. journalists, popular culture producers, and policymakers presented the internet technology as American and did not publicly discuss it as a transnational one until the late 1980s. In the early 1990s, when journalists and policymakers began to focus on the internet as a marketplace, the U.S. government began seeking to control that new market through domestic corporate powers. These efforts then helped construct the internet as a distinctly American space, or what I call an "American virtual nation." Therefore, while a number of agents began to acknowledge the internet's global reach, American institutions worked in conjunction to keep the dominant vision of the internet as "American," turning it into an American export to the globe and working to re-nationalize the internet in the face of increasing awareness of its global reach.

Representations: Media and Policy

The importance of discourse is not only in its capacity for erasing. News media, popular culture, and policy debates are discursive sites where ideas about new technology are hashed out and where relations of power are rendered visible. In other words, these sites are strands of discourse that come together in different ways and in different historical moments; charting the ways that they do offers a glimpse the way that power is enacted, resisted, and transferred through its articulation and alignment across many cultural locations. As Manuel Castells has written, the "media are not the holders of power, but they constitute by and large the space where power is decided."[43] Media—from news to advertisements and films—should be taken seriously as places where power over the internet, its users, and its possibilities is exercised, refashioned, and transferred. Still, media are not the sole locations where power can be glimpsed. Media distribute information and may flatten some hierarchies, but policy is the vehicle through which money, resources, and institutional attention is distributed. Policy is also a location where rhetorical and political shifts in national priorities may be observed.[44] As American studies and media scholar Melani McAlister has written, the "politics of culture is important, not because politics is *only* culture (or because culture is *only* politics), but because where the two meet, political meanings are often made."[45] In looking at such conjunctions of culture and policy, this book tries to strike a balance, as did cultural theorist Stuart Hall, between conceiving of power through "state domination" or through "free-wheeling discourse."[46] Governmental decisions about which way to regulate the internet or which institutions to fund are culturally defined and also materially experienced. They happen at an intersection of the state's power, popular discourse, and the materiality of technology and resources.

Taking into account a variety of ways that power is exercised in or over the internet's history is to acknowledge that certain agents and sites are more active and powerful in producing ideas about the internet as well as in controlling its infrastructure. Power is institutionally constituted and expressed through the state, nation, and corporations, and not everyone has equal access to these institutions or to the production of media and policy. As media studies scholars have long noted, power plays out in varying ways in particular cultural locations and through different media. An advertisement is not a film is not a newspaper is not a policy paper. Communication scholars have shown, for instance, how news media help set an agenda by determining what issues the viewing public should consider most important or by focusing attention on certain aspects of an issue by choosing how to frame it.[47] According to communication scholar Robert Entman, "To frame is to select some aspects of a perceived reality and make them more salient in a communicating text, in such a way as to promote a particular problem definition, causal interpretation, moral evaluation, and/or treatment recommendation for the item described."[48] Reporters make sense of new developments—including technological ones like the internet—using frames they imagine readers will understand.[49] In effect, then, the news frames our ways of seeing facts. Yet, because news frames are cloaked in notions of news objectivity, meaning they disappear into the functional imaginary of news as unbiased fact-conveyors, and because readers believe news media relay facts, frames are often unquestioned. Narrative tropes thereby disappear, becoming "completely familiar in their seemingly fundamental uncanniness, so much so that we rarely question the often fantastic conventions through which we conceptualize and engage these media."[50] Popular films serve as broadly accessible frames of reference and useful tools for journalists and politicians who draw on such material for common cultural context. Audiences know films are fictional, even as films work to make their narratives relatable and naturalized. Most films "unfold without acknowledging the presence of [their] viewing audience," effacing their own camerawork.[51] Both news media and film rely on attentive audiences convinced of the reality they are consuming. The power of these media emerges in part through that logic of consumption. However, the two media have different conventions, and in some ways film is a more flexible medium where power is less visible.

Combining insights from media and communication studies with attention to policymaking processes, these chapters map not only what understandings of the internet became dominant, but also how those ideas won the day and what forces were at work in the process. The first chapter in this book sets the tone by examining how journalists and politicians used the 1983 film *WarGames* as a frame through which to present news and policy debates concerning the internet. The use of *WarGames* in conjunction with news reports of young hackers helped politicians and the public to jointly re-imagine the internet as a weapon and as a domain of teenagers. Insofar as representations of the internet as a developing or "teenaged" technology and as a domain of teenagers dominated, these representations helped make parental rather than punitive policy options seem preferable for dealing with early internet crimes. Policymakers mobilized these particular visions of the internet in popular culture and news media to privilege some policy solutions over others, thereby influencing the internet's development. Cultural images helped determine "winners" and "losers" in internet policy debates by influencing which options policymakers deemed more reasonable, rational, or marketable to their constituents. However, the parental policy approach to internet crime was not merely an effect of culture. Policy worked as a cultural actor itself, one that helped further legitimize other representations of the internet as adolescent in news media and popular culture.

Here, the story of government action or policy enactment is a story about the state's response to a naturalized reality. That is, the U.S. government and others respond to what they imagine as the internet's essential structure and character, its users, and its productive or destructive potentials for democratic or economic health. This reality is made natural, in part, through media representations. As Bourdieu illustrated, the contest over meanings in the public sphere sets the boundaries of political debate.[52] In turn, those voices deemed legitimate by news media and governmental actors are reified in policy spheres. As political scientist Deborah Stone argued, cultural representations govern political reasoning, which then frames policy decisions. Culture works to help a population define its "problems" and to construct particular policy solutions as "in the public interest, or natural, or necessary, or morally correct."[53] Policy may dictate the protocols for technology use, such as the standards for fiber optic wire installation or the sanctions for online privacy violation.[54] It may also legitimize certain representations and codify that legitimization in documents and debates and through the establishment of rules governing the internet's use and growth. In other words, policy is both a participant in and product of discourse; it is a site in the discursive construction of the internet that also shapes the internet's technological development.

As the above preview of chapter 1 suggests and the rest of this book similarly supports, no one cultural artifact, person, or policy causes any particular shift. Instead, discursive power operates through layers of influence and in complex ways. People formulate and produce views about the internet using news media and popular culture content, political leadership, and their own interactions with technology. Neither media representations nor policy formulations operate in isolation. Rather, they interact with each other, shaping each other's vocabulary and working in tandem within the minds of the public. Media producers, policymakers, and everyday people read representations associatively. Therefore, this book approaches representations rhizomatically rather than hierarchically, reading popular film alongside advertising, policy statements, and regulations, arguing that they are all active (though often unequal) participants in the discursive construction of the internet.[55] This approach offers a window into central tensions of various historical moments, showing that discourses have formative effects on technology and on the society that produced it.[56] Visions of technology are strategic in that they serve the interests of journalists, users, policymakers, and cultural producers. Likewise, technologies are "never entirely revolutionary: new media are less points of epistemic rupture than they are socially embedded sites for the ongoing negotiation of meaning as such."[57] Focusing on what Sconce calls the "reoccurring fictions," or the points of overlap between content in various media, while simultaneously acknowledging the differences in media production forms, processes, intents, and consumption, this book sketches complex interrelationships among discourse, power, representation, and policy.[58] Each chapter in this book shows how ideas and images have productive power.

Networking the Nation and Going Global

While in some ways this book is about the internet, in other ways it is about cultural investments in particular sets of ideas about internet technology and how they have intersected with contemporaneous (if also fluctuating) ideas about nation, state, democracy, space, consumption, corporations, and globalization. For example as chapter 3 illustrates, news media reports that conflated the internet and the "World Wide Web" imagined the internet as what I call an "icon of globalization," in that they assumed the technology would inevitability facilitate changes in global market forces, merge or flatten the world's cultures, and/or replace the nation-state with a "global village" of "netizens." At the same time that corporate technological developments such as graphical user interfaces (GUIs) like Mosaic and Netscape helped produce the internet as a marketplace, corporate gateway browsers—specifically those used by America Online in the early 1990s—helped construct the internet as a uniquely American space. Thus, news media and, in particular, academic debates simultaneously mapped anxious and hopeful visions of globalization—as harbinger of post-national chaos or liberation, "Americanization" or multiculturalism—onto the internet at the same time as developments in internet technology facilitated late capitalism, transnational activism, and international media organizations. In this way, in news media and academic discussions of the internet in the 1990s, neoliberalist and globalization discourses dovetailed and competed.

As this illustrates, neoliberalism is a related but distinct concept from globalization. Neoliberalism assumes that humanity is best served through corporate and not state organizations. As a theory, neoliberalism "takes the view that individual liberty and freedom are the high point of civilization" and that "individual liberty and freedom can best be protected and achieved by an institutional structure made up of strong private property rights, free markets, and free trade: a world in which individual initiative can flourish." The suggestion here, according to David Harvey, is that the state should involve itself in the economy only to promote free markets. Globalization is less a theory than—a highly complex process that involves economic, political, social, cultural, and technological shifts away from nation-states and toward transnational organizations.[59] Would the internet facilitate the demise of the nation and the rise of the post-national corporation? Would we become cybercitizens or netizens or stateless surfers? Would America Online become the "new" America, the one that happens in online spaces and in which corporate America better serves consumers than the United States government serves citizens? These kinds of questions proliferated in the 1990s as globalization and neoliberalism battled and romped in cultural and political visions of the internet. These questions were also asked by academics, who interrogated the internet from a number of perspectives in a number of disparate disciplines, including political science, economics, cultural studies, communication, and media studies.

And these questions also proliferated outside the United States, often in different ways, with different social and political investments. Indeed, the primary project of the final two chapters is to contribute a comparative discursive analysis that investigates news media and popular culture representations and state policy initiatives in Europe (and, to a lesser extent, the Middle East). This comparative critical analysis remains grounded in technological histories of the internet, but illustrates the nationalist characteristics of visions of the internet available in cultural and policy debates. Imaginings of the internet mapped in the United States were by no means predetermined, uncontested, or the only options available. Analysis of European representations, for example, shows how the internet could have been understood and regulated quite differently, as a public good instead of a product of the private, corporate sphere. Although in U.S. news media, policy, and popular cultural spheres, the internet seemed self-evidently American, democratic, and capitalist, European cultural and political agents questioned all of these assumptions.

This comparison illustrates how particular voices helped to construct the internet as "American" both discursively and materially. It also suggests the work required to establish and maintain such a conceptualization. The assumption that the internet was and would always be an American virtual nation was, in fact, contested by European policies and popular culture, even as European policymakers actively attempted to Americanize their internet technologies. Although this is a story of American power, it is not one of simple top-down imperialism. The European Union was not overpowered by an invader, but instead willingly participated in the successful and attractive political and economic models that surrounded internet technologies. Rather than losing its national identity in this policy shift, Europe engaged and reversed U.S. economic tactics to Europeanize the internet. It was able to do so by creating a distinctly European space online imagined as an "information society" that Europeans could universally access and that would engender continental community and economic equality.

Although it is arguably one of the ultimate examples of transnationalism and is frequently cited as a force of globalization, the internet is still constituted through national policies unequally instituted by European Union member-states. Comparative work is imperative for dismantling both the technologically determinist and unflaggingly American nationalist common senses that the internet's expansion is "inevitable" and that corporate forces are the natural rulers of online spaces.[60]

Cached: A Preview

Each chapter of this book parses varying representations of the internet in popular culture, niche and news media, academic debates, advertising, and policy in a different historical moment. Beginning with the period preceding the Computer Fraud and Abuse Act of 1984, which remains the precedent for contemporary American regulatory internet policy, chapter 1 shows how *WarGames* (1983)—the first mass-consumed, visual representation of the internet—served as both a vehicle and a framework for America's earliest discussion of the internet. *WarGames* presented the internet simultaneously as a high-tech toy for teenagers and a potential weapon for global destruction. In the film's wake, major American news media focused on potential realities of the "*WarGames* Scenario." In response, Congress held computer security hearings, screened *WarGames* on the Senate floor, and produced the first internet-regulating legislation. As this chapter illustrates, *WarGames* engaged a "teenaged technology" discourse, which cast both internet technology itself and its users as rebellious teenagers in need of parental control. Although in the following year more than a dozen policies were proposed—some more lenient than others—the final policy tended toward the lenient pole. Ultimately, the teenaged technology discourse allowed policymakers to equate government internet regulation with parental guidance rather than with suppression of democracy and innovation. This was a crucial distinction in the context of the Cold War and especially in the year 1984, when George Orwell's *1984* reappeared as a news media focus.

Chapter 2 illustrates how in the decade following the release of *WarGames*, computing became a more common activity, and increasingly also meant networking. This chapter illustrates how computer networking emerged as a symbol of national economic power and productivity. Throughout the mid- to late 1980s and early 1990s, hopeful views of the internet and computer corporations began to gain resonance. These (often) corporate visions challenged previously threatening representations—like the anthropomorphized computer capable of overpowering or replacing humans—and helped recast the computer as a friendly co-worker. In recasting the internet, corporations, advertisers, and news media outlets also re-imagined the internet user. The out-of-control computer jockeyed by an antiestablishment teenaged hacker shifted to a "user-friendly" computer controlled by a knowledgeable, adult "user." The computer moved out of the teenager's bedroom and into the American workplace. This image of a productive, computer-using adult helped promote images of competent users capable of disciplining the computer in ways useful for American nationalist capitalist projects. The internet was thereby inserted into an established narrative of technology and human progress. Within this narrative, the internet was understood in political spheres as instrumental in helping America retain global economic dominance. With Ronald Reagan promoting a de-federalization climate, policy shifted away from protecting the internet itself or its users and instead focused on protecting U.S. internet dominance through the fortification of U.S. corporate power.

Chapter 3 examines the emergence of the "World Wide Web"—the internet's best-known hypertext system—when the global nature of the internet became an animating idea in news media and popular culture as well as for policymakers and academics. As such, the internet became increasingly understood as an icon of globalization, as a player in the perceived downfall of the state, and, often contradictorily, as both a space in need of state control and a liberating, democratic arena. At the same time, although the internet was increasingly understood as global, it was nonetheless identified as a distinctly American space, or what I call an "American virtual nation." This Americanness was visible in the organization of the internet, including the ways the U.S. government retained control over internet addresses and domain- name assignments; for example, U.S.-based websites did not have to use country identifiers like ".de" for Deutschland (Germany). The American virtual nation was also visible, however, in news media and policy language describing the internet as a "new democratic frontier" and an "information superhighway." These terms were enabling to and enabled by hopeful U.S. policymakers, who aimed to colonize the internet before competitors arrived. Major internet corporations also capitalized on this presumptive Americanness of the internet in their efforts to become what I call "American corpoNations," despite their transnational corporate structures. For example, America Online not only incorporated national identity in its very name; its software also served as a nationally bound entrance to the internet's "global" space. Just as users, policymakers, and media coverage imagined an internet controlled by or at least entered through the American virtual nation, corpoNations became cultural carriers for and constructors of the nation. Thus, these large transnational entities paradoxically functioned as online proxies for the state, even while academics and news media frequently described them as complicit in diminishing or undercutting state power. Ultimately, this chapter shows how discourses of globalization participated in the abstractions of both the internet and the nation, helping to construct both as virtual realities and spaces. Imagined as an American virtual nation, the internet was perceived as both a contributor to the destruction of the state and a preserver of the nation.

Chapter 4 compares American and European understandings of the internet—primarily those articulated through policy—and investigates how they functioned, how they converged and diverged, and how they were mapped across national boundaries. For much of the 1990s, member-states of the European Union regulated internet technology using the nationalist and protectionist models it used to regulate other media. This meant European governments assumed that publicly supported telecommunication corporations like the British Broadcasting Corporation or Deutsche Telekom would promote nationalist versions of the internet—like France's Minitel—and would control the internet just as they controlled the telephone and broadcasting. In short, Europe went about regulating the internet as if it were a public utility. This chapter shows that these initial policies were produced by and helped produce a discourse that imagined the growth and influence of the internet as a choice rather than an inevitability, as it was imagined in the United States. But Europe's statist policies did not last. At the turn of the century, the European Union proposed its eEurope 2005 Project, the language of which identified the internet as already a distinctly American space and a source of U.S. power. It suggested that for the European Union to compete, it would have to adopt policies that promoted competition, entrepreneurialism, and innovation, like those in the United States. In telling the story of failed efforts of European nation-states to put their nationalist stamp on internet regulation (or in other words, the story of Europe's regulatory "road not taken"), this chapter shows how the internet became a carrier of Americanness in that it was understood as increasingly synonymous with free-market capitalism. Although this is a story of American power, it is a story of the complicated ways visions of the internet flowed back and forth across the Atlantic. Europe did not lose its national identity in a wave of Americanization. Rather, it engaged in a version of what Reinhold Wagnleitner terms "self-colonization"[61] by adopting U.S. economic tactics to Europeanize the internet. To a lesser extent, U.S. policymakers attended to European concerns in addressing issues of equity and access and working to bridge the "digital divide," or the gap between those with and without access to the internet.

Chapter 5 focuses on the reemergence of representations of the internet as democratic and a vehicle of international freedom in the wake of blogs and social networking. This chapter argues that unlike radio and television, the internet continued to represent fluid and democratic participation even after it was commodified. Representations of blogs and bloggers drew on individualist and democratic rhetoric suggesting (or at least fantasizing) that individuals could fill the vacuum left by skepticism about global and commercialized mass media. Imagined in news media as "unmediated" proxies of the blogger's self, the individual user-rebel (described in chapter 1) and user-worker (portrayed in chapter 2) could blog their way out of both the American virtual nation and corpoNation (defined in chapter 3). As news media, policymakers, and Egyptian citizens began referring to the 2011 uprisings in Egypt as the "Facebook Revolution," they framed the internet as authentic, as democratic, and as a space where nation-building occurred. This reassuring strain of discourse suggested that the revolution would promote "the right kind" of democracy, one that would support capitalism and U.S. national interests, and in this way, it metaphorically extended the American virtual nation abroad through the corpoNation (Facebook). But through its focus on multiplatform and anonymous connectivity, this framing of the internet also highlighted not only the ways that Egyptians at home and abroad participated in diasporic nation-building, but also the messiness that constitutes a virtual nation in the face of a transnational medium.

In sum, this book is about the ways people made sense of the internet in news media, popular culture, and policy as it became a major player in the global economy. These ways of understanding the internet were hashed out in the pages of magazines, in the halls of Congress, and in teenagers' basements. The internet's meanings have multiplied and changed in accordance with culture and policy (and politics as culture) as much as with the capabilities of technology itself. The internet was understood in relation to the nation, the state, democracy, consumption, and capitalism. Telling the history of players who staked claims for the internet's future, envisioned alternatives for interacting online, and ultimately helped define the meanings and uses of a communications technology that has become central to daily life for millions around the globe gives us a better understanding not only of a now quotidian technology, but also of power, culture, and policy. The history of internet technology and the ways the technology has been understood and regulated did not have to develop as they did. The internet did not have to be regarded as a democratic space regulated by the forces of capital, as it was in the United States. In fact, it could have been seen as a public utility to be regulated by state forces, as it was in Europe.

1

The "*WarGames* Scenario"

Regulating Teenagers and Teenaged Technology

Many Americans "experienced" computer networking for the first time in 1983 by watching a young Matthew Broderick nearly blow up the world. In the immensely popular, Academy Award–nominated film *WarGames*, the teenaged computer-hacker David Lightman (Broderick) accidentally dials into the Pentagon's defense system while looking for a computer game company.[1] Lightman plays what he thinks is a game called "Global Thermonuclear War" and unintentionally brings the United States and Soviet Union to the brink of global destruction. Several weeks after *WarGames* was released, NBC aired a story that described the film as having "scary authenticity" since the North American Aerospace Defense Command (NORAD) contained computers that "occasionally go wrong."[2] Following NBC, every major American news media organization questioned government and military officials about whether the film's fictional plot, or the "*WarGames* Scenario," could actually happen. Congress responded to this media attention by holding subcommittee hearings on computer security in both the Senate and House, several of which included viewings of excerpts of *WarGames*; this coincided with preparation of reports that eventually led to legislation regulating what would be popularly known as the internet.[3] In this sense, *WarGames* not only helped American filmgoers understand the new and strange computer networking technology, but also served as a framework for the first widespread public discussion of computer networking.

This chapter examines why the fictional story of *WarGames* was so compelling in the early 1980s and why media organizations and policymakers could imagine the "*WarGames* Scenario" as a viable potential future event. It also discusses what policy responses emerged following the "*WarGames* Scenario" debate. Concerned policymakers offered more than a dozen ultimately failing proposals for regulating computer networking[4] which contained a variety of definitions of illegal computer infiltration and a corresponding variety of punishments. For example, one option proposed in November 1983 defined any kind of unauthorized access as an automatic felony and recommended severe punishment, including up to a $100,000 fine and/or ten years in prison.[5] A more lenient alternative proposed in August 1984 made infractions misdemeanors and recommended punishment only for "willful" intrusions on computers involved in "interstate or foreign commerce or operating on behalf of the Federal government or a financial institution."[6] Ultimately, the legislation that emerged tended toward leniency in that it made only deliberate, unauthorized access to government computers illegal and did not set monetary or incarceration penalties for infractions. This Counterfeit Access Device and Computer Fraud and Abuse Act of 1984—commonly referred to as the Computer Fraud and Abuse Act (CFAA)—defined an infraction as "knowingly access[ing] a computer without authorization or . . . access[ing] a computer with authorization for unauthorized purposes."[7] Penalties were restricted to those who accessed "computer[s] operated for or on behalf of the U.S. government" and could be either felonies or misdemeanors, depending on the intruder's intent (e.g., whether the intruder was intending to explore a network to satisfy curiosity or intending to do damage or steal information). Although the act was amended due to this vague wording, the CFAA remained and remains the precedent for American, and even international, regulatory internet policy.[8]

While *WarGames* catalyzed policy initiatives to regulate computer networks, the film also helped shape the way the American public envisioned this new radical form of technology and the perceived dangers associated with it. Both *WarGames* and the CFAA mobilized a powerful notion that associated computer technology and the military-industrial complex with generational divisions. This association—what I call a "teen technology" discourse—cast computer networks as dangerous and in need of regulation and individuals who were powerful on the networks as unruly, anti-establishment teenagers in need of discipline. In effect, both *WarGames* and congressional policy engaged the same dominant mass media representations of two separate but related categories—teenagers and hackers—and placed teen hackers in the context of two tensions already dominant in American culture since the 1960s: first, the Cold War and military expansion, and, second, anti-establishment youths and youth culture.

This chapter begins by sketching the contours of the teen technology discourse by illustrating how *WarGames* engaged dominant representations already present in American culture in the early 1980s. These include textual and visual representations in popular magazines, newspapers, advertising, industry and enthusiast magazines, television network news, popular literature and popular film. Through its engagement of these representations, the film helped viewers, media outlets, and policymakers imagine computer networks as simultaneously high-tech toys for teenagers and potential weapons for global destruction. But the film also anthropomorphized the computer itself, giving it human qualities and presenting it as an adolescent male, while presenting individuals with evolved computer skills as both "teenage" and "anti-establishment" figures. By placing hacking in the context of videogame play, this film framed hacking as an innocently rebellious and not a malicious act.[9]

WarGames did not necessarily directly cause policy change. Rather, it participated in a complex process through which meaning was made and remade in the cultural sphere. The film was a participant in a conversation going on among a number of agents in the cultural sphere. While the film is a text that makes a "statement," its textual meaning is "not the same as its historically constituted meaning." This means that *WarGames* was legible in its moment as a "cultural production" that made meaning through its "historical association with other types of meaning-making activity, from the actions of state policymakers to marketing."[10] Although it did not itself hold power, discursive power flowed through it as it participated in the construction of knowledge about the internet. To note that the film did not have directed power is not to argue that *WarGames* was just any cultural actor. On the contrary, it was exceptional. Extended and concentrated media attention on the film helped frame early government discussion about internet regulation in parental instead of punitive terms. Attention to the film privileged visions of computer network users as juvenile and anti-establishment and of the technology itself as a dangerous security risk in need of regulation. Policymakers echoed these representations in internet policy debates. The film's engagement of this powerful "teen technology" discourse may have ultimately helped news organizations align with government institutional power as this discourse disempowered images of the computer network as a benign tool, lending weight to policy images that viewed networks as a potential threat to domestic security and as a space in need of government regulation. In this view, computer technology and its users were keys to a bright future, but only if "successfully" regulated by the government. Thus, in the wake of *WarGames*, policymakers hoped to teach youths "appropriate" computer use that would not only allow them to keep their radical entrepreneurial spirit, but also simultaneously contain that spirit through government regulation and the forces of capitalism.

Real-World War Games: Cold War Context and Hacker Hysteria

In the late 1970s and early 1980s, both before and after the release of *WarGames*, articles and television news reports overwhelmingly claimed American dominance over the computer industry, but not control over the technology itself. That is, while reports on computing often noted that American corporations dominated the market,[11] they also often cited fears of Soviet use and theft of American technology, of computer crime, and of the possibility of technology going awry in the hands of the young and irresponsible teens who embraced computer networking.[12] Characterizing the computer and networks as products of military expansion and the military-industrial complex, these representations also suggested the technologies were increasingly uncontrolled by the military and therefore posed security threats.[13] In this moment, Cold War fears of Soviet power and technological supremacy converged with anxieties about teenaged rebellion.

Thus, public understandings of computer networks were part of larger ideas about political shifts at the end of the Cold War, economic shifts in relation to newly globalized trade patterns, and social shifts as Americans struggled with the rapid restructuring of communication and entertainment patterns. As historian Paul Edwards notes, the Strategic Defense Initiative (or "Star Wars" project) and military stockpiling during the Carter and Reagan administrations in the early 1980s worked in confluence with the cultural legacies laid by the previous decades' popular films—such as *Dr. Strangelove, Fail-Safe,* and *2001: A Space Odyssey*—to reinvigorate widespread public anxiety about military-industrial defense systems and technology itself.[14] Thus, when *WarGames* was released, it was both an update to an already established popular culture trope of weaponry and technology gone awry and a distillation of already established public anxieties connected to the automated STAR WARS defense program and American technology under siege. For example, in 1983, *Life* magazine ran a long feature called "Russia's High Tech Heist: The U.S. Mounts a Belated Effort to Halt the Theft of Electronic Secrets." This frenzied article reported that the Soviet Union began stealing, studying, counterfeiting, and mass-producing American microchips as early as 1978. Exhibiting language reminiscent of Senator Joseph McCarthy's, the article also noted ominously that "some 20,000 Soviet bloc agents" worldwide, including "scientists, technicians, trade officials, embassy personnel and professional spies," were already "devot[ing] themselves full-time to the so-called technology transfer." Representing the military technology race between the United States and the Soviet Union as a dead heat, the article stated, "the technological time lag between U.S. and Soviet weaponry has narrowed from 10 to two years in just a decade."[15] With a partnership of savvy scientists and stealthy spies being represented as threatening American technological and geopolitical dominance, the contest for power over networking technology was implicated in an older panic over information security and technological supremacy, as well as anxiety about inflation that helped sustain high military spending from the 1940s onward.

For several years after the film's release, newspaper, magazine, and television reports connected the fictional film *WarGames* to these Cold War fears of real-world "war games" between the United States and Soviet Union. News organizations also used *WarGames* to frame a number of reports on computing and networking technology. Most stories emerging in the immediate wake of *WarGames* investigated whether hackers could actually hack into defense systems. These reports reinforced Cold War anxieties tapped by the film by treating the scenario as if it could be real—interviewing hackers with the ability to hack into government computers—while simultaneously diffusing those fears by showing how it could never happen—interviewing national security advisors. By treating the fictional plot as possible outside the world of the movies, media organizations lent the film credibility in its message that computer networking threatens national security, as well as arguing that it might serve as a tool to ensure it. In their partnership and unity of message, news media and film cast themselves as important watchdogs over government and the public.

In early July 1983, just a few weeks after the national release of *WarGames*, the three major U.S. television networks aired a flurry of television reports using the film as a frame. The first report, featured on ABC, compared *WarGames* to that highly metaphorical icon of Cold War anxieties, the 1964 film *Dr. Strangelove*. Showing the famous clip in which a nuclear bomb was dropped while being ridden like a bucking bronco by a cowboy Air Force pilot, ABC followed up with a clip from *WarGames* that showed Lightman dialing into NORAD, thereby suggesting a parallel not only between the teen hacker and the Cold War cowboy, but also between a modem and a nuclear bomb. The second clip was introduced with the statement: "Another movie about nuclear madness…" The report went on to investigate the possibility that a computer or simulation could accidentally begin World War III. Reporter Rick Inderfurth interviewed NORAD spokesperson General Thomas Brandt, who claimed that checks and balances systems prevented computer errors of the magnitude portrayed in *WarGames*. In these systems, he said, "man is in the loop. Man makes decisions. At NORAD, computers don't make decisions."[16] Similarly, an NBC report argued, "False alarms and the dependence on computers make some people uncomfortable and that's what this film plays on." The reporter noted that the "*Boston Globe* had a computer expert analyze *WarGames* and he picked it to pieces. The kid couldn't do it in the real world. The movie has the kid playing a simulator and not NORAD's main system." Ultimately, NBC confidently addressed "all you computer geniuses with your computers and modems and auto-dialers" and taunted them to "give up," assuring potential Lightman-copycats: "There's no way you can play global thermonuclear war with NORAD, which means the rest of us can relax and enjoy the film."[17]

In these reports, news media outlets forced institutions of military power to answer to fantasy allegations lobbied by a fictional film. *WarGames*, therefore, offered news media an opportunity to engage and threaten governmental power, to cast themselves as both actively watching out for the public good and staying in touch with its public consumers. Some of this engagement was overt. ABC recalled past NORAD errors to dispute their claims that the system was flawless. The network also quoted Defense Secretary Caspar Weinberger, who acknowledged his concern over accidental nuclear war, and Senator John Warner, who called for modernization of communications systems along with weapons. Detailing President Reagan's efforts to upgrade emergency communication links between the United States and the Soviet Union, ABC reported that Reagan had recently announced that he would upgrade the hotline in order to allow the transmission of photos and to facilitate emergency contact between the Pentagon and the Soviet Union's Ministry of Defense. The report ended by saying, "While *WarGames* is a Hollywood fantasy, there is a real concern about accidental nuclear war triggered by computer error, human mistake or terrorist attack."[18]

A month later all three major television networks gave extended coverage to a story that challenged the assuring notion put forth by government sources that the "*WarGames* Scenario" could never happen. On CBS, Dan Rather opened his report on hacking by asserting that the "future-shock premise" of *WarGames* "came pretty close today to becoming shocking science fact." He then went on to report that young Milwaukee hackers had successfully tapped into a Los Alamos nuclear weapons center computer. Although sources said that "nothing secure was accessed" and that all new security measures were in place, the broadcast interviewed the hackers, who claimed "It's easy to do. There's no security or nothing."[19] *Life* magazine also described the incident: "A troubling side of the computer revolution came to light when FBI agents questioned a number of 'hackers,' including 17-year-old Neal Patrick of Milwaukee. Like his youthful hero in the summer hit *WarGames*, Patrick was able to break into what were thought to be secure computer systems."[20] The hackers became known as the "414," after their Milwaukee telephone area code. The FBI granted immunity to one of the hackers, Neal Patrick, in exchange for information about how the hack worked. The notion that the government needed help from a teenager to figure out weaknesses in its own computer system suggested that the government was incompetent, or, at least, less competent in some sense than a teenaged boy.

News media ramped up anxiety about hackers by casting the film as having the power to instigate devious behavior. Like *Life*, both NBC and ABC stories emphasized that the hackers had watched *WarGames* and were "inspired" by it.[21] One NBC report played a clip of *WarGames*, framing the film as "a story of a boy and his computer" that "fueled an idea within a group of computer whizzes in Milwaukee."[22] The network also reported that "millions of kids who yearn for their own computer sat enthralled" by the film.[23] These millions of would-be hackers, which raised the specter of national insecurity, tapped Cold War anxieties about the "enemy within"—anxieties that would only increase as computers became more ubiquitous and available to these increasing numbers of young rebellious hackers. NBC reported that "as more people buy home computers, the chances of using home computers to change or steal information from other computers increases."[24] Internet historians have noted that exactly this happened in the late 1980s and that the development "ushered in a new era of law enforcement: computer crimebusting."[25] On the one hand, publicity of hacking in particular reinforced the need for security organizations and policy interventions.[26] On the other, in these reports, Defense Attorney Paul Piatrowski, representing the hackers, downplayed the danger associated with these intrusions, describing his clients not as intruders, but as "hobbyists, like stamp collectors."[27] Journalist Ned Potter reported the hackers were challenged by entry and had not intended to misuse their access by engaging in theft. The hackers wanted to play games like those in the movie *WarGames*. Potter went on to explain in detail how modem networks function, using *WarGames* footage as illustration.[28]

As in the case of the 414 hackers, news media represented another hack the next year in similar terms. Teenager Robert Grumbles and three friends infiltrated NASA computers and printed messages like "you can't catch me" on office printers. The hack of a government office—especially of NASA which President Ronald Reagan featured in his "Star Wars" weaponry plan—further legitimized *WarGames* and the connections among hackers, military weaponry, and computer networks as posing a national security vulnerability.[29] As in the case of the "414" hacks, however, this hack was also presented as innocent tomfoolery and not malicious.

When CBS news interviewed Mr. and Mrs. Grumbles about their son Robert, both downplayed his indiscretion, comparing it to what they viewed as far worse infractions. Mrs. Grumbles said, "I'd rather he get into trouble with his computer than with drugs." Mr. Grumbles observed, "These boys are not the Mafia, you know."[30] Hacking, to these parents, was neither a "real" crime, like those perpetrated by mob criminals, nor more harmful to their son than drug experimentation. These parents imagined computer networks as separate from real life, meaning that what occurred in cyberspace was less important than transgressions they imagined as involving the physical body.

In sum, the release of the film *WarGames* helped merge Cold War anxieties with those involving teenaged rebellion. News media—regarded in the United States as observing conventions of truth and objectivity—lent the fictional film an air of scary credibility in the ways that they merged real-world hacking activities, fictional representations of hacking, Cold War popular culture representations, and coverage of actual Cold War conflict. Thus, news media's use of the film *WarGames* helped "frame" the first national debates about computer networking by "select[ing] some aspects of a perceived reality and mak[ing] them more salient in a communicating text." In using the film to discuss real-world hacking activities, news media portrayed computer networking as a teenaged, game-like activity.[31]

To research framing is to research "what people talk or think about by examining how they think and talk about issues in the news."[32] Coverage and particular characterizations of problems help create a "mass mediated reality."[33] Frames are important because they "promote a particular problem definition, causal interpretation, moral evaluation, and/or treatment recommendation for the item described."[34] Framing effects extend outside the cultural sphere in that they help establish "policy images," or the "public understandings of policy problems."[35] Policies are not determined necessarily by need, but are instead culturally determined. In turn, policy images are formed through the types, amounts, and locations of news coverage of particular issues.[36] News stories help frame policy by "influencing perceptions of an incident," calling "attention to matters of potential concern," and providing "cues to the public about the degree of importance of an issue."[37]

Popular films serve as broadly accessible frames of reference and useful tools for journalists and politicians, who draw on such material for common cultural contexts. But the power of frames is in their repetition. A particular event that changes the frames surrounding a story, narrative, or issue and then enables media to perpetuate those frames is the most powerful. *WarGames* persisted as a media focus as news organizations continued to use the film to frame a variety of hacking stories for the next few years.

This on-going framing helped construct computer networks in news media as simultaneously a danger of great proportions and a harmless game for rebellious youths—and, in some cases, a favorable alternative to other activities like experimenting with drugs. Although a number of news media and popular culture outlets presented hacking as a potentially serious threat to national security, hackers were simultaneously imagined as playing an innocent game, as not intending to cause damage, and as learning their lesson after being caught.[38]

Complex Computers, Hacker Mystique, and "Teenaged" Technology

Although it was often imagined as the key to America's future, the internet's future in the early 1980s was uncertain. In a 1981 *Life* magazine article, an unnamed "industry expert" was asked to predict the future of computer networking. He responded, "It's like trying to forecast the impact of the automobile on society as the first Model T rolled off the assembly line."[39] For this expert, once new computing technologies entered the market, they felt unstoppable: "Whatever its variations, there is an inevitability about the computerization of America."[40] The sense that computers and computer networks would determine America's future—the idea that they were in fact driving "progress"—emphasized the technology's importance and added political relevance to its perceived status as secure or insecure. This technological determinism, or the perception that technology drove American progress, dovetailed with anxieties about using and understanding new computer technologies. Because the computer was so important, those who controlled it also controlled the future. Images from film, television, news media, and policy discussions in the early 1980s show the battles that took place among hackers, policymakers, journalists, and computer corporations to determine the narrator or the expert on computer networking technology. Some tried to predict its future, while others tried to demystify the technology by instructing the mainstream on its uses. In either case, Cold War anxieties about computer networking as a security risk were enhanced by notions that the technology was complicated, mysterious, reachable only via impossibly specialized knowledge or skill, and yet key to America's future.

Internet technology (i.e., computers and modems) in the early 1980s was not easy to use, which, in some sense, helped set the parameters in which it was understood. Individuals had to purchase various parts separately (keyboards, floppy disk drives, processors, software), assemble these complex parts into a computer at home using only a manual, and then separately load, use, or create software compatible with the machine purchased. Although it was invented in the 1960s, the user-friendly mouse, for example, was not popularized until the mid-1980s with the release of the Apple Lisa. Thus, users in the late 1970s and early 1980s interacted with their computers using a "command line interface," or by typing a specific command after a blinking cursor. After mechanically assembling the parts, users had to constantly refer to complicated manuals or had to possess considerable knowledge of computer coding to use their machines.[41] Computer networking had a military sensibility. As early user and internet pioneer Janet Abbate said, being online in the early years felt "rather like taking a tank for a joyride."[42] As media scholar Lisa Gitelman recounts in *Always Already New*, although the internet would become an "informal" activity, "it would apparently take a few years for [its] countervailing military-industrial tenor to be forgotten or reengineered."[43]

As the first mass-consumed, visual representation of computer networking, the film *WarGames* served as a kind of instruction manual to audience members, thereby playing an especially important role in forming early assumptions about the technology. In the film, Lightman shows his love-interest, Jennifer Katherine Mack (Ally Sheedy), how to dial in using a modem. Lightman demystifies the computer networking process, making it less threatening and confusing for her by slowly and deliberately explaining how the technology works and how he connects his computer to other computers. The extraordinary lengths gone to by filmmakers to explain technological processes and to normalize networking through the film suggested the lengths they thought necessary to make the film's technical elements understandable. Computers, let alone computer networks, were still new mysterious technologies for the target mainstream audience. When the film was released, computer networking largely occurred through large and expensive mainframe computers located in military or university institutions and often consisted of work on "intranet" networks, or private networks accessible within organizations. As the next chapters detail, users did not regularly experience connections to homes and offices until the late 1980s and early 1990s, when personal computers (PCs) emerged and became popular in American domestic settings and workplaces and network providers like America Online and CompuServe began offering more affordable connectivity. As previously mentioned, the word "internet" was not commonly applied to computer networking until the late 1980s and early 1990s.

Like Ally Sheedy in *WarGames*, numerous news media outlets in the early 1980s tried to make sense of the new technological innovations in computer networking.[44] Both the *Washington Post* and the *New York Times* ran regular columns specifically designed to relay basic computing information to the pre-computer generation and to make computer spaces navigable to non-expert users. In an article about programmer Michael Wise, who wrote the video game Captain Goodnight, *Time* magazine wrote, "The lines of code Wise types into his Apple IIe may look like a meaningless string of letters and numbers, but they are the crucial link between computers and the people who use them. At the heart of every machine are thousands of on-off switches. Wise's 64K Apple has 524,288. Software tells the switches when to turn on and off, and those switches control the machine."[45] In this statement, journalist Philip DeWitt explained how code worked and the relationship between hardware and software for his readers. Like Lightman, he demystified the computer, offering home-users insight into the mysteries of the computer, showing the potential for each home user to understand and therefore to wield the technology for his or her own purposes.

The flurry of articles and columns in popular magazines and newspapers offering "expert" advice on how readers should use and purchase computing technology participated in struggles over its narration. Providing "newsworthy" material to readers, news media placed their publications on the "cutting edge" of technology, while also appeasing advertising industries interested in privileging explanation over exclusion in the interest of selling products. While these articles contained some descriptive element of the technology itself, they also simultaneously characterized it as too complicated for regular computer users to understand without help. Some even called computing magic.[46] For example, one article was titled "The Wizard Inside the Machines: Software is the Magic Carpet to the Future."[47] A similarly titled article in the April 16, 1984 issue of *Time*, "Computer Software: The Magic Inside the Machine," featured Bill Gates on the cover looking smug and levitating a floppy disc over his pointer-finger. Representations of computing as "magic" or as supernatural make the computer seem untouchable, sublime, and incomprehensible to the average person, and usable only by "magicians" like Bill Gates.[48]

Not only did computer users need special skills, or "magic," they needed to know a foreign language: "computerese." Computerese was spoken only by particular individuals described by *Time* magazine as the "'computer literate,' which was synonymous with young, intelligent and employable: everybody else is the opposite."[49] As a barrier of access to computer-mediated spaces, computerese helped form those online into an "imagined community" in similar ways that language functions in the formation of national identity.[50] Publication of computerese guides not only made the public aware of the community, but also helped reaffirm its boundaries by reinforcing the complexity in computing. One reporter characterized computerese as creating a culture of distinction and exclusion comparable to a religion: "Like the high priests of any new religion, these keepers of the computer faith like to rename familiar things. (How else could a TV screen become a monitor?) They like even more to give things names that are mystifying to an outsider as the secret password of an esoteric cult."[51] Computerese was also likened to race in its power to distinguish insiders and outsiders. One reporter compared it to language associated with African-American cultural groups, writing that "in black English, for instance, bad means good. So hacker, a term of contempt in ordinary English, becomes high praise when computer fanatics apply it to themselves."[52]

News media reported extensively on computerese, not only translating it to the public but also adding to the sense that most Americans were outsiders to that world and needed a translator.[53] Some journalists covered (sometimes in list format) the minimum vocabulary necessary to purchase a computer. Don Nunes, a *Washington Post* staff writer, published a series of articles he claimed could instruct potential computer buyers in the most important terminology. These articles used analogies to relate computing terms: the "disk drive" became the "record player," and the "Disk, floppy or hard" became the "45 rpm record on which information is stored magnetically."[54] Writers like Nunes often mocked the insiderism of computerese. But at the same time, these writers, like hackers, were invested in keeping the language and their corresponding technologies incomprehensible to their readers in order to protect their own credibility, market shares, and jobs. To some extent, industry leaders like Steve Jobs assisted in that project. *Time* magazine quoted Jobs as saying, "'Kids know more about the new software than I do.'" In this statement, Jobs suggested that the knowledge and computerese fluency of those he encountered surpassed even his, furthering notions of insiderism. Jobs associated this knowledge base with young individuals. He also suggested that program savvy, computerese, and accompanying membership in the imagined community—imagined as dominated and/or run by hackers—was only for the young.

In simultaneously (and paradoxically) dismantling and reinforcing the boundaries of access to computer networking technologies, news media, users, and computer industrialists continued a long history of power struggles. As Carolyn Marvin argues, the "early history of electronic media is less the evolution of technical efficiencies in communication than a series of arenas for negotiating issues crucial to the conduct of social life; among them, who is inside and outside, who may speak, who may not and who has authority and may be believed."[55] Thus, for example, Marvin demonstrates how electrical engineers deliberately constructed organizational institutions and hoarded cultural capital in a power play to create technological knowl-edge monopolies. They empowered themselves by preying on race, gender, and class constructions of the period in order to elevate themselves and were "as deeply involved in the field of cultural production as in the field of tech-nical production."[56] Similarly, although the public debate about computer networking was ostensibly about functionalism—what could these technol-ogies do or not do for us, and how could we unlock their potential?—the debate was also a platform in which traditionally powerful groups (re)nego-tiated power. Capitalist youth entrepreneurs, imagined as America's main economic drivers and key to the future of America's power, remain primary holders of cultural capital in this narrative. Established powers were not nec-essarily destabilized, even though the narrative about internet technologies often revolved around the notion that power was being destabilized.

Indeed, representations of computer networks as an exclusive and elusive technology were enhanced by the notions that it was the *domain of teenag-ers* and that the *technology itself* was teenaged. In the early 1980s, popular culture and news media increasingly represented home computer users, video game players, hackers, and computer network users as being the same, producing the cultural trope of the "teenaged user." This user was a teen-aged video-gamer and member of a new, computer-literate generation; in this trope, hacking itself was imagined as a kind of video game and there-fore innocent, not malicious. As Stephen Johnson would later argue, gaming and hacking were coconstitutive activities. Hacking skills developed in part because of a gaming legacy through which teenagers learned to "probe" sys-tems for weaknesses and "exploit" them. Hacking was a "natural extension of the mental skill set developed in gaming."[57] The tough technological realities of computing in the era made computing seem game-like. As media scholar Ted Friedman illustrates, the increasing complexity of computers, especially networked computers in the 1970s and 1980s, inspired some users "to experi-ment with ways to break into these networks."[58]

The crossover between teenagers and videogame play made sense in the early 1980s not only because computing was like gaming, but also because teens were primary users of home computers and because they used them mainly for playing video games. Indeed, according to some estimates, by 1983, over half of personal computers were used primarily for games.[59] While video games were invented in the early 1960s (SpaceWar), they did not become popular until the mid-1970s with the invention of Pong and the late 1970s with Space Invaders. After the release of PacMan, video games became commonplace in the early 1980s.[60] The video game industry grossed six bil-lion dollars in 1981, more than the film and gambling industries combined.[61]

In addition, beginning in 1981, the first video game magazine (*Electronic Games*) began facilitating the creation a larger video-game community. Although many games listed above were initially played in video arcades, as home computers became more popular in the early 1980s, games were frequently obtained online and then played offline or bought in stores and then traded online.[62] Home consoles and computing markets were big money. By 1982, Atari was the most popular gaming company, with revenues of over $2 billion.[63] The following year, the company entered the computing market with its "My First Computer," a $250 console which had a compatible keyboard that could be hooked up to a modem, printer, and disc drive and which was advertised as being ideal for teenage users.[64]

Like the figure of the teenaged gamer, that of the teenaged computer hacker was already firmly established in American popular culture by the early 1980s, even as the representation of the hacker was neither simple nor static. All major magazine and newspaper reports on hackers in the years before *WarGames*'s release engaged at least one of the following tropes: the hacker as an innocent and intelligent every-teen, the hacker as a menacing trouble-maker or criminal, and the hacker as the icon of a generation. All three competing representations appeared in the May 1982 issue of *Time*, which was devoted to computer networking and focused on hackers.[65] The cover sported a pixilated young male face in what looked like a blurred school picture. The blurred nature suggested both an innocent, school-aged individual and an unknown, unknowable, menacing criminal. The cover's text branded computing youths the "Computer Generation: A New Breed of Whiz Kids," suggesting computing was so significant that it merited a generational (if not biological) boundary. In his introduction to the issue, the publisher of *Time* wrote: "Where their parents fear to tread, the microkids plunge right in, no more worried about pushing incorrect buttons or making errors than adults were about dialing a wrong telephone number."[66] These teens had special, powerful abilities as a result of the mediated environment in which they were raised. For example, "Unlike anyone over 40, these children have grown up with TV screens; the computer is a screen that responds the way they want it to. That is power."[67] These skills were not shared by older individuals: "If many of us blanch and shy away from anything so formidable as an electronic brain, the younger generation is moving quickly to claim the computer as its own."[68]

Like this issue of *Time*, most media representations conceptualized generational difference mapped along lines of computer ability. The notion of a generational gap suggested older generations could not or could not easily traverse into the world of computers. These generations were not only represented as essentially different, but also described as located in different times and spaces. Older, pre-computer generations were in the "real world" of the past; the younger, computer generation was in a computerized space in the future. One report noted that hackers used the term "real world" as a disdaining way to define the "location of non-programmers and the location of the status quo."[69] Ten-year-old hacker Shawn Whitfield was quoted by *Time* as saying, "When I grow up it's going to be the Computer Age. It won't affect parents. They're out of the Computer Age. They had their own age."[70] Commentator Roger Rosenblatt quipped:

> A great deal of intellectual effort is therefore spent these days—mostly by the computer scientists themselves—trying to reassure everybody that, as smart as a machine can get, it can never be as intelligent as its progenitor. In part, this effort is made in order to see that the wizened, non-computer generation—which often regards the younger with the unbridled enthusiasm that the Chinese showed the Mongol hordes—feels that it has a safe and legitimate place in modernity.[71]

In his humorous account, Rosenblatt noted the generational difference between the older computer novices and the younger invading computer experts. At the same time, he not only recounted the terror with which the first greets the second and suggested a significant anxiety associated with both computing technology and youth, but also cited efforts to pacify those anxieties.

While explicitly denoting the boundary between generations and declaring it problematic, popular publications also offered help to parents wishing to bridge the divide. A 1983 *Time* magazine article reported that thousands of parents could attend the "Blue Ridge CompuCamp," where they could "catch up with their children's knowledge of computers." The children were characterized as "young-know-it-alls at home," with "home" being a space represented as a war-zone and suggesting that parents should go to (re) boot-camp to learn to "defend themselves in the computer world."[72] These magazine articles reinforced the notion that computers were the key to the future and that parents had better get on board or they would be left behind. Following suit, the camps were explicit attempts to bridge the computing generational gap and to help the older generation parent the younger. They provided parents with skill sets through which to model "appropriate" computer use and to discipline (or at least to identify) "inappropriate" use. These camps, then, helped soothe anxieties about mysterious teenagers and complex technologies.

The discursive connection among "youth," "computing," and "hacker sub-culture" was so powerful that computer-skilled individuals were represented, no matter their physical age or political affiliation, as teenaged video game players and as members of an anti-establishment, hacker subculture. Print descriptions of "typical computer users" generally resembled the following descriptions: (1) "In his pin-neat, Northern California bedroom, a bespectacled 16-year-old who calls himself Marc communicates with several hundred unauthorized 'tourists' on a computer magic carpet called ARPANET"; (2) "For Space Invaders whiz Frankie Tetro, as for thousands of teenage boys and girls, the first time he ever grabbed an electronic brain by the joystick was to play a video game."[73] Descriptions emphasized the age of the user and the "teenaged-ness" of the individual's appearance and almost always discussed computer use in reference to video game play.

Although they were no longer teens in the early 1980s, industry leaders were coded as such. In the case of Bill Gates, founder of Microsoft, his petite stature was generally noted along with his youthful in appearance.[74] In his 1984 *Time* article, "A Hard-Core Technoid," Michael Moritz noted that when a seventh-grade Gates began working with the computer that his Seattle Lakeside School bought in 1967 with proceeds from a rummage sale, he "devised a class-scheduling program so that he could take courses with the prettiest girls."[75] Not only was Gates repeatedly described as teenaged-looking, but articles also focused on his teenaged years. His interest and giftedness in computers were connected with his teenage years and his teenage interest in (and failure with) girls. The anecdote also gave Gates hacker credibility in highlighting his ability to use computer course schedules retained by the school administration. Nonetheless, the suggestion that Gates held "hacker ethics," which emphasize the free exchange of information, runs contrary to evidence of Gates' political persuasions.[76] Gates was one of the first advocates for treating software as a commodity and as intellectual property. He possessed a "shrewd business sense" early in life, and was clearly against the hacker ethic promoting free exchange of ideas without monetary exchange.[77]

Steve Jobs, founder of Apple Computers, was described in similar ways. Jobs's youth was also a focus of articles, and his early years were characterized as countercultural. For example, he was described as, at one point in his life, "headed for Reed College in Oregon," where "He lasted only a semester but hung around the campus wandering the labyrinths of postadolescent mysticism and post-Woodstock culture. He tried pre-philosophy, meditation, the *I Ching*, LSD, and the excellent vegetarian curries at the Hare Krishna house in Portland."[78] The article also noted that he lived in a commune in

1974. Another noted that Jobs named his company after a job he had working in an Oregon orchard and that he and his business partner got the capital to fund their first computer company from selling Jobs's VW van, an icon of the 1960s counterculture. *Time* quoted tech-investor Don Valentine's description of his first meeting with Steve Jobs. Valentine reportedly said to another tech-investor, "Why did you send me this renegade from the human race?" Like the notion that a "new breed of whiz kids" existed, this comment suggested that Steve Jobs was different biologically and at war with the previous generation. Valentine first saw Jobs wearing "cutoff jeans and sandals while sporting shoulder-length hair and a Ho Chi Minh beard."[79] The symbols connect him with the aging baby boomer generation. But the verbal cues also explicitly coded Steve Jobs as both anti-establishment and young by referencing icons of countercultural lifestyles and the "don't trust anyone over thirty" youth movements in the 1960s and 1970s. The Ho Chi Minh beard reference engages the memory of anti-Vietnam War movements; it suggested Jobs as a threat to mainstream power structures by insinuating he fought on the "wrong side" of the Vietnam War.[80]

To some extent, representations of industry executives as anti-establishment teenagers were tempered by representations of those individuals as "good capitalists." For example, several articles note that Jobs met Steve Wozniak, his business partner, in 1975 through a home-computer building club called "Homebrew Computer Club." The article described him as less interested in building than he was in selling what Wozniak was building.[81] In this sense, Jobs was more a salesman than a hacker. Numerous articles appeared in the 1980s about potential financial gains computer-skilled individuals could experience.[82] For example, when *Time* magazine profiled Bill Budge, who was one of the most famous computer-hobbyist programmers in the 1980s and wrote "two of the industry's biggest entertainment hits" (Raster Blaster, a pinball game, and Pinball Construction Set, a program for customizing their video pinball machine), the article focused on the $500,000 he earned in 1982 from his programs and how he turned his teenage obsession with gaming into a profitable career.[83]

Thus, Steve Jobs, Bill Gates, and others were represented as good capitalist industry leaders (i.e., as wealthy, successful businessmen), as teenagers, and as members of anti-establishment subculture. By focusing on the teenaged years of both Bill Gates and Steve Jobs and framing those years as countercultural, journalists suggest that their "radical" youth offered insight into their present activities. In other words, to understand why these individuals were computer, networking, and financial geniuses, you first had to understand their oppositional teenaged years. Representations of adult computer-skilled individuals as being "teenaged" and anti-establishment suggested they were both the key to the future of America and simultaneously a threat to American stability.[84] This focus presented the world of computer networking as a teenaged and countercultural space.

As in other popular media, *WarGames* explicitly marked computer-skilled individuals as video game playing teenaged, anti-establishment hackers. These individuals lived alternative lifestyles, and were creative, non-conventional thinkers adept at problem-solving. The main character, David Lightman, for example, was a teenager who spent much of his time playing video games at his local arcade. He rode his bike, as he was too young to drive. When asked if he was worried about his hacking activities, he mentioned that he could only be arrested if he were older than seventeen. For Lightman, youth was a shield against authorities.

Lightman also behaved in an explicitly anti-establishment manner. His room was disheveled; he avoided his chores and cut school to play games on his computer. He disrespected authority. When his chemistry teacher asked him, "Alright, Lightman, maybe you can tell us who first suggested the idea of reproduction without sex," Lightman snarkily replied, "Your wife?"[85] The teacher sent Lightman to the principal's office, where he snuck into the secretary's desk to view her computer password. He used this password to try to impress Jennifer Katherine Mack by hacking into their school's computer to change their grades. Burdened by ethical questions, Mack told Lightman not to change her grades. Lightman, unencumbered by such questions, went in after she left and changed her grades without her permission. Later in the film, Mack asked to have her grade changed after all, and Lightman told her he had already done it. The film suggested the corruptibility of youth and that hacker ethics—explicitly different from mainstream ethics—may be "catching" and may spread from one youth to another. Any good girl may be at risk if she came in contact with an anti-establishment, teen hacker.

Although the film presented the grade-change hack as a rather harmless rebellion, or a "kids-will-be-kids" infraction, the film also suggested that teen hackers were more susceptible to foreign infiltration and therefore threats to national security. In the film, one FBI agent, Nigen, described Lightman to his military colleagues: "He does fit the profile perfectly. He was intelligent, but an under-achiever; alienated from his parents; has few friends. Classic case for recruitment by the Soviets."[86] This description suggested that Lightman's hacking activities substituted for "more meaningful" activities, preventing him from being "safely" involved in community action and therefore inaccessible to infiltration. The description also suggested that while Lightman was hacking, he would never fully become a fully competent

American citizen. While he was a hacker, he would always be a threat to national security.

In *WarGames*, Lightman and Mack were literally teenaged. But as with Steve Jobs and Bill Gates, age did not determine a computer-skilled individual's "teenaged-ness." Like Lightman, his hacker friends were also coded as anti-establishment and teenaged. When Lightman needed help hacking into what he thought was the game company computer (but was really the Department of Defense computer), he went to two hacker friends. These two friends were both dressed casually, in T-shirts, jeans and sneakers. The first, Jim Sting, played by Maury Chaykin, was described in the script as "eating a junk food lunch" and as "a fat Rasputin with beard and long, stringy hair." He was shot working in a chaotic office space that resembled Lightman's bedroom in both its disorder and contents; it was filled with scattered papers and computer parts. Singer's T-shirt sported a 1960s-era smiley face. The second hacker, Malvin, played by Eddie Deezen, was skinny with a high-pitched voice and had acne, glasses, and slicked hair. He was socially awkward, interrupted conversations, and snatched papers out of Sting's hands. When Malvin did this, Sting told him he was "behaving rudely and insensitively."[87] The hackers demonstrated their creativity and computer knowledge by teaching Lightman about "back doors," or hidden passwords that allow software authors into programs after clients changed the official passwords.

Dr. Stephen Falken, former DOD computer programmer who wrote the Global Thermonuclear War game that Lightman played, was also explicitly coded as anti-establishment. When Lightman first found Dr. Falken to enlist his help controlling the Artificial Intelligence computer program named "Joshua," the eccentric Falken was living an alternative lifestyle in a cabin on an island unreachable by car. Falken behaved erratically and was unfriendly when Lightman arrived (via boat) at his house. Having faked his death, Falken lived a reclusive and Luddite existence full of books and stuffed big-game animals. Falken's house resembled a tree-house or backyard fort. Dr. Falken displayed his creative thinking and computer knowledge not only in his creation of the computer game, but also in that he ultimately saved the world by pacifying Joshua. Some trivia lists noted that writers of *WarGames* wrote the part of Dr. Falken imagining that John Lennon would play the role.[88] In *WarGames* the artificial intelligence computer program itself was also represented as a youth. The program was patterned after a real person (at least in the film's universe), Dr. Falken's deceased son Joshua. Thus the program was imbued with personality traits and anthropomorphized through the use of a computer-generated voice. The program enjoyed playing games, but was ultimately looking to its "father," Dr. Falken, for parental guidance.

In contrast to computer-skilled individuals, those who were unskilled were represented as older or mainstream members of society, in particular, military and secret service officers Lightman met at the DOD. These computer-unskilled individuals were explicitly marked as members of the dominant power structure. They wore uniforms, called the president, controlled nuclear bombs, and made the rules that Lightman had to break to save the world. They displayed not only more superficial understandings of computers than Lightman, but also an unwillingness or inability to learn. They were in control of the military's computer systems by mandate, but not in practice; they relied on the computer-skilled to enact their control. The military leaders themselves had few plans as to pacify "Joshua," the computer gone berserk. They refused to accept that the simulated war game that Joshua was playing was just a game and instead, like Joshua, believed the game was real and advocated bombing the Soviet Union instead of fixing the computer. These individuals could not think creatively or abstractly and instead adhered to a rigid moral and behavioral system based on chain of command and protocol. This group tried to enforce its moral system on computing technology and on the computer-skilled, whom the computer-unskilled viewed as undisciplined and dangerous. In the film, the military was the parent trying futilely to discipline unruly teenagers and "teenagers."

The film clearly favored the computer-skilled group over the computer-unskilled. Lightman, his hacker friends, and Dr. Falken were the film's heroes. This preference was evidenced by the film's ending, which abandoned apocalyptic visions consistent throughout the rest of the film in favor of idealism. In the end of the film, the computer, unable to distinguish between simulation and reality, was about to blow up the world in order to win global thermonuclear war. At the last minute, the computer came to the conclusion that "the only winning move was not to play."[89] The film suggested, then, that the Cold War was "un-win-able," that "peace was the answer," and that antiestablishment activists, hackers, and computers were all more capable than established leaders in the military and security forces. This ending not only reinforced messages of the countercultural and anti-war movements of the 1960s, it also reinforced the notion that technology was good only if used correctly—a notion that may have been especially resonant in the early 1980s during the rise of the anti-nuclear movement. At the end of the film, the computer, the icon of "rationality," used its powers of logic to determine that peace was the answer. Those with computer abilities and who had prevailing faith in computers were ultimately vindicated. Those without computer abilities were proven illogical, irrational, impulsive, incorrect, and obsolete. But, as Melani McAlister has argued, "the apparent 'statement' of a text is not the same as its historically constituted meaning."[90] Although the film promoted a "hackers are heroes" message, it was ultimately used to argue in favor of anti-hacking legislation.

Both teenaged users and "teenaged" technology were, therefore, represented as needing the government to step in to regulate them like "parents," but not to the extent that their radical (and marketable) creativity was stifled. In this sense, the teenaged user and the teenaged technology both functioned as Lauren Berlant's "pre-citizen" or "infantile citizen," in that each was "neither representative nor a participant in the nation, but [was] in need of its protection." This citizen, which Berlant described as central to "national fantasy," was produced by idealizations of national inclusion and participation, with the result that the proto-citizen was rendered child-like, or as "infantilized, passive, and overdependent" on the state.[91] As infantile citizens, teenagers and teenaged technology engaged long-standing hopes and fears about the "changing of the guard," or the future of America once the younger generation had power. As Leerom Medovoi argued, teenage rebels like Elvis Presley and James Dean served national ideological purposes in the Cold War in that they became symbols of democracy, self-actualization, and anti-conformity in opposition to constructions of communism as the antithesis of these ideals.[92] Because teens represented "America's future," and youthful computer entrepreneurs like Bill Gates and Steve Jobs represented the best parts of capitalist enterprise, they needed both direction and fostering. This simultaneous need for radicals to promote capitalist engines and fear of radical disruption of the democratic status quo presented one of the major contradictions in 1980s American notions of democracy and capitalism.

Political New Frontier or Dangerous Space?

Before and after the film's release, hackers were engaged in a cultural battle over what the nature of computer networking should be and who had power over it. Although some hackers clearly envisioned themselves as heroic pioneers, paving the way for individual Americans to self-actualize on the new computer network frontier, hacker subculture was more diverse and complex. Fittingly, news media represented hacker subculture in more ambivalent terms, noting its politics, but also questioning its ethical investments. Both hacker self-representations and news media, however, imagined the computer network itself as middle-class (presumably white), male space, a space in which men were simultaneously empowered and at risk.[93]

Early hacker self-representations revealed that early hacker subculture members believed their activities were heroic and leading America toward a utopian future. To be a "hacker" meant to hold utopian beliefs, or to be "not conventional programmers, but idealists absorbed in the pleasure of computing for its own sake."[94] Perhaps the most-cited "insider" source on hackers in the 1980s was Steven Levy's 1984 seminal work, *Hackers: Heroes of the Computer Revolution*, which provided the first lengthy, investigative history of "heroic" hackers and hacker subculture.[95] The book traced the origin of the term to MIT, where technological pranks were dubbed "hacks." The group called Tech Model Railroad Club (TMRC) began calling themselves "hackers" in the 1960s and 1970s. Thus, Levy's book on *Hackers* effectively discovered, publicized, and helped create the hacker ethic.[96] In *Mondo2000*, a 1980s magazine that attempted to create a lifestyle around hacking, early hackers saw their goal as what Vivian Sobchack calls "the dawn of a new humanism. High-jacking technology for personal empowerment, fun and games."[97] As the magazine illustrates, hackers saw themselves as having a distinct cosmology that combined "New Edge high-technophilia" with New Age "'whole earth' naturalism, spiritualism and hedonism." This combination "implicitly resolves the 1960s countercultural 'guerilla' political action and social consciousness with a particularly privileged, selfish, consumer-oriented and technologically dependent libertarianism."[98] Hackers, therefore, saw themselves as taking up failed counterculture projects of the 1960s, but adding a new twist, a "console cowboy" notion of American individualism and libertarianism.

However, this "rebellion" paradoxically relied on the status quo, on "male privilege, white privilege, economic privilege, educational privilege, First World privilege," and especially on capitalism, since *Mondo2000* revenues relied on a product list that was collected in a "Shopping Mall" on the back of the magazine.[99] Thus, while imagining themselves as ushers of true democracy and as guardians of the cyberspace where that they would solve the problems of financial and power inequity that they saw in the physical world, early hackers reinforced existing power structures. Additionally, while the hacker archetype espoused in *Mondo2000* wanted to be radical, he also feared social interaction and therefore desired the safety and remoteness of computer access, living in what Sobchack calls a state of "interactive autism."[100] Thus, hackers imagined themselves (to each other through their in-group publication) as political, social, and cultural activists and at the same time as solitary, isolated individuals. Like the news reporters who covered the advent of the "computer age," writers and publishers working on this magazine reinforced some existing power structures, like those discussed by Carolyn Marvin, in which male, white, middle-class dominance was attained through knowledge monopolies. But the publication also worked to create a subcultural consciousness or affiliation through a media product. Through this magazine and through social movements that arose in the wake of Levy's book, hackers were able to reimagine what was presented in news media and popular culture as an individualistic, antisocial, and potentially dangerous or anti-American activity as a social activity with a civic value. Through this reimagining and through these media and other media products, hackers began to sketch their own subculture, a subculture that defined itself in opposition to the mainstream representations of hacking detailed earlier.[101]

In most self-representations like *Mondo2000*, as well as in news media reports about hacking or hacker subculture, hackers themselves were exclusively male. These representations helped cultivate the space within computer networks as male space. Several historians have noted the paradox in this notion. For example, the very roots of the term "computer" lie in women's military history. One original use of the word was to identify the (mostly) women in charge of "computing" target coordinates for military assaults.[102] Nonetheless, only a miniscule number of magazine articles recognized women, despite the importance of women to this history of computing.[103] Those articles that did, noted the historical importance of women, but not their contemporary presence in the computing sphere. A few magazine articles noted that one of the first credited programmers was Augusta Ada, Countess of Lovelace and daughter of the poet Lord Byron. In 1834, she helped finance the analytical engine, a machine that used punch cards to calculate math equations; the idea for the machine came from the system used to determine woven designs using Jacquard looms operated by women.[104] Other articles refer to Grace Hopper, a pioneer programmer who created COBOL (Common Business-Oriented Language), a popular mainframe programming language in the 1980s. She is perhaps most famous for reportedly coining the "ubiquitous computer phenomenon: the bug" while working at Harvard in 1945, although the term was in existence in the days of Thomas Edison. She investigated a "circuit malfunction" and "using tweezers, located and removed the problem: a 2-inch-long moth." Although the word "bug" initially indicated a hardware problem (a literal bug in the hardware), the term was soon applied to software glitches.[105]

Representing computer networks as male spaces did not mean that they were viewed as safe for men, even male hackers. On the contrary, they were presented as spaces in which the computer-skilled were simultaneously empowered and at risk of isolation, addiction, or physical disabilities. Articles about Bill Gates often represented him as a workaholic: "In the past six years he has taken only 15 days' vacation, four of them at a Phoenix tennis ranch in 1982."[106] Programmers reportedly had "computer widow[s]."[107]

Because programmers might "spend 18 hours a day at a terminal working on a difficult problem," the "fanaticism allows very little time for ordinary human pursuits."[108] Fear of computer addiction leading to failed relationships dominated many interviews as well as popular culture representations of computer users. In *WarGames*, Lightman's only friends were fellow hackers, and he spent much of his time skipping school to play video games or play on his computer in his locked, unsupervised, suburban room. This notion of the hacker or computer nerd as an isolated teenager tapped into anxieties present elsewhere in news media in the early and mid-1980s—anxieties that were specifically produced by (or at least credited to) fall-out from the Women's Movement and that focused on latch-key teenagers and working mothers.

Not only were computers and hackers represented as threatened by addiction and isolation, but several doctors also claimed video game and computer use could cause physical or mental injury. For example, a *Life* magazine article cited doctor reports that joy-sticking "can lead to 'video elbow' and 'arcade arthritis.'" This story paired the human-ness of the tiring human body in opposition to the relentless energy of the computer. With the human unable to keep up physically or mentally, side effects of were potentially serious. For example, according to this article, computer use could change subconscious thought-patterns, in that "the proper sequence of command and letter keys insinuates itself into the subconscious rhythmically."[109] Many articles about video gaming noted the potential for "unfavorable" content to seep into the minds of youths. *Life* magazine wrote that U.S. Surgeon General C. Everett Koop felt, "there's nothing constructive in the games… Everything was kill, destroy, zap the enemy." Gamers disagreed; the "TEMPEST virtuoso Leo Daniels," for example, said, "I think Koop is a quack."[110]

In this sense, computers functioned as a new location for "moral panics," a moment when "a condition, episode, person, or group of persons emerges to become defined as a threat to societal values and interests."[111] The more sources that participate, the more entrenched the crisis becomes.[112] A moral panic emerged about computer networking largely because the technology was imagined in film, by policymakers, and by news media and popular publications as something used by youths in isolation and as empowering dangerously isolated and immature boys in ways that might have national (or global) consequences. The multitude of representations linking teenagers and computer networking not only reinforced the notion that many individuals may be at risk, but also that parents may not realize the risk due to the complexity of the technology. In this way, the confluence of media (popular and news) and policymaker attention helped convince what Stuart

Hall calls the "silent majority" that computers and computer networking were threats.[113] This moral panic followed a long history of moral panics surrounding youth, which some trace from Plato's apprehensions about the effects of "dramatic poets" to fears about television violence in the 1990s.[114] Hall saw a moral panic as "one of the key ideological forms in which a historical crisis is 'experienced and fought out.'"[115] Early moral panics focused more on the social and less on the political, mobilizing local organizing institutions of control. In the 1960s, however, the "increasingly amplified general 'threat to society'" that included "drugs, hippies, the underground, and pornography," bypassed local organizations and instead produced what Hall terms "control culture" intent on regulating media. Panic about networking emerged in the wake of this period and capitalized on cultural and historical links among 1960s counterculture members, rebellious youths, and computer network users.

While many sources reinforced this panic, occasionally news media provided the "other side" to the story, focusing on how perceived benefits of computer networks, or in Marshall McLuhan's terms, how the technology's extensions out-weighed its amputations.[116] By this, McLuhan meant the ways media extended the human senses. The telephone, for example, could extend the human capacity to hear across the country. At the same time, it might be an amputation of writing abilities and cultures in that individuals wrote fewer letters as telephoning became easier. McLuhan pushed for recognition of amputations, which he felt were often overlooked in the face of sexy new technological capabilities. In the case of early computer networking, though, with its morally panic-laden reporting, amputation was the focus.

Nonetheless, a few early stories about bulletin boards did suggest that normal people (not anti-establishment teenage hackers) enjoyed computer networks for legitimate (not hacking) purposes. For example, a *Time* magazine reporter wrote, "Increasingly, as more home terminals are hooked into the telephone system, the lines that connect computers are being used for personal networking, carrying the raw materials of human intercourse: gossip, elephant jokes, pesto recipes and even the murmurings of long-distance seductions."[117] The article was framed around a thirty-two-year-old "bureaucrat," who was "neither a computer professional nor a thrill-seeking whiz kid," but instead "just an ordinary citizen who yearns to communicate." The article reported that "tens of thousands of other computer owners who share that urge" were online.[118] But such instances in which the social benefits of online communities were highlighted were rare. For the most part, bulletin board users' activities were marginalized until the late 1980s, and participation in these communities was presented as a threat to and not a facilitator of social interaction.

Still, the future held solutions to these perceived threats, and the solutions for the most part were to be found in education. For example, *Life* magazine featured Clarkson University, a private university in Potsdam, NY, in which the almost 900-member class of 1987 was issued computers in fall of 1983.[119] Images accompanying the article featured a photograph of a monitor with works of literature like *The Scarlet Letter* piled on it and a religion quiz on the Book of Genesis on the screen. The quiz featured the question: "God expels Adam and Eve from the Garden of Eden because..." The answer was given: "God fears that they will eat of the tree of life and coupled with their knowledge of good and evil, become godlike."[120] The article reported that "Carnegie-Mellon in Pittsburgh hopes to have all of its students' personal terminals linked to the school's computerized library system within two years."[121] By connecting religion, knowledge, and computer use, news media presented Clarkson University as one appropriate place to begin unseating computer misuse by teenaged hackers and to teach appropriate use. The university's board already assumed the computer was central to America's future success and therefore computer-skilled teenagers were also central to this future. If teenagers learned how to use computers legally, under the watchful eyes of university professors, these teenagers would be less likely to learn to hack or to become a part of "dangerous" anti-establishment organizations. These teenagers would not fall victim to Soviet infiltration (as Lightman was thought to have to have done) or obsessive video gaming (as Lightman did), but would instead develop into controlled, self-policing citizen-subjects and would support rather than threaten the American government.

Educational institutions were potential safety valves, or a means of re-grasping control over the computer age and empowered youths. Education (and education corporations) and capitalism, then, were the means for controlling unruly teenagers. Placing the disciplining of the teenager in the context of the school system implied that the government was not the agent of discipline. Rather, it would be up to educational institutions to mediate youthful rebellion, teach appropriate computer use, and stave off the potential harmful effects of computer networks, such as hacking, isolation, and addiction. This solution allowed universities to discipline teenagers and simultaneously allow their creativity to unfold for the public good. This notion reinforced the belief that computers, combined with the next generation's disciplined creativity, were the key to America's idealistic future.

Reining in Teens and Teenaged Technology

In their debates about the first major internet policy, policymakers mobilized tropes from news media and film. These tropes linked Cold War security anxieties with generational concerns and engaged what I call a "teenaged technology" discourse, which focused on computer network technology as both itself teenaged and as the domain of anti-establishment teenaged hackers. Because the first policy discussions took place in the context of these cultural tropes, policymakers could present the "computer network problem" as involving "rebellious teenagers" instead of "criminals," thereby allowing them to cast their regulatory measures as parental, or designed to discipline while fostering individual talents and productivity. In this sense, policymakers could present their policy as the epitome of democratic success because it was designed to re-incorporate rebels into society productively without oppressing them.[122] Thus, film, news media, and hacker self-representations not only helped construct the networking as a teen technology problem; they were also instrumental in constructing the imaginable and winning policy solutions.

WarGames in particular was a primary part of the argument for the first internet policy, the Counterfeit Access Device and Computer Fraud and Abuse Act of 1984.[123] Policymakers used the film for fear-mongering about global destruction and to lobby for controlling measures over cyberspace. The use of film in the policy arena is not uncommon. As media scholars Murry Edelman and Anthony Downs have shown, politicians overtly pick up issues dealt with in a popular film, seeing in them winning or popular policy options. These "active" policymakers then use a film, for example, as a frame to argue their cases.[124] In this case, *WarGames* made it visually imaginable that a teenage hacker could access military weaponry, even by mistake, and bring the world to the brink of destruction. This example, fictional as it was, proved a powerful tool for the policymakers who were looking to demonstrate that government control over computer networks was a matter of national security. *WarGames* dramatized "bad" computer use and characters like "the hacker," placing both in a Cold War context in which immature people and technology might be susceptible to infiltration either by innocent hackers or sinister Soviets. Positioning the establishment as unprepared and ignorant, the film represented non-governmental individuals as the world's saviors, as the only ones able to use technology for good.

But the film was especially compelling in this policy debate because of how it functioned in the news media sphere. As noted earlier, especially in conjunction with the "414" Milwaukee hacking events, the film provided media outlets with a sensational and usable news hook, or a timely reason to publish stories on computers and networking. The film's political slant, its apocalyptic representations, and the real-world events—especially those concerning failures of the military-industrial complex and successes of hackers—directed the kind of questions those media outlets using the film as news hook would likely ask institutional sources. The 1984 legislation offered policymakers an answer to these media inquiries. It allowed policymakers to represent policy and the government as responding to pressing issues and to represent themselves as not only serving timely and important needs of their constituents, but also as a branch of the government separate from the demonized and inept military. In short, *WarGames* and the 414 hackers brought news media attention to the dangers of hackers and networking and helped to discursively produce both as teenagers. Thus, policy solutions that were clearly necessary to address dangerous activities were focused on regulating teenagers instead of controlling online spaces.

WarGames itself and the issues it treated were legitimated by policymaker attention. During the Computer and Communications Security and Privacy Hearings that Congress held in 1983, members, witnesses, and experts all validated the film.[125] A four-minute clip was shown at the beginning of the first hearing, and speakers referred to the film throughout the hearings. Although these institutional sources downplayed the film's military scenario, they simultaneously labeled the film as an "accurate representation." In his opening statement, Representative Dan Glickman, Chairman of the Subcommittee on Transportation, Aviation, and Materials, introduced the four-minute clip by saying, "'I think [it] outlines the problem fairly clearly.'"[126] He went on to say, "'While this ultimate disaster is not likely possible, the film does illustrate, I am told, certain break-in methods that are factual.'"[127] Glickman recognized the film, then, as both a realistic and unrealistic representation of potential future events. He reinforced the security of defense systems, but also admitted that hacking occurs in ways similar to those represented in the film. As if following the same script, Representative Timothy Wirth introduced the clip later in the hearing by saying it "'is quite realistic in terms of what real hackers do.'"[128]

But this validation of the film did not only come from government officials. It also came from computer industry representatives. Stephen Walker, president of Trusted Information Systems, Inc., a company describing itself as involved in "Computer Networking, Computer Security, Information Systems, Telecommunications," said that he thought that "'the highly popular movie *WarGames* should be required viewing for all who were concerned with protecting sensitive information on computers.'"[129] Glickman presented this *fictional* film as a source for knowledge for policymakers. Walker, who was invited to the hearing as a "computer expert," endorsed the representation of hacking in *WarGames,* even ratcheting up anxieties by testifying that "'our vulnerabilities in this field are not limited to hackers. The widespread connection of major information processing facilities by communication networks is inevitable with our ever growing needs for rapid communication.'"[130] In this statement, Walker raised the specter of bigger threats to national security than juvenile hacking and suggested that vulnerabilities would increase in the future unless action was taken.

Some policymakers, like Representative Wirth, were overt in their hopes that the anxiety generated or tapped by both the film and the "414" Milwaukee hacking events would cause such action. In a statement read at the hearing directly after the *WarGames* clip was shown, Wirth said, "'Perhaps the combination of the recent hackers, which were exposed in Milwaukee, coupled with the popular movie *WarGames,* will move the discussion into the public eye and help to force debate on the implications of the changes that are occurring across the country.'"[131] Wirth hoped to open what political scientists call a "policy window," a period when a problem, a policy solution, and political powers align enough for policy change to be enacted. When policy windows open, some form of policy discussion also emerges. The discussion may be carried on in traditional veins, but it may also branch into new ones. Thus, policy windows are moments when new ideas may enter the policy arena or when new sources may gain credibility and discredit old ones.[132]

The policy window that opened via *WarGames* and its attendant press coverage did represent a transfer in credibility, namely to hackers like Neal Patrick, a 414 Milwaukee hacker who testified at the hearings. Policymakers were overt in their use of the film and Patrick together, reinforcing parallelism between the real-life event and the film and suggesting Patrick (a 414 hacker) and Lightman (character from *WarGames*) were equivalent. Not only did Patrick's testimony directly follow the film clip, but Patrick was also represented in the hearings in ways similar to Lightman in *WarGames.*[133] Both were imagined as simultaneously being teen video-gamers, members of the computer-capable generation with power over cyberspace, and participants in hacker subculture. Policymakers questioned Patrick directly about the film *WarGames.* Congressman Bill Nelson asked: "'Was anything gleaned from the movie?'"[134] Patrick answered: "'That didn't instigate us at all'"; "'the only connection'" was that "'we added another account with the name "Joshua" which was used in the movie, just as another little game that we played.'"[135] Although Patrick legitimated the film by suggesting his activities

were similar to those in the film, Patrick also represented the film as material for a practical joke and not as inspiration for or instructional on hacking
methodologies that intended to threaten national or international security.
Hacking was a game to Patrick and his teen cohorts and, just as for Lightman
in *WarGames,* breaking into computer systems was similar to beating a video
game. But the specter of anti-establishment hacker subculture entered the
debates nonetheless when Representative Glickman detailed the "414" hacking incidents and described the "underground" hacker culture as made up of
"'computer hackers who continuously try to defeat the security programmed
into modern computers.'"[136] The exaggerated relentlessness of hacker activities and the implied monolithic nature of hackers demonized the subculture
and simplified its belief system. This kind of representation reinforced Glickman's ultimate goal to implement controlling policy.

In contrast to the way that Glickman focused on dangerous hackers,
Congressman Thomas Piaskoski downplayed potential political motivations
for the 414 hacks and focused instead on Patrick's potentially bright future,
saying, "'He is human. He is 17 years old. … He is a National Merit Scholar
semifinalist. He is a bright kid.'"[137] He further normalized Patrick in describing him as a warning to other teens:

> "Neal is not here today …as an information-age Robin Hood, as we've seen
> him called on occasion. He disdains that folk hero label, and probably the
> media attention, too. He is here, I think, for the same reason that you've
> called this hearing. He's accepted the invitation so that he can let the public
> know, and especially other young computer hobbyists, that there are pit-
> falls, there are dangers, that there is potential harm that can be done, and
> that intellectual curiosity perhaps does not outweigh that risk."[138]

In contrast to Glickman, who amplified anxiety by connecting Patrick to
an underground and anti-establishment network, Piaskoski suggested that
Patrick had neither a political agenda nor a desire for fame. Patrick, in Piaskoski's formulation, was not part of a dangerous subculture intent on sub-
verting the system and was no communist (a Robin Hood). Instead, he was a
teenager who made a mistake and who wanted to help correct the weaknesses
on which he previously capitalized. Thus, Piaskoski represented Patrick as a
reformed rebel, a former hacker and current computer expert now on the
same side as the policymakers. He suggested the committee should listen to
Patrick's testimony with appropriate respect and treat him as an authority
figure. Like Joshua, the teenaged computer-gone berserk in *WarGames,* Patrick had grown up and was now a capable, self-regulating citizen subject.

And like Joshua, computing technology itself was an out-of-control child in need of some regulation for Congressman Glickman. As he asked in his opening statements, "'Are we, in effect, the modern-day Dr. Frankenstein?'" and as he promised further, "'the hearing today will try to dramatize the problem and also deal with the ways to prevent it from becoming a national catastrophe.'"[139] In Glickman's metaphor, the U.S. government may have "fathered" an uncontrollable, self-animating menace instead of the technological creature-citizen it had hoped to create. The menace could cause destruction on a national scale. However, Glickman reinstated human agency in his representation, suggesting that although the state created the unruly technology, problems may be ultimately solvable through further engagement by the "father" or state.

Proposals for what this engagement would look like often included programs comparable to the one at Clarkson University, which was designed to teach appropriate computer use. Congressman Ron Wyden explicitly advocated that education about appropriate computer use be incorporated into public schools, saying that "'Whenever a school offers basic courses in computer instruction, those courses should contain an ethics component.'"[140] Education measures were preferable to other types of legislation, because, as Senator Bill Nelson said, "'There is an inventiveness among computer operators that we do not want to stifle. And as we approach the problem evident in the computerization of society, we want to try to draft any legislation response without discouraging that inventiveness.'"[141] For Nelson, the computer-skilled generation possessed a valuable creative skill and, although misdirected, computer hacking represented one incarnation of that creative energy. Thus, while young people might need some guidance from government policies that would ensure national security, it was also important not to smother them, as their creativity was also important to national success and security. (This statement foreshadowed a primary education concern of the late 1980s, which was ensuring that U.S. children had a competitive edge over the children of Japan.)

Educational proposals were lobbied for not only because most policymakers felt that no technological security measures would ultimately ever be enough to protect security interests, but also because they were disturbed by the perceived ethical violations of hackers. Hackers were represented as simply not possessing the "right" ethical framework. When asked when he began to think about the ethics of his activities, Patrick quickly answered, "'When the FBI knocked on the door.'"[142] Wyden said, "'I think one of the things that concerns committee members the most is that this is an area that has attracted some of the best and brightest young people and that in so many instances we're not talking about hardened criminals, but really the country's future."'[143] His concerns stemmed less from criminal activity and more from his perception that the younger generation possessed significant character flaws or that they were corrupted by their computer network-use. This "changing of the guard" anxiety suggested that policymakers saw youths as developing or operating under an alternative, or anti-establishment, moral structure. Attempts to enforce educational programs suggested that (re)education could provide the nation with stability and protect the status-quo. Like Patrick (and Lightman in the cinematic world of *WarGames*), this generation of computer-abled unruly teens could be rehabilitated and formed into the next generation of "appropriately" self-regulating citizen-subjects.

But Wyden's educational proposal was aimed not merely at hackers; he also wanted to send the computer-unskilled generation to computer camp to learn self-defense. Wyden suggested educating the population at large about computer vulnerability, because, he said, "'we cannot ban computer crime. What we can do is educate our citizens about the risk.'"[144] Congressman Don Fuqua, Chairman of the Committee on Science and Technology, added that "'today's youngsters are a computer generation. They have the same kind of passion for computers that their parents had for cars when they were growing up. So, it doesn't take much of a projection to forecast the day when we will be completely comfortable with computers as an integral part of our daily lives—just as the automobile is today.'"[145] Although he reinforced the notion of a generational divide along the lines of computer capability, Fuqua also downplayed anxieties about youth rebellion by noting the cycle of hysteria over interest in and control of new technologies by younger generations. Just as rebellious behaviors associated with the automobile in the 1950s were domesticated through driving schools and licensing policies, so would computer use be controlled in the future.

With the focus on education, the government was clearly the preferred leader over industry, despite numerous references to Orwell's *1984* in the post-hearing report (which was released in 1984). However, perhaps in defense against the Orwellian critique, most proposed measures differed in valence from the report in that they advocated a government-industry alliance over a government-only model. While the government would provide "evaluation criteria" and would vet security measures proposed by the computer industry, it would not be entirely accountable for protecting corporate computers.[146] Corporations would need to "realize the commercial value of security, and build it into their systems."[147] In a historical year when big government was a cultural focus, security and governmental control would not be left unchecked by industry. Indeed, industry executives testifying at the hearing demonstrated their hesitation to involve government at all in network security measures. For example, "computer expert" Walker said he felt that the "'government should limit its efforts to a major education and awareness program concerning vulnerabilities and available solutions.'"[148] Clearly skeptical of government involvement, he advocated free-market solutions, which, he said, "'should be sufficient to advance the state of the art for at least the next few years.'"[149] In this statement Walker foreshadowed developments in the late 1980s and early 1990s, when corporations took the lead from the government for computer security.

In sum, news media reports, popular culture outlets, hackers themselves, and policy hearings leading up to the first internet legislation were all framed by a "teenaged technology" discourse that imagined both computer networking technology itself and its users as teenagers, and focused on the teenage users as being in need of regulation. This discourse engaged longstanding cultural anxieties connected to both Cold War military security—the specters of global destruction and uncontrollable technology—and antiestablishment youths—the changing of the guard responsible for America's future. Securing computer networks and containing or redirecting rebellious spirit into productivity became securing the nation. As with many Cold War threats, the scariest and most significant came from within, in this case in the form of computer-savvy, anti-establishment teenagers who were joyriding or "gaming" the military's computer network. Adding to this anxiety were notions stemming from hackers themselves and from news media covering early computer networking technology which presented this technology as complex, mysterious and unknowable and thereby suggested that there would always be those out there with more knowledge, skill, and access. These visions positioned established authorities—parents, policymakers, and members of the older generation—as obsolete in relation to young hackers and gamers, the holders of superior knowledge, magic, language, and skills.

The film *WarGames* engaged this teenaged technology discourse and framed both the first public debate about computer networking and the first federal internet policy. The engagement, elaboration, and dramatization of this discourse by *WarGames* allowed policymakers to use the film to push arguments for policies designed to teach youths "appropriate" computer use and to cast this regulation as democratic and not repressive. The resulting first policy regulating what would be popularly called the internet ultimately mobilized tropes from news media and *WarGames* and helped establish the legislature as the official "parent" of the teenaged internet and its users (instead of the military, its birth parent). The state, then, cast its regulation as the epitome of democratic success, suggesting this policy helped re-incorporate rebels into society productively without oppressing them. In 1984, when Orwell's book and the Cold War cultural battles served as frames for many discussions about technology, government, and power, this distinction was especially important.

These first news media and policy debates about internet policy formed the roots of how journalists and policymakers imagined the internet in the future. Although teenaged-ness remained an oft-mobilized trope, in the late 1980s it was no longer mobilized in the same ways. The internet still had teenaged domains, but it was no longer represented as being the domain of teenagers or as being teenaged itself. Instead, by the late 1980s, the primary user shifted from the "mischievous teen gamer" to the "productive adult worker," and images of the computer as a user-friendly tool replaced the visions of it as a rebellious juvenile technology. Both, in essence, "grew up." Mapping this shift, and shifting itself, legislation focused more extensively on economics. Thus, securing the nation's future became less about making the internet secure from and for teenagers and more about securing dominance over the increasingly global computer industry.

2

The Internet Grows Up and Goes to Work

User-Friendly Tools for Productive Adults

Beginning in 1983, IBM launched an extensive advertising campaign featuring Charlie Chaplin's Little Tramp to market the PCjr, the company's first major foray into the home computer market and ultimately the best-selling computer of the period.[1] IBM's massive magazine, newspaper, and television campaign featured the Tramp as a Depression-era worker and average man in his recognizably oversized suit-tails, jumbo shoes, bowler hat, mustache, and characteristic playful smirk interacting with IBM's computing and networking technology.[2] Perhaps the most-discussed and -successful corporate representation in the early 1980s, the campaign itself became a news hook.[3] One *Time* magazine article concluded that "the Tramp campaign has been so successful that it has created a new image for IBM." Instead of previous images that characterized IBM's technology as "efficient and reliable," "cold and aloof," this campaign gave IBM a "human face."[4] It was significant not only because it helped redefine IBM's corporate image in the home computing market, but also because as computing became increasingly popular in the mid- to late 1980s, this campaign helped form conceptualizations of what home computing and networking were and were for. This chapter asks why the Tramp—an icon of the Depression-era worker and of the rough adjustment to industrial modernity—made sense as a corporate symbol for IBM. Understanding how this anti-modern icon was logical or effective reveals how the public engaged with computers and ultimately the internet. The broad home-use of the internet was made possible by the prior acceptance of the home computer. Representations of the computer are vital to understanding those of the internet in the mid-1980s and thereafter because the two blended together conceptually.[5] Of course, to argue that computing increasingly also meant networking is not to argue that all images of the computer were inherently linked to the idea of the networked computer. It is to say that there were connections.

While Cold War and hacker anxiety shaped the first internet policy in the 1980s and continued as a major part of public debate for the next two decades, more hopeful views of the internet and computer corporations began to gain resonance in the mid-1980s and early 1990s.[6] This occurred in large part because of corporate efforts to commodify computing. Corporate visions took on previously threatening representations like those present in *WarGames* and elsewhere of the anthropomorphized computer capable of overpowering and/or replacing humans and helped recast the internet. What was conceptualized—in popular culture, news media and policy images in particular—as an out-of-control technology jockeyed by rebellious teenagers was re-imagined as a "user-friendly" tool controlled by productive adult "users." By 1990, the *Economist* wrote, "The Internet has grown up."[7]

In this chapter as in others, the story of government action or of policy enactment is a story about the state's response to a naturalized reality created in part through the history of representations. Thus, government responded to a new view of the primary internet user as a productive adult and the internet as a key to the United States' economic future. Although perceived threats to internet security, like hacking, remained topics of public discussion, threats to the United States' economic future posed by international powers like Japan rose on the public agenda in the mid-1980s. As news media and policymakers began to shift their focus from security to economics, ensuring U.S. economic progress and dominance became the primary goal instead of securing national military infrastructures. At the same time, news media cast the government as incapable—and corporations as quite capable—of regulating the internet and leading America toward global dominance. Unlike the early hands-on or parental approach to internet problems that emerged in the early 1980s, in the latter half of the Reagan era, the U.S. government focused on market-based instead of policy-based solutions. The rise of conservative politics and of optimistic images of both the internet and its users as grown-up and as economically productive allowed the government in the mid-1980s and late 1980s to begin handing the reins over to the market and corporate America. The government, then, turned its focus from the protection of internet users to the protection of internet corporations and the production of the computer-literate workers deemed necessary for success in the global marketplace.

The New User Takes on the Anthropomorphized
Networked Computer

In the late 1980s and early 1990s, both computer use and computer networking significantly increased in popularity. The release of the Commodore 64,
the Apple Macintosh, and the IBM PCjr in the early and mid-1980s made
computing radically simpler than it was with earlier mainframe computers
and thereby enabled users with less experience with computer programming to access the technology.[8] These technologies helped popularize computers in workplaces and personal homes, and the emergence of companies
like America Online made connecting those computers easier. Still, computer uses and skills varied widely between users. Some simply used isolated machines for word processing and accounting, while others networked
their computers and used them to participate in online chat rooms or bulletin board systems.[9] During this period, news media began applying the
technical word "internet" to computer networking. This term was derived
from "Internet Protocol" or the technology used to connect the variety of
computer networks that existed by the late 1970s and early 1980s.[10] The term
"internet," then, describes a network of networks. Although the term "internet" was in use in military and academic circles as far back as 1974 to describe
mainframe computer networks (not home computers) that were networked
between universities and military research institutions, the term was not
widely used in popular culture and news media until the early 1990s.[11]

In the wake of these product-releases and industry shifts, most popular
media representations imagined the computer either as a human or as a
tool.[12] These competing representations presented a paradox for the user. As
an anthropomorphized substitute human, the computer was either uncontrollable and a threat to the user or it was a replacement for the human and
a threat to humanity. In contrast, as a useful tool, the computer was controlled by a user and was an asset to the worker, especially the office worker.
Throughout the 1980s and into the 1990s, representations of the computer as
a tool waxed and those of the computer as an anthropomorphized human
replacement waned.

As research has long shown, notions of machine-human assemblages and
the sentient robot or mobile computer emerged in the period before and
during industrialization.[13] One place where mythologies and anxieties about
technology were produced and perpetuated was in science fiction literature,
and many cite Mary Shelley's *Frankenstein*, published in 1818, as one of the
first examples of anxieties about the blending of humans with technology.[14]

By the late 1940s and 1950s this kind of machine-human vernacular had spread to mainstream culture, where computers were called "electronic brains" and broadly discussed as replacements for or extensions of the human mind.[15] Electronic brain imagery appeared in a variety of sources. For example, the April 2, 1965, *Time* magazine issue titled "The Computer in Society" featured a large, humanoid computer with a face (eyes, nose, mouth and ears) on the cover, with an enormous human-looking brain in the background.[16] Science writer Roger Rosenblatt noted in 1982 the centrality of the computer to historically shifting conceptions of the human mind: from Plato's mind as a cave, to Freud's mind as a house, to the mind as a computer.[17] This notion was also debated in the 1981 book *The Mind's I: Fantasies and Reflections on the Self and Soul*, a popular study of human consciousness edited by Douglas Hofstadter and Daniel Dennett, which discussed the relationship between the mind and computer programs and implied that computers would ultimately simulate the mind by developing consciousnesses. This book debated whether humans "are" or "have" brains or souls and the potential for computers to have consciousness.[18] Contemporary debates have revisited this theme in large part due to Ray Kurzweil's book *The Singularity Is Near: When Humans Transcend Biology*, in which he predicts that by the 2020s, humans will have reverse-engineered the brain, meaning scientists will have studied the structure of the brain enough to understand how it works with an eye to recreating it. By the 2040s humans and machines will have merged into a singular entity. In Kurzweil's thoughtful yet techno-utopian future, "the knowledge and skills embedded in our brains will be combined with the vastly greater capacity, speed, and knowledge-sharing ability of our own creations" to create a new civilization in which hunger, pollution, illness, and death will be optional.[19]

Between the late 1960s and the 1980s representations of computers as sentient beings dominated much of popular culture. A number of films and television programs featured cyborgs or computers as main characters, and as both heroes and villains. These included *2001: A Space Odyssey* (1969), *Star Wars* (1977), *Battlestar Galactica* (1978), *Star Trek: The Motion Picture* (1979), *Buck Rogers in the 25ᵗʰ Century* (1979), *Blade Runner* (1982), *Terminator* (1984), and *Robocop* (1987). Treating computers as potential human substitutes and companions, these films and shows represented computers as sentient and human-like or as intricately integrated into human life. As computers were increasingly networked in the 1970s and 1980s (in people's lives and in cultural representations), they became more threatening in science fiction. Networked to one another, computers could theoretically easily unite against humanity. For example, in the film *2001: A Space Odyssey*, the supercomputer HAL 9000, who expresses emotions like concern or embarrassment and has a human voice, is networked deeply into human life aboard a spaceship. HAL's networking power grants him almost complete control over the needs of his human counterparts (e.g. food, movement aboard the ship, air on and off the ship), and he ultimately uses this power to kill them. Similarly, the computer in *WarGames* is not just a metaphor for the mechanics of the human brain or human thought; rather it is an electronic person, patterned after Dr. Falken's deceased son Joshua (a real person in the film's universe). Like HAL, "Joshua" is all the more powerful because he is networked. His access to nuclear defense systems of the most powerful country in the world makes him a threat not just to individuals as in *2001,* but to the entire world.

To complicate matters, later representations of computers and robots in films such as *Blade Runner* and the *Terminator* render computers increasingly more difficult (or impossible) to differentiate from humans and therefore more threatening. The central plot elements in *Blade Runner* and *Terminator* focus on this notion. In *Blade Runner,* for example, humanoid machines known as "replicants," escape and disappear into the general population, while in *Terminator,* a mechanical assassin from the future returns to kill the leader of the human resistance in the future war against the machines.[20] In both cases, the invisibility and ceaseless violence toward humans corresponded to Cold War anxieties about "the enemy within" and with fears of hackers relentlessly using computers to infiltrate networks from remote and hidden locations.

But outside the realm of popular film, companies invested in selling computer technology and news media covering technological developments began countering these images in the mid-1980s, when they started representing the computer and internet as helpful to humanity, as a source of efficiency at work and fun at home.[21] These advertisements imagined the adult user as the competent controller of the computer, which was in turn a "user-friendly" extension of the user. News reports offering this same perspective often associated user friendliness with efficiency, ultimately connecting the computer to capitalistic national goals of worker productivity and competitive advantage.[22] For example, one *Newsweek* article reported that one major U.S. industry goal was to have "no paper," or "an all-electronic office where white-collar productivity is sharply improved by a constellation of machines based on microprocessor technology that uses electronics to replace virtually every office function now done on paper." This "no paper" strategy often incorporated "intranets," or private networks (like ARPANET) accessible only within a particular organization, and was designed to increase worker productivity.[23] Connecting national economic productivity to the productivity of individual workers, these images suggested that helping workers be more efficient would benefit the nation as a whole. Ultimately, the overlap between advertisements and news media helped establish computer companies and their advertisements as trustworthy sources of information.

But the connections among national interest, business interest, and individual efficiency did not appear overnight. During the early to mid-1980s, corporations like IBM sought to convince individuals, government agencies, and other companies that they needed computers and computer networks. The winning advertisement tactic involved taking the computer out of the teenaged boy's bedroom—the locus of the hacker and gamer—and moving it instead and into the workplace of the "average" American.[24] In addition, these campaigns directly countered tropes that characterized the technologies as threatening with tropes about labor, efficiency, and progress and recast computers as friends and co-workers rather than menacing machines. Situating the computer in the context of narratives of progress, the advertisement campaigns ameliorated Cold War anxieties about computer technology's destructive capabilities and potential risks to national security by focusing on the belief that technological innovation had and would continue to propel America toward an idealized future.

Some advertising campaigns even directly employed the computer-as-human trope, but represented the computer as a co-worker that would improve working conditions instead of threatening workers as in *2001*. Most notably, the U.S. Postal Service used the friendly co-worker trope in its 1983 advertising campaign for its "E-COM" electronic mail system, which showed an image of a computer with a smiling face on its screen. The monitor had seven arms extending out of the base. All arms performed separate tasks, like typing, putting money in a piggy bank, or holding a stopwatch. The advertisement described E-COM, as a cost- and work-saving system that would "Let your computer transmit directly to ours. So you can send announcements and invoices, for example, while you bypass a lot of work—and expense."[25] This advertisement resembled the *Time* magazine cover from 1965, but in a way that presented the computer as helpful and not frightening. Anthropomorphized into a worker like HAL, this computer acted only if you "let" it. In this way, the advertisement suggested that the user ultimately controlled the computer and that the computer was a helpful and dutiful assistant.

Although the Postal Service system ultimately failed in the marketplace, IBM's computers and networking systems thrived using similar advertising tactics and tropes to position the company's products as aids to the worker.

For instance, one advertisement pictured a telephone, fountain pen, paper-clips, and a personal computer on a desktop. The title of the image read, "Office Heroes in the War of 9 to 5," and text at the bottom of the advertisement read, "At IBM, we know that pencils, memo pads, and even telephones are no longer enough to win all the battles in the War of 9 to 5. IBM office systems can help." Although IBM could not "guarantee that people who work in offices will win every battle they get into," it would guarantee that "at least they'll be in a fair fight."[26] In this advertisement, the computer was not only a weapon wielded by workers against their work (or against their competitors), but it was also a weapon for IBM to demonstrate that it sided with the worker. Moreover, the advertisement celebrated the American value of fair play, with IBM's technology offering the possibility for a "fair fight," suggesting without it the worker was engaged in a losing battle. Here, then, the computer became a tool to help humanity, not a sentient being to rival or undermine it. In its pairing with the worker, the computer also became linked to the human body and forming a new kind of hybrid, the effects of which have been hotly debated in academic literature. These images presented this hybrid worker as physically adapted, or, as media scholar Marshall McLuhan wrote, the human nervous systems of workers were linked through "extensions."[27] For others, such as theorists Gilles Deleuze and Félix Guattari, this kind of linkage, or "machinic assemblage," has the potential to oppress the individual, especially the worker. The human body becomes part of a machine as it operates machinery in, for example, a factory. In addition, human bodies become "machines" in their participation in organizational systems as in an assemblage of humans working to make a hotel operate, for example. For Deleuze and Guattari, assemblages include not only the units created by humans and machines ("bodies"), but also the ways they are used ("actions and passions," "an intermingling of bodies reacting to one another") and the ways in which they are represented or understood (the corresponding "regime of signs or enunciations").[28]

Feminist scholar Donna Haraway has called the resulting formation of the human-as-machine/machine-as-human a "cyborg." While Haraway—like McLuhan, Deleuze and Guattari—sees the cyborg bridging the divide between human and machine physically, emotionally, spiritually, and politically, she focuses on the liberating potential of this formation and argues that the cyborg "can suggest a way out of the maze of dualisms [i.e. man vs. woman] in which we have explained our bodies and our tools to ourselves."[29] In these models, humans and tools are not only mutually formative in that they eventually require one another, but are also not necessarily contemporary: "A knight [chevalier] without a horse [cheval] is no knight at all."[30] Like the knight's horse in medieval times, in the 1980s computers became increasingly "required" for American workers. Theorist Bruno Latour, however, offers an oppositional perspective to the theorists above who mark their terminology—assemblage or cyborg—with an air of novelty. For Latour, technology is not a new mixture of symbol, flesh, and steel; rather, it has always been "hybridized," simultaneously worldly and an object of discourse.[31]

Newness is, by definition, a primary feature of news reports and so not surprisingly news reports about the computer departed from staid representations of the computer as anti-human in favor of alternate representations that cast it as pro-human. In this sense, news reports were useful to computer corporations in their endeavors to cast computing technology as friendly and computer corporations as on the side of the user.[32] Because news reports are constructed (or construct themselves) as objective, the overlap between reports and advertisement information can help certify that the advertisements are accurate and therefore not merely propaganda. Thus, for example, one article directed computer buyers to consult advertising to inform themselves before heading to the computer store, stating that "choosing a computer, like selecting a spouse, can be a daunting undertaking" and that "once you make a choice, you are stuck with the family it comes with."[33] Representing the process of computer selection as partner selection implied not only the importance of computers, but also that the computer possessed a morality, humanity, and family. This report heightened anxiety about choosing a computer before it offered the promise of relief. Making selecting a computer like selecting a spouse raised the stakes because it suggested you could not just buy another if you did not like the first one you selected. But with the help of computing corporation and news media information, you would choose the correct one in the first place and you would have a pleasant addition to your family.

These images competed with those created by hackers and science writers—both of whom were invested in the specialization of knowledge—which presented the computer as unintelligible to and uncontrollable by the layperson. And these news reports that positioned the journalist as the reader's guide to a manageable and understandable technology dovetailed with advertisements. For example, one advertisement featured a businessman in a suit and tie working on a computer at what looked like a dining room table. The text emphasized the simplicity of the home computer pictured, stating, "The people who were writing our literature were adamant that an encyclopedia of 'computerese' *not* be required reading."[34] In presenting computerese as an undesirable competitor to computer-friendliness, IBM presented itself in similar ways as the news reports, or as invested in democratizing knowledge to the average user.

At the same time, this "average user" also became a common focal point of IBM's campaigns in the mid- to late 1980s and remained front and center thereafter.[35] Thus, one IBM advertisement in 1984 showed prominent outlines of two hands (left and right) with text between the hands stating, "Only average people fit their hands here.... Yours probably aren't a perfect match." The advertisement claimed the company eschewed designing its products for "'average' people of 'average' size," and focused instead on designing products to be "flexible so they can contribute to the comfort and productivity of all the individuals who use them." In this representation, the computer was a versatile and malleable tool for a wide variety of people, and as an infinitely adaptable technology, IBM computers were not only easily understood, but also able to be mastered physically by myriad body types. The advertisement also claimed IBM aimed to "accommodate both the diversity of the human form and the work humans do."[36] In this vision, computers and computing were designed to help humanity become more efficient, happy, and productive, a notion in competition with those dominant in popular film of computers as potentially damaging to humanity.

Advertisements do not operate in a cultural vacuum. Their cultural meanings compete and intersect, or "associate," with other cultural actors dominant in the historical moment.[37] One important element in the cultural production of the internet in this period involved George Orwell's *1984*. As the year 1984 approached, computer corporations and news media alluded to Orwell in advertisements and stories, often using anecdotal evidence to illustrate how Orwell's vision had or had not come true.[38] For example, in his article "Your Plug-in Pal," Jed Horne noted efforts on the part of advertisers to directly address anxieties of technology expressed in Orwell's work, specifically those connected to surveillance and government conspiracy. Horne wrote, "On the eve of 1984, the folks who write the manuals and programs for the home computer market are at special pains to allay any Orwellian anxieties you may bring to the contemplation of that future."[39] He described and defined the term "user-friendly," as "nice" and "accessible," noting advertisers promoted the computer as a helpful ally that would not "allow you to suffer the humiliating Rosemary Woods syndrome."[40] Rosemary Woods—President Nixon's secretary who was blamed for erasing the 18½ minutes from the Nixon tapes that many speculated would have directly linked Nixon to the Watergate scandal—claimed the erasure was an accident, a result of her having to balance too many technological devices in her office.[41] In a post-Watergate historical moment when anxiety about security and competence permeated American culture, this article and the reference to Woods laid bare the efforts by advertisers and the computer industry to address public anxiety about relying on computers—anxiety that also included the fear, emerging in the 1970s, that technology would cause information overload and "a state of intellectual enervation and depletion hardly to be distinguished from massive ignorance."[42]

The placement of computing technology in the context of Orwell and Rosemary Woods inserted it into an established American cultural formation in which industrialization was anxiety-causing, especially for workers.[43] As Ithiel de Sola Pool writes, the "electronic revolution" is one element in a long history of worker dehumanization, as both mass media and technology were part of "a great historical process in which work by hand is replaced with work by the brain. The human role in production becomes that of information processor, reaching decisions and giving instructions. Work becomes the moving and processing of signals, not objects."[44] This long-standing cultural anxiety about technology and labor was enhanced by economic downturns that began in the 1970s when fears of declining jobs due to recession and globalization were augmented by fears of automation. The mid-1970s and 1980s were characterized by a "litany of growing federal deficits, accelerating inflation, slow economic growth, factory closings, gasoline shortages and price hikes, and rising rates of crime, divorce, welfare, single parenting, and drug use."[45] Economic recession combined with inflation ("stagflation") caused by a variety of factors including OPEC's oil embargo in 1973 led to drops in industrial stocks, factory closings, and high unemployment rates. Germany and Japan became effective competitors, particularly in "bedrock" steel and electronics industries.[46] Between 1970 and 1990, the percentage of workers employed in manufacturing declined from 26 percent to 18 percent, and increasing inequality in income distribution also marked the period.[47] Not only were factories closing, but companies were also looking for cheaper means of production. One of the primary ways to eliminate costly labor was to replace human workers with automated machines, which could work tirelessly and would not unionize or call in sick. Given this historical legacy, computers and other "digital systems" lent themselves to comparison in news media to Orwell's work particularly well because, as Lisa Gitelman noted, "anxiety, like alienation, was one response to dehumanizing bureaucracies with dehumanizing machines."[48]

If computers could not replace workers completely, they could disempower workers by disrupting union activity. Thus, for example, in 1983, when AT&T workers went on strike, CBS reported that strikes were having the "opposite effect" of those in the 1940s and 1950s because "workers strike and companies realize they don't need them because of computers and telecommunication." Newscaster Dan Rather went on to state that "anytime a company can transfer data electronically, it may be able to break a strike." That is, because networked computers and working from home allowed workers to avoid participation in union activities without significant harassment, companies could rely on these "scabs" to perform the work of strikers, or to "telescab" from home.[49] In reporting on such stories, news organizations publicized the plight of the worker, focused on anxieties about computing technology, and, in a sense, sided against the corporate controlling interest in favor of their employees in that they undermined efforts by computer corporations to cast the computer as worker-friendly.[50]

In addition to being represented as a potential worker-replacement, the networked computer was also represented in news media as a possible supervisor, displacing and oppressing management as well as laborers. Again, this scenario tapped Orwellian anxieties and emerged as the focus of several news stories about automated supervisors in which "Big Brother" iconography informed the presentation of the internet as a surveillance tool.[51] ABC, for one, ran a report called "Computer Monitoring" about mechanisms corporations used to monitor employee behavior. The report noted that managers could increase productivity if they monitored how many breaks individual workers took. Several workers were interviewed (all female) and all complained the monitoring mechanisms were "dehumanizing." The network reported that psychological ailments "apparently linked to computer monitoring, like anxiety, exhaustion, heart disease" could potentially diminish the quality of work and that one state was considering banning the practice. Here, using computers to monitor humans treated humans like machines, expected humans to be machines, and created anxiety as humans tried to please machines. The report concluded that the practice could "turn the office of the future into an electronic version of yesterday's sweatshop" and noted that the *New York Times* newspaper guild filed a grievance against the newspaper.[52] As with union activity, notions of the computer as oppressive to the worker were only enhanced by the increased networking in the late 1980s because fewer supervisors could monitor computers remotely and more efficiently.

Labor concerns, Orwellian anxieties, and the fears of being taken over by computers did not go away, then, despite the earnest attempts of advertisers and the sometimes-enthusiastic news accounts that presented computers as tools. In this contested environment and in the context of an advertisement war between Apple and IBM, Apple represented itself as the solution. Throughout the 1980s, IBM competed with Apple computers for a share in the market and, ultimately, for the shape of computing to come. Each company presented different styles of computers, and each one tried to present itself as the more user-friendly. This war was in the subtext of their advertising campaigns, which played on the audience understanding what each company "meant" in terms of brand image. In *Life on the Screen*, Massachusetts Institute of Technology sociologist Sherry Turkle identified this war as part of a larger cultural tension between modernism and post-modernism. IBM presented a textual platform, which required users to understand code and the logics of its operating system, but it also provided a transparency in that if users knew the logic. Users could manipulate the computer at a base-level and adapt it to suit their needs. Apple's Macintosh, on the other hand, provided a visual, graphical user-interface (GUI). Users did not need to understand the computer's inner workings to use it, but they also could not manipulate the computer at the same base level if they wanted to. For Turkle, IBM represented modernist ideals of epistemology: control, rationality, and linear logic. Apple represented postmodernism in that it stood for the culture of simulation: non-linear exploration, creativity, and flexibility. In addition, the ease with which users could use Apple gave the company a populist flavor in opposition to IBM's corporate one.[53] The cultural legacy of this battle continued to play out in global "I'm a Mac/I'm a PC" campaign of the mid-2000s.

In Apple's most famous (and most written-about) series of advertisements, the company presented itself as being antithetical to Orwellian scenarios, while simultaneously painting IBM as Big Brother. In January of 1984, Apple aired an advertisement during the Super Bowl that depicted the Apple Macintosh computer as the ultimate tool of individuality and as a weapon against corporate and governmental surveillance. Ridley Scott, who had just finished *Blade Runner*, directed the advertisement, which cost an astounding $900,000 to produce. The advertisement generated considerable attention at the time, was named 1980s Commercial of the Decade by *Advertising Age* magazine, and "garnered millions of dollars' worth of free publicity, as news programs rebroadcast it that night." With this advertisement, Macintosh pioneered "event marketing," setting the precedent of airing high-profile advertisements during the Super Bowl.[54] In the advertisement, gray, clone-like people march toward a large figure on a screen preaching about the benefits of unity and "information purification" and the harms of "contradictory thoughts" to the "worker."[55] This narrative and the imagery exploited tropes of conformity or loss of individualism that pervaded science fiction representations of sentient computers and robots.[56] Interspersed with images of the gray people are shots of a blond, tanned, athletic woman dressed in red and white, carrying a hammer, and running from officials in face guards. Spinning, she hurls her hammer at the screen and blows it up. The advertisement concludes with the following text: "On January 24ᵗʰ, Apple Computer will introduce Macintosh. And you'll see why 1984 won't be like 1984."

This advertisement dealt directly with notions of oppressive or dangerous technology present elsewhere in American culture, tackling "the specter of HAL head-on" and positioning itself as the antidote to the technology represented in *2001*. The advertisement imagined computing and networking technology in binary terms in which "bad technology—centralized, authoritarian—which crushes the human spirit and controls people's minds" opposes "good technology—independent, individualized—of the Mac."[57] In this sense, Apple simultaneously cast its computers as the tools of independent and free-thinkers, and IBM as the Orwellian computer company. In addition, the advertisement presented the computer user as a female athlete instead of the teenage boy or adult (generally male) user that had been so common. In a historical moment when computers were considered part of the "male-gendered sphere of the workplace," Apple worked to be included in the more female-gendered domestic sphere through its self-promotion as "soft, curvaceous, user-friendly," and "personal."[58] This re-identification presented Apple as supporting gender equality, Apple technology as female-friendly, and the Apple Corporation itself as a more user-friendly corporation than IBM.

Such early battles over the market and over consumers—especially like this one between IBM and Apple in these early years of public computer use—had important material and cultural effects. Early corporate representations are especially important because when media are new, "their protocols are still emerging and the social, economic, and material relationships they will eventually express are still in formation."[59] This, then, is when multiple agents have a chance to tease out and create meanings that may become dominant and persistent (although not uncontested) through the technology's history. Such agents include news media, advertisers, consumers, and indeed the "whole social context within which production and consumption get defined—and defined as distinct."[60] In short, IBM users may not have pursued the "modernist" ideals of linear logic and rationality when choosing their computers, and Apple users may not have intended to explore their "postmodern" creativity through their computing. They may have imagined themselves as creative-types and "therefore" Apple users or they may have imagined themselves becoming more creative on account of their computers. Or they might not have even thought about it. The categories were by no means necessarily purposefully practiced by users or deliberately produced by corporate brand-makers, but were instead much more flexible and complicated. The cultural meanings of both computing and computer networking were unconsciously engaged, contested, and reframed by corporations, advertisers, and consumers as much as they were lived.

In sum, in the mid- to late 1980s, the "user" became increasingly an adult worker and not a teenaged hacker. This adult worker was imagined as being able to use computing and networking technology easily and doing so in order to increase efficiency. In part in response to the reemergence of Orwellian anxieties about technology, to the continuation of anxieties about labor, and in the context of an advertising war between IBM and Apple over the computing market, advertisements and news articles directly countered representations in popular culture that focused on computers and networking as complicated, self-directing, and dangerous. Moreover, advertising and news media helped construct an image of computer companies as serving the interest of productive users in control of their computers. The "productive adult user" was imagined as a solution to American economic struggles in that it created efficient engines to drive capitalism. But at the same time these users were also imagined as potentially problematic, as over-productivity could produce Orwellian clones antithetical to democratic and American ideals of self-expression and individualism. Apple, in particular, developed advertising strategies explicitly to ally those anxieties and to promote its vision of the individual using the computer for leisure in addition to work.

The Little Tramp and America's Progress Narrative

In the great IBM-Apple battle, the Little Tramp campaign for the IBM PCjr was part of IBM's attempt to crush Apple's success in the home PC market. (IBM already dominated the corporate market thanks in part to government contracts with the company.) The campaign pictured Charlie Chaplin's Tramp interacting with the IBM technology with his characteristic smirk and as the iconic everyman and fool. Since the Tramp was a figure that critiqued industrialization and technology as dangerous to the worker, the character may seem an odd choice for IBM, a corporation hoping to engender favorable brand images and increased sales. Moreover, print advertisements and three widely released television commercials featuring the character did not use the Tramp generically, but instead incorporated the well-known film *Modern Times*, in which the Tramp appears as a newly-hired factory worker facing threats of technology.[61] This film, regarded by some scholars as "overtly political" and "didactic," engaged anxieties about industrial technology in American urban environments in the 1930s.[62] A well-known and active communist, Charlie Chaplin wrote and directed the film to comment on the trials of workers in the Depression Era, indicting industrialization and the efficiency of factories for causing the Great Depression.[63] Both on and off screen, Charlie Chaplin's "loyalties lie with those persons in and out of work, just trying to survive the Depression."[64]

The IBM advertising campaign worked, however, because it focused on the Tramp as a fool and not as the embodiment of any meaningful critique. The advertisements implied that if the Tramp could use a computer, anyone could. The campaign also worked because it inserted computing technologies into an established American narrative of progress, suggesting through Chaplin's Tramp that transitioning from one electronic technology to another may be uncomfortable, but it was possible and profitable for both the individual and the nation. For example, one advertisement pictured the Tramp wearing slippers, sitting in an easy chair, and peering into the computer screen with a surprised expression on his face and his hand on his chest—all of which suggested that computing was a surprisingly easy, leisure-time activity, something one could do at home in a relaxed environment. An opened PCjr box pictured at the Tramp's feet suggested the instant usability of the computer, as did the accompanying text listing "Eleven things you can do on the very first day." With phrases like "friendly little mouse" and "short-cuts to help you," this advertisement emphasized that "PCjr makes it easy... You can start using PCjr as soon as you set it up."[65] Another advertisement stated you could "plug your family into Modern Times" and that "hooking up the new IBM PCjr isn't much harder than plugging in a lamp. But you should find it much more enlightening."[66] In this vision, although the Tramp had to cope with industrialization, or the incorporation of machinery into his otherwise "manual" life, a less serious transition would be necessary from the lamp and television to the computer. IBM used both the film *Modern Times* and the Tramp's comic nature to gently make fun of those resisting the transition from paper to computer networked communication, as well as to reinforce the notion of technological development as "inevitable," as something that humanity must deal with, and as a major part of American "evolution" or "progress."

But these images used only selective aspects of *Modern Times*. They did not, for example, tap Chaplin's critiques of industrialization by incorporating memorable depictions of the Tramp struggling with technology. Nor did they allude to situations in which the Tramp was literally and physically processed through a machine in the factory since doing so would have tapped into popular representations of technology as uncontrollable and as humanity's enemy. The campaign also omitted references to scenes in which the Tramp is stuffed with food and physically attacked by an out-of-control eating machine designed to keep workers at their posts even during their lunch hour. These images would have engaged Orwellian notions of technology as oppressing the worker by monitoring behavior and productivity, by increasing efficiency through overwork or making workers obsolete. IBM instead cultivated a particular representation of the Tramp, one that ultimately showed the character whimsically profiting from adaptation to technology. The campaign used the "signifiers of the Tramp" but not the "reference system in which the signification took place." Through this process, the campaign "recontextualized the Tramp in its own narrative, which supports computer technology itself" and "leaves the negative elements behind."[67] IBM capitalized on vague memories of Charlie Chaplin's Tramp as a friendly or happy character living in the age of industrialization, and perhaps hoped that most consumers would not remember, have seen, or have understood the critiques in *Modern Times*. Ultimately, through its advertising campaign, IBM "transformed Chaplin's tramp into a yuppie."[68]

According to Lord, Geller, Federico, Einstein, the advertising agency responsible for the IBM campaign, the choice of the Tramp was a deliberate attempt to deal with computer anxiety.[69] As a *Time* magazine article reported, the agency searched for "someone or something that would attack the problem of computer fright head on." In the process, the agency had also looked to the Muppets as an alternative and one that avoided the Tramp's "anti-technology sentiment." Ultimately, however, the agency's creative director, Thomas Mabley, decided that the Tramp "stands anxieties of technology on its head and would help the PC open up a new technology world for the non-technician." In other words, adopting an icon of technological ineptitude would make a positive statement about IBM's usability and friendliness.[70] By contrast, although Mabley did not explicitly mention it, bringing the Muppets into the campaign would not have served the goal of moving the computer to the profitable adult office market which IBM wanted to reach. The advertising executives were apparently correct in their choice. Public sentiment during the Tramp campaign was positive, and the campaign itself became a topic of news reports in what amounted to "free advertising" effect highly cultivated by advertisement (and political consulting) firms. By placing computing and networking technology in the context of industrialization, IBM successfully recast Charlie Chaplin (and his film *Modern Times*). A figure used to critique industrialization and of technology became not only a figure representing the positive gains new technologies offered, but also a figure that mocked and thereby undermined the anxieties about technological transitions. In the midst of the IBM battle with

Apple, the Tramp helped recast IBM as a corporation with personality and heart that produced usable technologies.

By using a historical figure, IBM's Tramp campaign placed new computing and networking technology in the context of older media technologies. In several Tramp advertisements, the PCjr was pictured on or near a stack of books bound with a leather belt and reminiscent of early 1900s schoolbooks. The juxtaposition underscored the greater power of the computer to store information and to serve as an educational tool.[71] The contiguity of the modern CPU and the schoolbooks suggested a continuum, insinuating a narrative of progress and evolution from the book to the computer. As scholars have long argued, such treatments of technology are "deeply entrenched in American culture" and "American national consciousness."[72] But many have also noted how problematic this progress narrative is.

For example, French theorist Bruno Latour has critiqued the modern notion of time "passing" as an "irreversible arrow" of progress. This progress narrative constructs an essentialized and static "past," "present," and "future": the past dies, the present lives, and the future becomes as we are drawn into ever-better and new existences.[73] Latour found this model problematic because it ignores the ways that ideas function transhistorically. The past does not die; instead, it exists in a mash-up with a variety of presents and futures to imbue objects with meaning. Latour proposed a revolutionary poly-temporality that would still allow us to measure time (in hours for example) for practical purposes, but would not look at time as progressing from a confused past to an enlightened future. Similarly, media scholar Joel Dinerstein has also noted the constructed-ness of "progress," which meant social progress when the United States was founded, but shifted to mean technological progress in recent decades.[74] Like Latour and Dinerstein, French philosopher Roland Barthes observes that the naturalization of concepts like progress occurs primarily through culture or "myth," which "transforms history into nature."[75] In the case of the IBM Tramp advertisement, placing the computer into the same historical trajectory as books makes the computer's individual history and the complex ways in which the technology emerged "evaporate," ignores the ways the past continues to operate in the constructions of the computer's multiple meanings in the present, and effectively naturalizes its place in a progress narrative. Through its use of the Tramp, "IBM attaches itself and its computer to the traditional American values—country, community, and family. The purchase of this totem allows one to enter this nostalgic mythical U.S. community." This recontextualization, however, not only denies Charlie Chaplin and the Tramp's representational past, but it also "denies the urban industrial past depicted."[76]

Other popular media representations in the mid-1980s worked in similar ways to help produce computer and networking technology as the next inevitable chapter in the history of human progress.[77] Represented as the result of a natural evolution, the computer simultaneously embodied the future and emblemated the past in that it was a stage in history even as it was also a radical step toward a new future. News media were particularly complicit in constructing computing technology as the next stage in a progress narrative. For example, one journalist wrote: "Since the invention of the primitive hand ax, humanity has turned to tools as a way of making life easier or work more productive.... Computer software is only the latest of those tools, and programmers are only beginning to understand the true potential of software."[78] Like the wheel or ax, the computer was enabling "civilization" to "progress" toward a predestined utopian future. Both the ax and computer are seen as beneficial here, even though both also have the potential to further war and destruction.

Networking was a major part of this progress narrative and these visions of ever-increasing efficiency.[79] A 1988 *New York Times* article opened with the "Pony Express, telegraph, telephone, overnight letters, computers and modems—a constant progression of communications technology, fueled by the belief that faster is better."[80] The networked computer was lauded by news media as the vehicle that would improve quality of life for users by allowing them to work where they wanted, free from urban congestion; they could be anywhere and still be productive agents in capitalist ventures. For example, a 1981 *Life* article stated:

> Computers, not granola or wood stoves, are the first real promise of an end to centuries of intensifying urbanization. Forty acres and a mule—and a desk-top terminal. With one of these babies there's very little anybody ever got paid to do in a downtown office that can't be executed just as efficiently in a farmhouse or cabin. Tie your computer in with the phones lines and you can conduct live interviews by computer and join conferences.[81]

The statement referenced one of the first reparation efforts to repay newly freed African Americans for their unpaid slave labor with plantations confiscated during the Civil War—forty acres and a mule, or the minimum the U.S. government deemed required to live at the time. Updating this allotment for the computing age, the article implied that networking was essential to contemporary life. By referencing slave liberation, the article also suggested computers could free workers from the slavery of the urban office and allow them to telecommute from the natural splendors of the suburban home.[82]

The increasing numbers of representations in news media and advertising that imagined computers as networking media and not merely stand-alone information storage devices often placed computers in the context of traditional, even artistic modes of communication. These images stripped potential anxieties about new technology by couching it in terms of great human achievement. One such advertisement taken out by Northern Telecommunications discussed a code invented by Benedictine monks to preserve Gregorian chants that formed the roots of contemporary musical notation. The advertisement's imagery showed Benedictine musical and textual notation alongside beautifully intricate Benedictine artwork on one page; continuing on the mirroring page, the images took the form of computerized analog and digital data. Below the image was written: "Merging the analog and digital codes is changing the way the world communicates."[83] This advertisement engaged notions of high and divine art to present computing as not a purely scientific endeavor. Advertisements such as this engaged technological progress narratives, implying that the computer was the latest step in human communication technology that found its roots as far back in "Western" history as Benedictine monks in 1066.

Perhaps in a space-clearing maneuver to differentiate themselves from bigger companies like IBM and Apple, other companies not only showed the computer as engaging the past and thereby driving the future, but also represented the computer as ahead of its time, as actually containing the future, or as an artifact from the future. A Toshiba advertisement in 1982 showed a computer cord as a road leading to a floppy disc under the headline "Take a trip to the future. Right now." Both the imagery and the text focused on networking technology and on the computer as a vehicle for travel. The text below the images reassured purchasers that they would no longer have to worry about "obsolescence," "standardization," or "compatibility" because a Toshiba would offer "futuristic capabilities."[84] Similarly, a 1985 AT&T advertisement campaign showed a computer CPU (central processing unit) open and glowing inside with the words "The AT&T PC. The Computer with the Future Built In" written on the side.[85] The advertisement assumed the reader understood and feared the exponentially increasing obsolescence that had already begun in the 1980s. According to this progress narrative and corporate advocates pushing images of the user-friendly and efficient networked computer, without the right machine, the user (or company) might get left behind.

In sum, IBM's Tramp campaign not only worked because the computer was increasingly characterized as a user-friendly asset to the common worker, but also because it placed the computer and networking technology into an established progress narrative. In representing the technology as key to America's future, as the next step in the evolution of human communication, and as actually embodying the future, advertisements and news media helped cast computing and networking as essential, natural, and as self-determined. Thereby, corporations also promoted themselves as friends of workers—not manufacturers of their replacements—as well as those holding the key to America's future.

Placing the computer and networking in the context of human evolution and the container of the future made it seem organic or natural. Yet, at the same time, it implied a "technological determinism," or "hard determinism," a world-view in which "inventions and technological systems have primary agency."[86] This notion was (and is) common and powerful in part, as Susan Douglas has noted, because technological determinism is a "rather large stream in the journalistic reservoir of how to explain societal change."[87] Technological determinism drove media to focus, for example, on the video games played by the Columbine shooter. Technological determinism erases the investment individual actors make in developing, regulating, consuming, and resisting, technology. As Andrew Ross writes, to "cleave to an epistemology of technological determinism" is also to "dismiss the capacity of people to make their own uses of new technologies."[88] This problem persists in public, policy, and academic debates. Instead of technological determinism, Siva Vaidhyanathan uses the term "techno-fundamentalism," meaning a "blind faith in technology as a simple solution to complex social and cultural issues," and suggests how it has "colored the discussions of public concerns ranging from pornography to piracy to national security."[89] To say this reductive concept was present and dominant in a variety of cultural locations—advertising, policy, news media, and academia—or to insinuate it is deeply intertwined with American national identity is not to say that it completely mistaken. And the stakes of technological determinism in, say, advertising, are not the same stakes as in policy. While technology is clearly important, it is not self-propelling. To assume it is obscures the ways technological change happens through human action, which, as Gitelman notes, can have disastrous consequences for policy decisions.[90] To solve the problem of technological determinism—to reinsert humans and their institutions into determinative positions—Douglas builds on work by Leo Marx and Merritt Roe Smith and ultimately advocates "soft determinism," a perspective in which "technologies are seen not as the prime movers, but as having some agency in the mix of how individuals, institutions, and political-economic systems respond to and shape technological change."[91] Policy decisions based on soft determinism would theoretically acknowledge the formative power of technology, but at the same time recognize that humans have the power to determine their own history in the ways they regulate technologies.

Governmental Incompetence and Pro-Business Policy

As in the early 1980s, so in the mid-1980s, U.S. government policymakers responded to the reality made, in part, through media representations. As French theorist Pierre Bourdieu has illustrated, the contest over meanings in the public sphere helps set the boundaries of the political debate.[92] Accordingly, those voices deemed legitimate by news media and governmental actors presented particular images of the internet that were then reified in policy spheres. In other words, popular filmmakers, journalists, internet and computer users, advertisers, industry executives, and members of Congress "spoke" to one another—debated in a sense in and through media—about what the internet was, what it was capable of, and what it should be. Clearly these voices neither agreed nor presented static visions of the internet. As dominant visions shifted, the ways policymakers envisioned internet technology's potential problems and solutions did, too. Insofar as progress was a goal to be realized, this would be possible only if the internet developed in the "right" way. In the early 1980s, the right way was imagined as involving direct government action to parent both the "teenaged" internet and its teenaged users and to help shape both into self-regulating citizen-subjects. Although more optimistic images of the internet rose in prominence in the mid-1980s in part due to advertisement campaigns like IBM's Tramp series, these campaigns by no means universally dispelled anxieties about computing and networking technologies. Cold War security and hackers concerns continued to receive news media and government attention.

By the mid-1980s, however, the internet and its users were increasingly imagined as "grown up," dissolving the rationale driving parental government involvement. Like news media, policymakers placed internet technology within a narrative in which it became a key to American progress. By associating themselves with the development and spread of computing technology, then, news media, corporations, and government agencies could cast themselves as serving the nation and as democratizing knowledge. They would be spreading a technology that would help users rather than one that individuals, like teenaged hackers, could use for their own selfish devices. In addition, by placing the internet within this progress narrative, policymakers helped legitimate notions presented in advertising. Individuals with symbolic capital, like credibility, prestige, or education, help legitimate particular ideas over others, and, in this sense, policymakers—with access to news media and policy decisions—helped shape mainstream assumptions and knowledge.[93]

Imagined as "adults," both the internet and its users were constructed in advertising, news media, and policy debates as vital to the U.S. economy and future productivity. During a series of economic recessions that hit the United States in the 1980s, economic threats posed by foreign countries—especially Japan, Germany, and the Soviet Union—increasingly became a policymaker focus.[94] A series of high-profile hacks in the late 1980s, along with government scandals (like the Iran-Contra affair) that involved computing technology helped cast the 1984 Computer Fraud and Abuse Act as a failure. The government was imagined as an incompetent parent, incapable of disciplining or securing the internet.[95] These events and Reagan conservatism in the mid-1980s helped produce the new "right" government action as a more hands-off policy.[96] This policy shift began with a federal lawsuit in 1981 that disbanded AT&T's century-long monopoly over the telephone industry, resulting in the creation of "Baby-Bells," or new providers and companies. With this reconfiguration of U.S. telecommunication policy, Reagan opened telephone and therefore internet providership to market forces. Reagan "carried this [deregulation] policy much further because the president and his advisors saw virtually all government regulation as anticompetitive."[97] Instead of focusing directly on internet security as it did in the first internet regulation, the state began to hand responsibility to corporate entities. In short, the government focused on protecting American economic dominance over the internet by protecting the American corporations newly deemed responsible for protecting internet security. This division of spheres was consistent with Reagan conservatism in that it kept market-making in the government's sphere, but left consumer regulation to corporations.

During the late 1980s, the number of news media reports about the internet in general skyrocketed.[98] Economic downturns were a major reason for this jump, as a debate erupted in policy and media spheres about whether other countries were threatening American command over computing technologies.[99] While technological dominance had become an icon of a healthy economy, news media explicitly noted the beginning of a new era of uncertainty in which American technological dominance was no longer a viable assumption.[100] And because American dominance in technology was no longer certain, American global dominance in general was also at risk. As the *Washington Post* put it in 1985, "the current growing sentiment is that technological momentum is the force that will determine whether America brightens or fades as an economic power.… This pace and pervasiveness of innovation throughout the [computing] industry has [*sic*] made technology as powerful an economic force as capital, labor and government regulations."[101]

To some extent, the threat of losing power stemmed from the notion that countries were "ganging up" on the United States to undermine its economic and technological prowess. For example, in a 1985 article titled "Germany is West's Worst Security Risk," the *Washington Post* reported that West Germany was the Soviet Union's leading supplier of Western, primarily American, technology. The article reported that between 1966 and 1982, Germany was responsible for half of the "probable high-tech leaks," which amounted to three times more leaks than engineered by the next highest country, Japan.[102] A popular nonfiction book entitled *The Cuckoo's Egg* (1989) reinforced this notion through its recounting of the discovery of a West German spy ring that fed information to the KGB.[103] Increasing transnational trade and global capital flows, as well as growing government cooperation were sources of wealth, but also threats to domestic and economic security. As this book also illustrates, in the late 1980s and early 1990s the internet was viewed as a major driver in these global shifts, as well as construed as a deterritorialized, post-national, and contested space over which states began vying for control. Beginning in the late 1980s, the U.S. government began identifying Germany, Japan, and of course the Soviet Union as its main rivals. This competition was particularly fierce with Japan in terms of technology production, and with France and Germany in terms of connectivity, as the latter two countries already had widespread computer connection systems (the Minitel in France and Bildschirmtext in Germany).

Because computing and the internet were understood as key to the future of the United States, recovering technological dominance and control of the technology market became a national priority. As focus shifted from security to the economy, the American worker was increasingly culturally constructed as a part of the computer and controller of the computer. The U.S. government also linked its technological research and development efforts with those in universities, investment communities and businesses, an approach considered new, or a "marked contrast to the industrial behavior as recently as a decade ago, when America's overall superiority in technology was unquestioned."[104] While this was perhaps true for technology as a whole, it is a historical overstatement about the internet in particular as the government linked with universities and corporations several decades before.[105]

President Reagan made securing the technology market one of his priorities, and in January of 1985, he met with Japanese Prime Minister Yasuhiro Nakasone in Los Angeles to discuss the computer industry and international economics. At the time, "many Americans accused Japan of launching an economic offensive against the United States."[106] Some argued that Japan was effectively protecting its domestic computer technology markets while simultaneously aggressively pursuing inroads into American markets.[107] As one *Washington Post* reporter remarked: "U.S. policymakers and several industry leaders say the fear that the growing economic success of Japan, the Pacific Rim countries and West Germany comes at the expense of U.S. industrial growth. Japan, in particular, has enjoyed impressive economic growth and competes with U.S. companies in the vital area of information technology."[108]

This anti-Japanese sentiment also pervaded American culture in the late 1980s and early 1990s. In the wake of a flurry of Japan-bashing books, "some bookstores created a section all on their own."[109] Part of this flurry was Michael Crichton's 1992 bestselling book, *Rising Sun*, which dramatized a Japanese corporation's plan to buy up U.S. technology companies made vulnerable by economic recession. In their "relentless drive for world domination," these corporations also "bought and sold American politicians and companies and made whores out of white women."[110] According to the *New York Times*, the book "catapulted the debate—who are the Japanese, and what do they want of us?—from remote think-tanks and C-SPAN into the popular culture."[111] The paper characterized the book as "spirited call for vigilance in the face of growing Japanese power."[112]

In an attempt to wrestle economic power back from Japan, Reagan explicitly made Japan's computing and networking markets targets of American economic policy. Telecommunications was considered especially important because of the perception that Japan was taking advantage of AT&T's break up to "flood" the United States with its technological products. This Japanese aggression in American markets was seen as compounded by its own closed-market strategy and reluctance to buy American-made products. According to the Reagan administration, this strategy "denies American companies access to a lucrative market in which they have a competitive advantage while Japanese companies have full run in the United States."[113] To make matters worse, in January of 1992, George H. W. Bush vomited during a state banquet in Japan and slumped over Japanese Prime Minister Miyazawa Kiichi's lap, and the episode was televised in the United States. In the aftermath, the Japanese prime minister remarked that American workers were "illiterate," "lacked a work ethic," and were themselves responsible for the U.S. economic downturns. The episode helped spur the already-present wave of anti-Japanese sentiment in policy and news media spheres and served as a "metaphor for the unraveling of America's Cold War dominance."[114]

The U.S. government began passing legislation designed to maintain its lead over communication technology. The main policy, the Omnibus Trade and Competitiveness Act of 1988, was based on a series of hearings and reports which took place or were produced between 1985 and 1988 and contained elements designed to help U.S. telecommunications corporations gain market shares and U.S. workers gain technical skills to increase their productivity.[115] The economic elements, specifically called the Telecommunications Trade Act and the Technology Competitiveness Act, were designed to enhance U.S. economic power in the telecommuting and computing markets by sanctioning Japanese firms and promoting U.S. firms. For example, the Telecommunications Trade Act improved enforcement of U.S. rights under trade agreements and strengthened America's ability to respond to what it viewed as foreign countries' harmful trade practices. The act stated that U.S. officials should "achieve improved market access for U.S. manufacturers of supercomputers and end predatory pricing activities of Japanese companies in the United States, Japan, and other countries"; officials were also to "monitor the efforts of U.S. manufacturers of supercomputers to gain access to Japanese markets while recognizing that Japan may continue to manipulate the government procurement process to maintain the market dominance of Japanese manufacturers."[116] Under the act, the president was explicitly directed to negotiate with Japanese firms on behalf of U.S. trade interests; the act also required the secretary of commerce to "study the competitiveness of the U.S. telecommunications industry" and advise Congress and the president "what actions might be necessary to preserve such competitiveness." Meanwhile, the Technology Competitiveness Act promoted U.S. firms within U.S. borders by establishing the National Institute of Standards and Technology, which was designed to help industries design, commercialize, and manufacture new technologies quickly. This act specifically mentioned the development of "fiber optics" and "advanced computing" technologies.[117]

Policies were designed not only to help corporations, but also to assist American workers, both present and future, in gaining technological skills. For example, the Education and Training for a Competitive America Act of 1988 gave the secretary of education up to $20 million annually to establish "eligible telecommunications partnerships for the development, construction, and acquisition of telecommunications facilities and equipment" in a variety of educational contexts. While some initiatives aimed to help schoolchildren, others focused on adults in order to "assist their entry into, or advancement in, high technology occupations or to meet the technological needs of other industries or business."[118] Moreover, the act authorized establishing partnerships between government and corporations and funded computing technology in libraries, thereby making it available to the public. Thus, policy initiatives in this period authorized the U.S. government not only to work protectively in international spheres to support U.S. computer technology corporations, but also to work domestically to facilitate the training of the American worker in computing and networking technologies.

A major idea supporting this legislation was that corporations were better able to retain control over technology and the technology market than the state and that they would thereby serve as an effective, albeit informal, arm of national defense. For example, the *New York Times* reported "A strong IBM serves the national interest by keeping the Japanese from invading the United States market with computers the way they did with autos and steel."[119] In this sense, IBM was a protector of the American economy and defender against economic invasions and should, therefore, be supported by the U.S. government.

A series of scandals involving the U.S. government and computing technology reinforced the view that the state should focus on economics and promoting corporations rather than more hands-on control of the internet it advocated in the early 1980s. For example, during the Iran-Contra scandal, the Tower Commission discovered hundreds of emails containing details of the scheme. The *Washington Post* reported that Robert McFarlane, Oliver North, and John Poindexter, who were "vaunted experts on security matters," mistakenly viewed computer-mediated messages as more secure than other types of messages and that they used "computer messages because they weren't sure that telephone calls would remain secret." The article mocked the three government officials by stating that one would think "the guardians of a nation's deepest national security secrets" would understand how computers work. The article ultimately concluded that the government's "lesson learned" was the value of computer knowledge and that "For the country's sake, it's probably fortunate that the National Security Council's leading lights proved to be dim bulbs on this point."[120] This sarcastic piece pointed out government incompetence with new networking technology, implying that post-Watergate fears of telephone security pushed government officials into a false sense of security in email communication. Although email existed since the 1970s, government officials were still unfamiliar with its security, and, in the case of the Iran Contra scandal, computer incompetence was a means of discovering other governmental deficiencies.

In the context of government incompetence, corporate security solutions like encryption programs became a focus of news media and policy debates. But encryption technology was not only necessary for national security; it was also a commodity for sale. Although the government was generally the main source of funding that produced security measures, most news reports focused on the ways corporations implemented or sold them and often called attention to the market advantage computer corporations gained from the use of government-funded technology.[121] For example, the *New York Times* noted that the new encryption technology was based on "techniques developed in the late 1970s by federally financed researchers at the Massachusetts Institute of Technology," but that the adoption also would provide security companies, in this case RSA Data Security, Inc., and the Digital Equipment Corporation, with a "competitive edge."[122] In effect, security fixes funneled potential profits toward private corporations and away from government institutions, even though federal funds enabled the fixes to begin with. This maneuver, which allowed the U.S. government to cast itself as proactively protecting the internet, also provided a way for it to shield itself from criticism or blame if and when the technology failed.

In sum, although the security anxiety dominant in the early part of the 1980s continued as a major part of public debate, from the mid-1980s to the early 1990s the focus on the destructive capabilities of computers and the internet began to shift toward their economic potentials. Rather than parenting the juvenile internet and internet user, the U.S. government became increasingly concerned with protecting American computer corporate interests in the increasingly globalized marketplace. This redirection, from security to economics and from the protection of users to the protection of corporations, was enabled by a discourse that imagined the computer moving out of teenager's bedroom and into the American workplace. The individualism and isolation previously stigmatized and identified with hacker-troublemakers became associated with economic productivity and identified with office workers efficiently laboring. This "productive adult" user was imagined as an office worker capable of disciplining the computer and computer networks in ways that would serve the state and its economy. The productive adult user figure represented the user longed for in the political and news media debates in the wake of *WarGames*. As part of a tool-user combination, in news media, advertising, and government constructs, or as a component in an "assemblage," to use Deleuze and Guattari's term, the productive adult user figure overcame popular cultural ideas of machines oppressing humanity.[123] Once the anthropomorphized computer was disciplined and squarely under the adult user's control, users became self-protectors rather than potential victims.

As a goofy adult, the Tramp in the IBM advertising campaign functioned as a stand-in between the teenager and the adult user. The Tramp worked because he linked new technology to the past so that economic change looked familiar, funny, and awkward, and ultimately helpful and non-threatening. Focusing on the inevitability of new technology and acknowledging the discomfort in adapting to it, the campaign reinforced the view that the transition was possible and profitable for both individuals and the nation. Inclusion of computing and networking into a national narrative of progress and naturalized technological change presented the computer as a stage in history, even as it was also understood as a radical step toward a new future. Inserted into this established progress narrative of technology, the computer-human-network assemblage was cast as instrumental in helping America retain global economic dominance. In keeping with Reagan's defederalization policies, the government recast itself as the protector of internet corporations rather than of the internet itself. In the hands of business and disciplined by productive adults, the computer and internet became tools integrally linked to national progress.

3

From Computers to Cyberspace

Virtual Reality, the Virtual Nation, and the CorpoNation

In 1996, economist, techie, and writer Carl Malamud teamed up with one of the inventors of the internet, Vint Cerf, to set up the Internet World's Fair.[1] Called the "most ambitious undertaking on the Internet to date" by *Newsweek* magazine, this fair had over 5 million visitors from 172 countries, garnered over $100 million in contributions from a variety of industry and governmental sources, and received letters of support from a dozen governmental elites like Bill Clinton and Boris Yeltsin.[2] The fair changed the infrastructure of the internet through its establishment of the "Internet Railroad," a global networking backbone that used trans-oceanic cables to substantially increase connectivity around the world.[3] Each participating country had its own "electronic theme pavilion" or website, which could feature events such as concerts and art exhibitions or contain information about the country, its government, and its people. But the fair was also open to individuals from any country who wanted to establish sites. As a result, some pavilions were more complex than others, ranging from the official German pavilion, which claimed to be "more than Wurst and Kraut" and featured web pages on many topics including German "Arts & Culture," "Media," "Science and Technology," and "The Virtual Pet Cemetery," which was (and is) the world's first "on-line pet mortuary."[4] Although the fair's participants came from a variety of places, the entrance to the fair was an online "Central Park," a digital recreation of the main park in New York City. As a transnational event, with material effects on the internet's infrastructure, the 1996 Internet World's Fair helped literally and figuratively to construct the internet as a *global* space. Paradoxically, however, imagined as an English-language, democratically constructed space entered through Central Park, the fair also helped literally and figuratively to configure the internet as an *American* space. This chapter investigates why this seemingly contradictory representation of the internet—as simultaneously global and American—made sense in the mid-1990s.

One significant factor was internet technology itself, which along with its best-known hypertext system, the "World Wide Web," functioned as an icon of globalization. For reasons discussed later, news media, popular culture producers, policymakers, corporate institutions, and academics imagined the world as not only increasingly interconnected in the 1990s, but also increasingly organized in a new global order that operated independently of natural or state boundaries. In this "new global order" or "globalization" discourse, academics in particular tended to view the state as being in decline, becoming increasingly irrelevant, archaic, and inadequate to dealing with shifts in global power brought on by late capitalism. The corresponding view was that the corporation, imagined as ideally suited to deal with globalization, was on the rise.[5] Academic debates and news media in the 1990s envisioned the internet as a global, virtual marketplace, as an engine and product of globalization, as both its driver and its destination.[6] In these visions, internet technology that stretched around the globe was liberated from the state and, therefore, a major contributor to the perceived loss of governmental power. Thus, functioning as an icon of globalization—paradoxically both its driver and its product—the internet tapped fears of anarchy and the loss of government control that emerged in the late 1980s and were increasingly dominant in the 1990s.[7]

At the same time, though, spatial metaphors in news media and U.S. policy initiatives not only helped contribute to the construction of the internet as a global phenomenon, but also as a distinctly American one. Enabled by technological advances like Mosaic, which brought images to the internet in 1993, U.S. news media in the late 1980s and early 1990s increasingly represented the internet as a space through which one moved instead of a computer network one utilized. Metaphors such as "virtual reality," "new democratic frontier," and "information superhighway" became dominant in news media and policy debates. Although these visions were different, they did similar work in abstracting the internet, conceptually removing it from the hardware, software, wires, servers, and other infrastructures that made networking possible.[8] Such abstractions had ramifications. Just as the U.S. government facilitated and pushed settlement of the western frontier and the lunar landing, so it pushed exploration and ultimately economic control of what it imagined as new frontier of global space and marketplace.[9] During most of the 1990s, the U.S. government retained controls over the internet that had been in place since the 1960s, such as the assignment of internet addresses and domain names (e.g. .com, .edu). This meant that, unlike websites in other countries, those based in the United States would not have to use country identifiers after web addresses (e.g., .uk for United

Kingdom). These state practices and culturally forged links between internet and nationalist American frontier narratives meant that cyberspace in the 1990s was cultivated as, and presumed to be, both a new frontier space and, simultaneously, an "American virtual nation." This enactment of American imperial power over the medium was a "new type of colonization," for "one way to colonize public terrain is to forget that it is a shared space, shared with others who may have different needs, different concerns, different expectations than oneself."[10]

Major internet corporations participated in this Americanization by functioning as what I call "corpoNations," corporations that embodied the nation and served as its cultural carriers into online spaces. For example, not only did America Online incorporate national identity in its name, but its software also served as a nationally bound entrance to the internet. As the internet became increasingly corporate in the mid-1990s—websites dedicated to commercial-use rose "from 4.6 percent of the total in 1993 to 50 percent by early 1996"—corpoNations functioned as stand-ins for the diminished state, even while they were imagined as drivers of globalization that undercut state power.[11]

W.W.W.: Icon of the New Global World Order

The early 1990s was a period of increasing public attention to both the internet and "globalization." Indeed, during this period, the internet became one prevailing metaphor through which news media, popular culture producers, academics, and policymakers understood globalization. Imagined by these sources as both a product and driver of globalization, internet technology itself was understood in similar utopian and dystopian terms as globalization. Although news media did not consistently feature the transnational character of the internet until the 1990s, the internet was in actuality transnational almost from the beginning. That is, while internet technology technically originated in the United States with the Department of Defense's creation of ARPANET in 1969, during its debut at a conference in Washington, D.C. in 1972,[12] Vint Cerf, one of the original designers of ARPANET, founded the International Networking Group (INWG) with representatives from England and France. This group wanted to create an "international network of networks,"[13] and they did, indeed, accomplish this goal as early as 1974, when a satellite system linked computers in Britain, France, Germany, Italy, Norway, and the United States. Thus, only five years after its invention the internet was already a transnational (albeit Western) technology.[14] For Americans, the first international internet connections were to London in

1973. Queen Elizabeth began emailing as early as 1976. She, not a U.S. president, was the first state leader to do so. By 1987, twelve countries were online, and by 1990, thirty four were connected, although connections were primarily among university campuses and government institutions.[15]

Despite these early transnational connections, the internet was not generally represented as global outside of governmental arenas until the mid-1990s, when reports about the "World Wide Web" began to dominate news media.[16] Although the two terms are often used synonymously today, the "Web" and the internet are not the same. The "Web" is a hypertext system that *runs on* the internet to link sites. Developed in 1991 by Tim Berners-Lee and Robert Cailliau at European Organization for Nuclear Research (CERN) in Switzerland, the system introduced many tools standard to today's internet. The Web "made it possible to retrieve and contribute information from and to any computer connected via the internet."[17] The development of the Web was one of the most formative events in the internet's history. Internet historian Manuel Castells called it "the main event that led to the constitution of the internet in its current form: that is, as a global network of computer networks made user-friendly by the World Wide Web."[18] Before the Web, the internet was used by few people; those who did, used it as a "system for the exchange of text messages." After the Web, it became "a way to publish information, to incorporate multimedia formats, and to quickly and easily connect previously discrete clusters of information."[19]

While the World Wide Web helped construct the internet as an icon of globalization, because the internet was always global already, the shift represented not a structural but a cultural change. News coverage of the internet increased substantially in the wake of the Web's emergence in 1991; at the same time, other metaphors or terms for the internet—information superhighway, cyberspace, and computer with modem—began to decline. In effect, then, not only was the Web a primary focus of news coverage in the mid-1990s; it also shaped news media understandings of the internet. My survey of major U.S. news sources shows that reports in the *New York Times,* the *Washington Post, USA Today,* and *LA Times* (combined) about the World Wide Web increased from one story in 1992 to 84 stories in 1994 and then to 1,940 stories in 1996; reports about the internet increased from 24 in 1992 to 982 in 1994 and to 5,329 in 1996.[20]

This period—the period leading up to the Telecommunications Act of 1996, the first major revision to telecommunications policy since the 1930s—saw the largest single increase in coverage of the internet until the "Y2K" scandal and the burst of the "dot.com bubble" at the end of the century.[21] Alongside newspaper coverage, reports on the major TV networks

(ABC, CBS, NBC, and CNN) increased 600 percent between 1994 and 1996, from 17 to 104.[22]

Thus, in a moment of increased news media attention on the internet itself, coverage of the name "World Wide Web" and its origins in Switzerland focused news media attention on the nationally neutral and already global nature of the internet.[23] Because it simplified the searching process, providing easier access to online information, news reports represented the Web as a major driving force in the popularization of the internet. It was credited with significantly increasing the number of internet users globally, with the surging amount of content available online, and with the increasing number of corporations interested in investing in the internet.[24] In the first three years after its development—that is, between 1991 and 1994— World Wide Web traffic grew tenfold annually; thereafter, the number of worldwide internet users doubled from 20 million in 1995 to 40 million in 1996—and that the number was expected to double again by the end of 1997, which nearly happened.[25] At the same time, the number of networks connected through the internet also doubled, from 48,000 in 1995 to more than 95,000 in 1996.[26] In a 1996 article about the Web, *U.S. News & World Report*

Lexis-Nexis Graph -Newspaper Coverage
Searched headline, lede, highlight, and body for: ("computer highway," "computer superhighway," "information highway," "information superhighway,") "internet," "cyberspace," "world wide web," & "computer and modem"

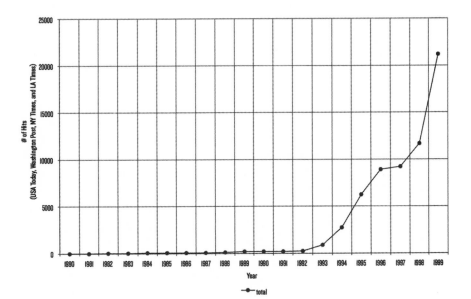

stated that "every 30 seconds, nearly 20 Internet novices log on to the global network" and that "every 10 minutes a new corporate or academic network is added to the maze of digital byways."[27] News reports presented corporations, especially U.S.-based media corporations, as racing to get control over access to the internet.[28]

Emphasis on the World Wide Web and on the internet's reach represented the internet as a technology that would draw the world together, as a force of globalization. The very structure of the internet made it a logical site of and metaphor for economic and cultural changes during this period. Because the technology was initially conceptualized as a Cold War weapon by the U.S. DOD, the internet was designed to be decentralized in order to ensure that it could operate after an attack to any one military headquarter.[29] The internet, as a rhizomatic, "nonhierarchical and noncentered network," was understood as a model for how the post-globalization world would function.[30]

But what exactly was globalization? American Studies scholar Melani McAlister describes it as a "phenomenon" with a variety of "symptoms and engines" including the "increased role of international organizations like the

Lexis-Nexis Graph -Newspaper Coverage
Searched headline, lede, highlight, and body for: ("computer highway," "computer superhighway," "information highway," "information superhighway,") "internet," "cyberspace," "world wide web," & "computer and modem"

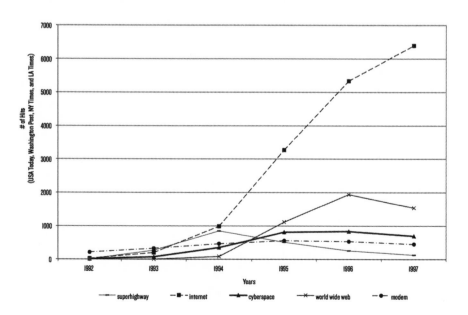

WTO and IMF; the movement of transnational capital and the continual relocation of production to chase lower labor costs; the extraordinarily rapid global flow of information, culture, and ideas enabled by new technologies like the internet; and the development of diasporic communities as loci of emotional affiliation."[31] In this description, globalization is both a cause and an effect, a highly complex process that involves economic, political, social, cultural, and technological shifts. Economic engines often have primacy in discussions of globalization. As scholars Michael Hardt and Antonio Negri argue in their foundational text, *Empire,* globalization was part of economic transformations that began occurring in capitalist countries in the 1970s as "modernization" became "postmodernization." In this model, modernization is coterminous with "industrialization," or the shift from agricultural production to industry; postmodernization corresponds with "information-alization," or the shift from industry to services and information-processing.[32] While Hardt and Negri acknowledge the multiple historical layers in the history of capital, they see post-1970s globalization as distinctly new. Any similarities to the past, they argue, should not "blind us to the rupture or shift in contemporary capitalist production and global relations of power" that produce a "properly capitalist order" and bring together economic and political power.[33] Yet, even as economics are clearly a major part of globalization, globalization in itself is not only an economic phenomenon. Rather, it involves the complex and growing interdependence and integration of the world's societies, cultures, and governments, as well as its corporations and markets. Moreover, in Hardt and Negri's model, the "unmooring" of "communication points in the network" is credited with "intensifying the process of deterritorialiation."[34] Much of the contemporary literature about globalization is concerned with a number of elements, including globalization's cultural, political and economic impact.

In contrast to these more contemporary views, in the 1990s policymakers and academics focused more narrowly on globalization as a cause for declining in state power in the face of a newly global economy. States "would melt away, their citizens lured back form archaic party-based politics to the 'natural' agora of the digitized marketplace."[35] For example, for former U.S. Secretary of Labor Robert Reich, globalization meant the formation of a global economy. He wrote that as "almost every factor of production—money, technology, factories, and equipment—moves effortlessly across borders, the very idea of a national economy is becoming meaningless." In his view of the future, there would be "no national products or technologies, no national corporations, no national industries," and there would "no longer be national economies at least as we have come to understand the concept."³⁶ Globalization, therefore, was imagined as both facilitating and requiring a new global world order in which nation-states declined in opposition to rising transnational forces like the United Nations (UN), the North Atlantic Treaty Organization (NATO), and the Group of Eight (G8).³⁷ President George H.W. Bush propagated this notion in his January 1991 national address announcing the invasion of Iraq:

> We have before us the opportunity to forge for ourselves and for future generations a new world order—a world where the rule of law, not the law of the jungle, governs the conduct of nations. When we are successful—and we will be—we have a real chance at this new world order, an order in which a credible United Nations can use its peacekeeping role to fulfill the promise and vision of the U.N.'s founders.³⁸

In addition to the rise of transnational organizations, perceived breakdowns in state power corresponded with the ascendance of international corporations. As academics in the 1990s increasingly maligned the government as irrelevant, absent, or inadequate to deal with global capital flows, they imagined corporations as better suited.³⁹ These academics noted that whereas before the 1990s, most public and private industries corresponded roughly with nation-states, thereafter, as corporations became more powerful, they also became more globally oriented and actively worked to avoid being tied down by the state and its regulations (e.g., labor laws, union activity, taxation). Because state borders did not restrict transnational and multinational corporations, these corporations could "exploit the different economic and political conditions among the current nation-states" and "ignore the borders to their own advantages."⁴⁰ Although they could ignore *state* (governmental) boundaries, these corporations could ignore neither *national* (cultural) boundaries nor, in particular, language boundaries. Consumers and audiences had to understand—both linguistically and culturally—a corporation's products. The boundaries of nation-states were, then, theoretically replaced by the boundaries of "geolinguistic markets," like the "Middle East" and "Latin America."⁴¹

Some academics in the mid-1990s argued that global corporations still needed state infrastructures for security and to maximize profits. Nonetheless, corporations found operating outside state controls more profitable, and, therefore, transnational corporations worked to unravel the state.⁴² Others argued that the nation-state was a tool of global business, but that the nation remained culturally powerful. The nation-state was "thoroughly appropriated by transnational corporations" and persisted only as a "nostalgic and sentimental myth that offers an illusion of classless organic community of which everyone is an equal member." Where global corporations operated under the banner of "American" and stood for "America" abroad, corporations like Disney traded on and therefore supported the myth of the nation.[43] Thus, although the *state* was imagined as in decline, the *nation* was imagined as continuing to be a powerful cultural construct, one through which other identities—like religious, regional, and political—could be understood, and one that could provide a sense of historical continuity in light of the imagined stateless future.

In addition to corporations, academics in the mid-1990s also imagined media technologies—computer networking in particular—as engines of globalization, especially its structural, economic, and cultural components.[44] Because it connected individuals across time and space in new ways, the internet was imagined as a primary driver in the globalization of culture, including homogenizing, fracturing, localizing, and/or hybridizing existing cultures.[45] As Lisa Gitelman has noted, because of its flexibility and its potential to be in continual flux, World Wide Web technology in particular helped configure the internet as both global and timeless, and, as such, as able to support a new global world order in the wake of globalization.[46] Likewise, in his 1995 bestseller *Being Digital*, Nicholas Negroponte wrote that the internet would "flatten organizations, globalize society, decentralize control, and help harmonize people."[47] Discussing the effects new communication technology would have on global culture, Marshall McLuhan speculated about the "global village," a (then) future reality in which the world would be connected by electronic nervous systems.[48] He believed that computer networking technology itself, in addition to the content available via the technology, would fundamentally change the ways individuals interacted, thought, and functioned within their nations and social organizations. He also argued that people would evolve because of their relations to and through informational systems.[49] Academics like McLuhan, who "correctly" predicted the future of computing network technology were and are influential forces in the production of ideas about of globalization and the internet. Indeed, predictions by individuals like McLuhan stood in for the internet's history, meaning that "intellectuals of previous generations" and "their role as prophets or architects of what is to come" replaced historical understandings of what actually came. This "history of prognostication" was shallow and inaccurate, obscuring the actual history of the complex processes and range of actors participating in the formation of a technology.[50] Visions of how the internet would drive globalization obscured historical understandings of how it actually did or did not.

This historical obfuscation has in part led to a sense in academic communities that the internet "failed"—and failed, in particular, in liberating oppressed peoples. Focusing on the internet as a decentralized technology, academics saw it as a driver of political reorganization in the 1990s, which, some believed, would lead to a new and more democratic world order. In their review of the 1990s literature, internet scholars Jack Goldsmith and Tim Wu argue that the internet was envisioned in that historical moment as being able to "challenge the authority of nation-states and move the world to a new, post-territorial system."[51] The assumption was that the internet would change the political status quo by replacing outmoded democratic practices like voting, for example, with "flexible, consensus-driven rules, created by informal communities organized by interest and expertise rather than the arbitrary condition of location." In particular, "internationalists" dreamed that the internet would cause governmental power to shift "downward from nation-states toward individuals and private groups," and thereby "eliminate the parochialism of territorial legalism." This new world order would become the manifestation of a transnational, hybrid dream in which international, non-governmental organizations would assemble and merge the finest governing methodologies from around the world. This new world order would "not only clear up confusion and conflict, but also wash clean the prejudice and ignorance hiding in the basement of national governments."[52]

But as some scholars noted, instead of being the means for the creation of a cyber-utopia, the internet as an arm and product of globalization could also usher in a imperialist dystopia or serve as a domestic threat. In much of the 1990s literature, "media serve as instruments of Western cultural imperialism and mature finance capital, creating a global village of increasingly Americanized consumers."[53] The 1995 Oklahoma City bombing was a particular moment of news media focus on the internet as a container of dangerous information. After the bombing, many reports focused on how the bombers researched bomb construction online.[54] One article reported, "The yellow-brick road to a dazzling future of instant information and global interconnection is now a dank pit of sleaze, murder and terror. 'People would be shocked to know what is out there' in the Internet's 'dark back alleys,' Sen. Herbert Kohl said somberly."[55] Similarly, Leslie David Simon, a senior policy scholar at the Woodrow Wilson International Center for Scholars, noted that "parents and teachers were expressing concern about the amount of pornography easily available to children on the Internet," as well as citing well-publicized "cases of electronic stalking by child molesters," "the use of the Internet by militias and hate groups," and "the killings at Columbine High School in

Colorado in the spring of 1999" as all making "many people aware of the violent content available to anyone on the Internet."[56]

Part of this anxiety about the internet stemmed from the same decentralized structure that made it an imagined model for globalization. The internet seems uncontainable by governmental forces. In contrast to its ability to oversee other communications means, such as the telephone or postal system, the U.S. government could not monitor online activity. As journalist Steven Levy noted, "The Internet has no president, no police and no blueprints for organized growth" and was imagined as containing a "destructive ideology that celebrates the decentralized, semi-anarchic structure of the internet."[57] In other words, news media still viewed the internet as a domain for individuals with non-mainstream persuasions and as a hotbed for dangerous activity. To make matters worse, news media presented the U.S. government as being unable to keep pace on the treadmill of technological developments.[58] Churn, or the time it takes for a technology to become obsolete, was therefore an issue raised by news media.[59] For example, one *U.S. News & World Report* article reported: "For the next few years, anything you buy will be obsolete two years later. Technology is like a moving bus that just won't stop."[60] Thus, the internet became a national vulnerability, a way for foreign nations to infringe on American economic dominance.[61] A front-page *New York Times* article from 1996 positioned the internet as a major participant in America's impending economic decline and suggested that Japan, Europe, Russia, India, and China would step into positions of economic dominance.[62] Here the internet became evidence for an already well-established argument that the United States was in decline and that other world powers were in ascendancy.

It all came together on the big screen: globalization, the internet, the rise of corporate power, the downfall of the state, the dangers and potentials of online spaces. As illustrated in previous chapters, notions of computing and networking were not only produced in news media, academic and political debates, but also by and through popular culture. Film featured computer networking increasingly throughout the 1990s, and in this decade the internet became a part of James Bond films.[63] In both *Golden Eye* (1995) and *Tomorrow Never Dies* (1997) struggles for control over the internet are central to the storylines.[64]

In *Golden Eye*, for example Bond (Pierce Brosnan) needs the internet to dominate his foe because controlling the internet means controlling the Golden Eye, a powerful satellite weapon that emits electromagnetic pulses that can disable electronic devices. With the United States already so reliant on computers by the mid-1990s, the Golden Eye weapon seemed both plausible and frightening. Bond and his enemy team up with computer hackers, with the female hacker, of course, on Bond's team. The two battle throughout the film both on- and offline, reinforcing ways that cyberspace conflicts participate in material political conditions of dominance. The first Bond film produced after the fall of the Soviet Union, *Golden Eye* reinterpreted and reinvigorated the series for the post–Cold War era.[65] In it, this historical transition is dramatized overtly. During the opening credits, women bathed in communist red use hammers to destroy stars, sickles, and statues of Lenin and Stalin, thereby making way for a new villain. In the post-Soviet era and in the context of globalization, this villain was not state bound. Corporate assets and Mafia connections became means for wielding geopolitical power and funding terrorism. Operating transnationally in Russia and Cuba and with their headquarters in armored train, Bond's foe is in perpetual motion. The villain's only stable "space" is that which is located online. Thus, it is by hacking into the system that Bond saves the world. In the on-screen battle between nation-less terrorists and seemingly obsolete arms of the state, Bond trounces the villain and rehabilitates state power by working as an arm of the British government and collaborating with a CIA agent to stop the global terrorists.

In the following Bond film, *Tomorrow Never Dies*, 007 teams up with a (female, of course) Chinese government agent and a CIA agent against a transnational media corporation called the Carver Media Group Network. In an effort to expand corporate holdings and news market coverage for his company, the evil media mogul, Elliot Carver (Jonathan Pryce), tries to initiate war between China and the United Kingdom. Like Bill Gates, Carver operates outside state control to interfere with international affairs; however, in the Bond world, states combine powers to fight this transnational corporation. The film also comments on the technological and the political climate of the later 1990s. For example, when the Carver Corporation releases new software deliberately programmed with bugs to "force people to upgrade," this plot twist sardonically plays on the concerns over obsolescence during the period. Mimicking democratic rhetoric, particularly as expressed by then-President George W. Bush, Carver pronounces that electronic media are a force for good, resulting in "higher understanding" amongst the world's peoples and "launching" a "new world order." For the villain, "words are the new weapons and satellites the new artillery." Internet iconography permeates the film. In the opening credits, female bodies made of digital code smash through screens.

In these Bond films, images of both the internet and of globalization dovetailed with those in academic scholarship, news media, and policy

debates. Both the internet and globalization were simultaneously dangerous and desirable, and the internet was a site for and a player in the contest
between the state and transnational corporate power. While including the
internet updated the James Bond genre's well-established focus on technology, these films also participated in a larger shift in discursive constructions
of the technology. The internet itself became both a weapon and a battle-
field, control over which became a major struggle in the plot. As a sphere of
conflict, internet technology itself became "a terrain that must be dominated
before it can be put to use."[66] Following this logic, the film makes Bond not
a hacker-hero himself, but the brawn and brains that allow the hacker on his
side to work. The villain meanwhile became the corporation rather than a
country in these 1990s Bond films. Because corporations were not contained
by the state, but still powerful and representative of the nation, corporations
were doubly threatening and, unlike Bond's previous Soviet nemeses, uncontainable through familiar political channels of election, diplomacy, or war.

In sum, the logic of globalization that dominated academic, news media,
popular culture, and policy spheres in the 1990s and the technological emergence of the World Wide Web helped construct the internet as an icon of
globalization. As such, it was imagined in academic and political spheres in
particular not only as a product of the shift toward a new world order, but
also as holding causal power in that shift. As globalization and the internet
merged conceptually, news media, academics, and popular culture producers imagined the internet and globalization in binary terms. They stressed
the internet utopian or dystopian potential as part of a process that would
destabilize the state or as one that would embolden and empower the transnational corporation; as a means for connecting individuals around the
globe or as way for them gain access to potentially dangerous information.

Hardware Erasure: Constructing the Virtual Frontier

As the internet became an icon of globalization in media and academic
works, it also became an alternative universe or a virtual reality, separate
from the physical world of computers and wires, endless and overwhelming in its complexity. Although such images certainly existed previously,
they reached a new dominance in the 1990s.[67] Between 1988 and 1995, *Time*
magazine published six cover stories about the internet that demonstrate the
significant cultural shift between representations of the internet as located in
computers and as liberated from them. The 1980s cover images represented
the internet as located in or accessed through a computer, but cover images
after 1990 showed the internet as an abstraction, as disconnected from

screens, central processing units (CPUs) and other hardware.[68] For example, a 1988 issue on "Computer Viruses" featured a large computer monitor
and CPU which were covered by cartoon "virus" molecules that appeared
to be eating the computer.[69] This materialist representation of the computer
itself and the anthropomorphized image of the computer virus were typical of the 1970s and 1980s. In contrast, the cover of a 1995 issue featuring a
story entitled "Welcome to Cyberspace" represented the internet as infinite
doorways made vaguely of silicon circuitry extending inward to the horizon.[70] Both the image and the issue title presented the internet as an infinite space, an alternative sphere, or a gateway that a user entered through
a number of different avenues, none of which explicitly involved telephone
wires or modems—even though these were still necessary to connect to the
internet. The contents of this alternative space were not explicitly revealed.
Instead, the series of doors disappeared gradually into a white circle, suggesting that enlightenment (or transcendence or God?) was within the internet.
While the earlier *Time* magazine image presented the internet as a computing activity, the later one conflated computing with representations of virtual
reality and implied that computer networking provided access to a space that
humans could enter and potentially reach enlightenment.

Imaginings of the internet and virtual reality blended together so completely in mass media in the late 1980s and early 1990s that reports on virtual
reality almost always involved the internet.[71] This is not to say that users for-
got that computing was real. Virtuality was always "a construct more of the
imagination than of technology," but one "profoundly invested in the fantasy
that such substitutions might take place."[72] The connection between virtual
and real helped reconfigure the internet as a "cyberspace," a term coined by
William Gibson in his 1984 dark science fiction novel, *Neuromancer*. In this
book, the main character, Case, is an "interface cowboy," or a man who "jacks
in" to a "conceptual hallucination" and "non-space" made of high-definition,
graphical data. This "cyberspace" is a virtual space into which individuals
insert their consciousness, suggesting that the mind could (and should) be
deterritorialized from the body. Power over virtual reality means power over
reality since as nearly everything is networked and connected to cyberspace.
In turn, exclusion from cyberspace means powerlessness. When Case is prevented from entering cyberspace by "mycotoxin," a chemical that renders his
central nervous system unable to connect, he is trapped in his body (or his
"case"), cannot earn a living, and becomes severely depressed. Once repaired,
cyberspace liberates Case from his body and allows him to battle the primary
villain, which, as in the James Bond films discussed above, is a multinational corporation. Empowered by a dystopian free market, the corporation

is ultimately more powerful than any traditional nation-state.[73] Thus, ideas about virtual reality and the internet not only merge, but also blend with notions of the internet as driving globalization and shifting power away from the state and toward transnational corporations.

Gibson's vision was especially important in the conceptual formation of the internet because his book became a cult classic read by individuals who would become powerful voices in articulating the idea of the internet as a new frontier.[74] In 1990, John Perry Barlow—science fiction fan, cyberspace-activist, author of the "Declaration of Cyberspace Independence," and founder of the Electronic Frontier Foundation (EFF)—applied the term "cyberspace" to computer networking technologies of the time, which were increasingly merging telephone and computing technologies. As was the case with the early images of computer networking, news media representations of virtual reality that emerged in the late 1980s and early 1990s connected cyberspace to the countercultural movements of the 1960s and 1970s, and specifically to LSD trips and to other "out-of-body experiences," valued by countercultural internet users and builders.[75] The techie magazine *Mondo 2000,* which eventually became *Wired* magazine, made this connection explicitly when it published Barlow's article "Being in Nothingness," in which he recounted his first visit to virtual reality in 1990.[76]

While the conflation of the computer, the internet, and virtual reality was increasingly present in popular culture in the early and mid-1990s, it reached what some view as its Aristotelian perfection with the 1999 film the *Matrix.*[77] The mid-1990s marked a cultural fascination with the internet as seen in the number of major films released in the period, including *Johnny Mnemonic* (1995), *The Net* (1995), and *Hackers* (1995), as well as *Golden Eye* and *Tomorrow Never Dies.* While these set the stage for the *Matrix,* the 1999 film, regarded by many as groundbreaking, had an important precedent in *The Lawnmower Man* (1992).[78] Lambasted by some reviewers for its derivative plot and excessive demonization of technology, *The Lawnmower Man* nevertheless drew high box office pulls of $8 million in the first week.[79] Reviews credited this success to its special effects, which, according to one, "provide at least the first public glimpse inside an imagined VR world, what computer wizards call 'cyberspace.'"[80] Both the film and its reviewers actively helped formulate the connection between virtual reality and the internet made graphic in the *Time* magazine covers.

The Lawnmower Man's plot centers on Dr. Lawrence Angelo (Pierce Brosnan), a scientist working for the U.S. government, who uses virtual reality and a "neurotropic" drug cocktail to transform Jobe Smith (Jeff Fahey), a gardener with a cognitive disability, into a godlike and hyperintelligent individual. Although Dr. Angelo initially works with Jobe using a video game version of virtual reality in his basement, the scientist eventually moves Jobe to a government laboratory, where Jobe can jack into a networked virtual reality through a "full cyber suit," which permits its wearer's endocrine and nervous system to be "in sync with the computer system." Although it is a "virtual" space into which Jobe enters, it can affect "real" space as well as the biology of the human mind. Dr. Angelo can change Jobe's actual brainwave patterns by sending imaginary lightning bolts into his virtual brain to unlock his latent human potential.

In the film, virtual reality technology is represented as unstoppable in its global adoption and as a natural or organic evolution in communication technology. As Jobe says, virtual reality technology would "grow just like the telegraph grew into the telephone, as the radio into TV. It will be everywhere … by 2001 there won't be a person on the planet who isn't hooked into it." Tapping counter-culture iconography, the designers of the film's computer interface made it into a trippy, colorful, boundless, kaleidoscopic space in which images, symbols, and letters zoom, shape-shift, collid, and merge with human bodies. Describing the network in exploratory terms, Dr. Angelo says, "Sometimes I feel I've discovered a new planet… I'm only on the shore of one of its vast continents." Jobe describes the experience similarly: "Virtual reality isn't just a simulation. It's a whole other world. An electronic dimension. The utopia men have dreamed of for 1,000 years." In the end, Jobe disappears physically from the "real" world, leaving an empty cybersuit as he transforms into "pure energy" in the mainframe computer's virtual reality program in the "final stage" in his evolution. While Dr. Angelo attempts to contain Jobe by taking the mainframe off-line, Jobe hacks into the internet and uses it to travel into and explore global virtual space. In its emphasis on the internet as a parallel world, the film helped characterize the space as infinite, yet comparably complex to the physical world.

Notions of the internet as a cyberspace and a virtual reality present in works of popular culture like *Neuromancer* and *The Lawnmower Man* were enhanced by real-world technological developments such as Mosaic, which emerged in 1993, the year after *The Lawnmower Man*'s release. Designed by Marc Andreesen and Eric Bina at the University of Illinois's National Center for Supercomputer Applications, Mosaic was a ground-breaking program that had "an advanced graphics capability, so that images could be retrieved and distributed over the Internet, as well as a number of interface techniques imported from the multimedia world."[81] Because Mosaic was so visual and easy to use, "for most people, for business, and for society at large, the Internet was born in 1995."[82] By making the internet visual instead of just textual, Mosaic made the internet seem more like a space into which users could transport themselves and in which they could project their personalities through their websites. This development shifted the material properties of the internet and thereby helped reconfigure the internet conceptually, as Lisa Gitelman argues, writing that media's "material properties do (literally and figuratively) *matter*, determining some of the local conditions of communication."[83] Thus, Mosaic was a technology that helped reconfigure being online from "taking a tank for a joyride" in the early 1980s to exploring a space in the 1990s.[84] Instead of using the network, users could "be online," in a manner resembling Martin Heidegger's concept of "Dasein," which concerns the way humans make sense of the world through experiential beingness.[85] That is, for Heidegger, humans are always formed in relation to their environments, including mediated environments, and must therefore be understood as co-producing reality through interaction with its materials. The introduction of new technology, then, has the potential to reconfigure the nature of existence. In the case of Mosaic, experiential re-imagining and the addition of visuality to the internet helped configure the technology and the experience of navigating the technology as non-linear.

In addition to Mosaic, language drawing on modes of transportation helped construct the internet as space and assisted in the conceptual erasure of the internet's infrastructure. Jean Armour Polly, a librarian from New York known online as "Net-mom," is widely credited for the first published use of the phrase "surfing the internet."[86] However, she readily admits on her website that it was actually Mark McCahill, an avid windsurfer, who coined the expression. Regardless of its origin, the phrase caught on. Suggesting that individuals steer themselves through an ever-changing and tumultuously unpredictable environment, "surfing" implies the very opposite of navigating a highly structured system of data code traveling across organized, national infrastructure wires. As Gitelman notes, digital media require "a vast clutter of tangible stuff—the monitor on which it appears, but also the server computer, the client computer, the Internet 'backbone,' cables, routers, and switch hotels." At the same time, digital media are "strikingly intangible." This intangibility helps create the internet as having "no body."[87] As evidence of the prevalence of the assumption that the internet is a space liberated from wires, Gitelman points to the "frequency with which the word *material* appears between scare quotes" in academic writings.[88]

In combination with (and in part because of) new technological developments like Mosaic, news media and popular culture began to use metaphors like "virtual reality" and "cyberspace" in the 1990s and thereby helped culturally constitute the internet as an endless, complex universe that breeched physical conventions and was removed from the physical world. In this conception, the internet had no structure or organizing mechanisms—like wires, modems, software, meta-tags, search engines, surveillance programs—but was structure-less and self-determining. Differing significantly from dominant 1980s views of the internet which tied it to the physical world (computers and telephone lines), material structures of power (governmental agencies and policies), and a historical context (the Cold War), later representations erased the internet's material history, suggesting that the technology simply appeared in a historical vacuum and existed in a space separate from physical world. In news media and popular culture representations of the internet, technological structures were increasingly erased. The internet's origins in the United States military that had once dominated representations of connectivity were no longer the focus, and instead the internet was imagined as having appeared on its own. The internet was abstracted and deterritorialized, viewed as self-perpetuating, inevitable, and global.

From Virtual Reality to Virtual Nation

Deterritorialization of the internet served national goals as American policymakers, activists, and academics projected American "new frontier" narratives onto this imagined internet space, producing it as a potential tabernacle of democracy.[89] In the early 1990s, John Perry Barlow—the pioneer who originally applied the term "cyberspace" to the internet—called the internet an "electronic frontier," or "an imagined space in which individuals could recreate themselves and their communities in terms set by New Communalist ideals ... beyond government control."[90] This frontier, Barlow wrote, was similar to "the nineteenth-century West. It is vast, unmapped, culturally and legally ambiguous, verbally terse.... Hard to get around in, and up for grabs."[91] According to historian Fred Turner, by the mid-1990s Barlow's rendering of the internet as a frontier was "the single most common emblem" for describing the "leveled forms of social organization and deregulated patterns of commerce," as well as for combating views of the internet as being dangerous and filled with criminals.[92] Whether in the Electronic Frontier Foundation (EFF), created by Barlow in the 1990s to protect individual rights online, or in Howard Rheingold's famous book about computer networking, *The Virtual Community: Homesteading on the Electronic Frontier*,[93] the internet was envisioned as a new, egalitarian, nationwide, democratic public sphere. Similarly, *Time* magazine called the internet a "communicopia."[94] These voices in academic and news media fantasized an idealized space like that discussed by theorist Jürgen Habermas in which individuals could voice their opinions without the influences of cultural or literal capital. In this vision, the internet could fix problems that "refeudalized" the public sphere, meaning it could reverse state and corporate public oppression.[95] Key internet users and theorists, then, imagined the internet as a democratic virtual frontier in which individuals could self-actualize.

Focus in the mid-1990s on the internet as a new and democratic frontier suggested that any explorer around the globe could enter and set down stakes. (Several years later, digital divide debates would rage and weaken this notion of universal access.[96]) These "techno-physical fantasies" of electronic-frontierism placed the internet into an established narrative of democratic interaction that looked to "technological energies to realize human potential."[97] The terminology used to discuss the internet was important because, as French theorist Pierre Bourdieu notes, language not only reinforces existing power hierarchies, but also helps determine the shape of resistance to those hierarchies. In Bourdieu's model, "fields"—in this case, news media, popular culture, and policy—intersect to form visions of the internet that consumers make part of their *doxa*—that is, the unconscious beliefs that form the boundaries of what is thinkable and thus determine a conscious set of dispositions or "common sense" assumptions. In short, representations are key in the formation of what people assume about the internet. The power to set doxa is the power to determine the boundaries of opposition, for to be understood, the language of the opposition must speak in language understood or "legible" dominant forces.[98] For example, as the previous chapter argued, corporations hoping consumers would reimagine computers as useful tools had to engage notions of the computing as threatening— as anthropomorphized threats to humanity, as impossibly complex, and as a dangerous game played by teenagers—already present in news media and popular culture. In another example, by tapping frontier rhetoric and American national mythology, those early 1990s voices perpetuating the representation of the internet as a virtual frontier not only helped to construct its importance to American national identity, and vice versa, but also helped (temporarily) to inoculate it against the critique that it produced a stratified social structure. However, the "common sense" notion that the internet was essentially democratic did become a target in the late 1990s, when news media and policymakers invested in focusing on the digital divide.[99]

Even as the name allotted a particular medium or activity sets cultural attitudes surrounding it, the name also often informs how this medium or activity is regulated.[100] Thus, the use of particular metaphors for computer networking had policy implications and vice versa. As a budding "new frontier," the internet contained the potential to democratize the world, but only if the United States could "settle" this global space first. Hence, the internet was simultaneously a Cold War ideological battle and a focus of U.S. government attentions. Just as the government had pushed the settlement of the western frontier and the lunar landing, so it pushed the exploration and colonization and ultimately the economic control of what was imagined to be a new global marketplace. But then of course, since early American history, the frontier myth has "been the cover for capitalist territorialization, turning the wilderness into resources for the factories back East,"[101] as historian Richard Slotkin has noted. The push for regulation of the internet as a national infrastructure dedicated federal funding to the wiring of the nation with the explicit intention of beating other countries to the punch.[102]

Thus, in the early and mid-1990s, the frontier metaphor contributed to a kind of "land rush" as agents like the U.S. government and computer corporations rushed to "colonize" and control online spaces. In 1991, the much-hyped "Gore Bill"—officially titled the "High Performance Computing and Communication Act"—was designed to create a nation-wide, high-speed fiber optic network. Al Gore referred to this network as the "information superhighway" in his push for legislation.[103] In an illustration of the sometimes circular usage of metaphor through history, the internet's "nineteenth century precursor, the electric telegraph, was dubbed the 'highway of thought.'"[104] This new "highway" was officially called the "National Information Infrastructure" (NII) and was built by the Defense Advanced Research Projects Agency (DARPA), formerly ARPA or the government office responsible for originally developing internet technologies. NII differed from ARPANET in that it was envisioned as a publicly accessed network, rather than one available only to military and academic institutions. The Gore Bill also required the National Science Foundation (NSF) to provide networking infrastructure support to government and academic institutions as well as public libraries. The bill included provisions for educational networking, training students in networking skills, hardware and software development, as well as enhancing the security of commercial networks and ensuring intellectual property protections. Part of the argument for the creation of the information superhighway was securing American dominance over potential future markets.[105] As Gore said, "This is by all odds the most important and lucrative marketplace of the 21st century" and this marketplace would "give our companies and our citizens an advantage in worldwide competition."[106]

The metaphors of highway construction on new cyber-frontiers reached campaign politics as well. During their 1992 presidential campaign, Bill

Clinton and Al Gore made building a "data superhighway" central, arguing that just as the U.S. government had created the interstate highway system of asphalt in the 1950s, so must it create the information superhighway of fiber optic cable. According to *Time* magazine, the two politicians "repeated the information-highway metaphor so often that many voters—and industry leaders—were left with the impression that the government actually planned to build it, to use taxpayer dollars to construct a data freeway that anybody could ride." But as the article also reported, what Clinton and Gore actually intended was to "cut through the thicket of state and federal regulations" to free industry to create the highway.[107] This policy option departed from more statist legislative precedents. For example, federal telephone legislation "explicitly set a goal of 'universal service,' which meant that nearly everyone had access to a dial-tone and that rates were regionally uniform no matter how disparate the actual cost of wiring different locations."[108] In contrast, not only did the Gore Bill require "reasonable rates" instead of uniform rates, but it also required them only for "schools, libraries, and most hospitals" instead of the entire population.[109] These politicians saw corporate institutions as more suited to create the network than government institutions in a historical moment in which "regulation" was a "dirty word."[110] But the Clinton administration worked hard to associate itself with new technology and computer industries. Hillary Rodham Clinton even sat next to John Scully, who was at the time president of Apple Computers, during Bill Clinton's first State of the Union address.

Like the frontier metaphor, "information superhighway" imagery pervaded popular cultural representations of the internet in the early 1990s.[111] The metaphor was so ubiquitous by 1994 that humorist Art Buchwald recommended a "5-day jail term for anyone who uses the term."[112] In 1993, an issue of *Time*—"Coming Soon to Your TV Screen: The Info Highway: Bringing a Revolution in Entertainment, News and Communication"—pictured a symbolic road paved with a variety of images like telephones, magazine covers, music notes, and *Star Trek* images extending endlessly into a large human eye.[113] Again, the internet was not represented as contained within a computer, modem, or telephone wires, but was instead envisioned as infinite, stretching toward the horizon. The horizon, however, was a large human eye. The image echoes *The Lawnmower Man*'s visuals and plot line in insinuating that the human brain can absorb the boundless information provided by the internet and that the internet can extend the human mind's boundless potential. The cover image suggested an unmediated connection between the internet technology and the human mind—that is, one that occurred without technological, government, or corporate intervention.

Although news media and the U.S. government were active participants in re-casting the internet as a virtual reality and a boundless, global space, the "superhighway" idea did not preclude government control. On the contrary, the "information superhighway" presumably could have speed limits, blocked exits, and an atlas. "Cyberspace" presumably could not. And, indeed, the U.S. government did work to establish itself as the authority on the internet. One mechanism was through its protection of U.S. control over domain name assignment. Domain names are the addresses that lead a user to a particular website, which is actually identified by a string of numbers. The creation of the domain name system meant that what had been the unwieldy Internet Protocol (IP) address 63.161.169.137 became "whitehouse.gov." In 1984, five "top level" domain names were created—.com, .edu, .org, .mil, and .gov—in order to give domain space to commercial, educational, organizational, military, and governmental institutions, respectively.[114] U.S. control of this new system made sense given that it had controlled address assignment for most of the internet's history and given that the world could access the internet because the U.S. government had invented and developed the technology. From 1972 until his death in 1998, the responsibility of assigning unique addresses to individuals around the world belonged to one computer guru, Jon Postel, Director of the Internet Assigned Number Authority (IANA), an organization subsidized by the Nation Science Foundation (NSF). As director, he "guided the creation and refinement of the structure of the internet."[115] Jon Postel was characterized in histories of the internet and by news media at the time as a (or the) god of the internet.[116] U.S. control of the domain name system in the late 1980s and early 1990s meant that the United States was logistically the center of cyberspace. Since the beginning of domain name assignment, countries other than the United States had to use country code top-level domain names (ccTLD). The European Union's official site, for example, is europa.eu. Because the United States retained control of the system, however, the U.S. government did (and does) not need to abide by the same rules. The main U.S. government site is usa.gov and does not incorporate a country code domain name component like .us. This suggests a presumed Americanness to the internet built into the domain name system itself.

The U.S. government was not the only one configuring the United States as the center of cyberspace. Users did as well. As previously mentioned, the online World's Fair in 1996 had 172 participating countries with their own "electronic theme pavilions," but "Central Park" was the main entrance.[117] In short, the internet world fair was accessible only through the American virtual nation. As Benedict Anderson has argued, nations are to some extent always media-constructed and virtual in that they represented "imagined communities," or cultural systems formed by mass media that foster the sense of commonality out of which nationalism crystallizes.[118] In a simple, micro-level example, individuals who independently read the newspaper are aware that the "ceremony" takes place throughout their imagined community.[119] Individuals reading imagine the community in which they live as partaking in the same media rituals, and then this feeling of community is reinforced as they see others reading the newspaper or discuss newspaper content with others during the day. These communities unified individuals within conceptual boundaries roughly paralleling national ones and thereby excluded other individuals as belonging to other nations. According to Anderson, media "laid the bases for national consciousness" by creating "unified forms of exchange" and by both formalizing and stabilizing languages.[120] But because individuals increasingly interacted in online spaces and with internationally based individuals, the sense of nationalism in Anderson's model shifts. Cyberspace's virtual nation, with its not-necessarily-state-identified-but-assumed-American locations and governmental regulators, as well as its adoption of English as the primary language, became American flavored. Of course, practicality prevented multi-lingual textual interfaces at that stage in the internet's development as did the fact that more American users were online than elsewhere. But still, the use of Central Park and of English challenged notions of the internet as a culturally hybrid mediated space that was promoted by academic voices as well as limiting access for non-English speakers.[121] The fair also presented the internet as a democratic technology, tapping the notion of the internet as a frontier "where anybody can open a pavilion, where anybody can participate."[122] By including individuals and making them equivalent to corporations and government, the fair promoted in the internet as the public sphere imagined by academics in the early and mid-1990s, and that idealized by theorist Jürgen Habermas.

But the World's Fair also helped literally construct the internet as global. The fair's welcome page placed it in the context of other fairs—London's Crystal Palace of 1851 and the 1939 New York World's Fair—which "introduced people to the new technologies that came to define the industrial age." While the page compared the internet to a variety of technologies premiered at world fairs, including electricity, the ice cream cone, the hamburger, and the postcard, this fair and internet technology itself that made it possible would usher us "as we leave the industrial age and enter a new age of information."[123] As fair organizers Carl Malamud and Vint Cerf envisioned, just as previous fairs ushered in the technological icons of modernization, the 1996 World's Fair would usher in technologies of postmodernization and informationalization. Similarly, in a "Letter of Support," President Bill Clinton wrote, "Just as world's fairs in earlier days popularized the electric light, the telephone, and other technologies that dramatically reshaped our lives, this Exposition will help people everywhere to realize the promise of the future."[124] These terms placed the internet in the history of American technological progress.

The fair differed from many other representations like *The Lawnmower Man* and *Neuromancer*, which positioned the internet's virtuality as offering an escape from physical reality. In their mission statement, fair producers argued that "cyberspace is part of the real world" and that the fair itself was "real" and not a "virtual project." One of the mantras of the fair was "bring the real world into cyberspace and cyberspace into the real world," which, while it assumed the two were discrete spaces, also assumed they should not be.[125] Boris Yeltsin drew connections between this fair and the real word in his characterization of the fair as "humanitarian" and as having the potential to "bring people closer together, facilitate their mutual understanding, and deepen their knowledge of each other and of their environment."[126] The fair was conceptualized as being in "places in the real world," and although cybercafes were scarce in the period, the fair organizers hoped to create infrastructure and demand for public access.[127] Like Gore, Malamud wanted the fair to affect material change. He said, "World's fairs create huge sites, which are often turned into public parks and other permanent improvements to the local infrastructure when the fair is over ... my idea was that a world's fair might give us a common focus, a lever we might use to raise the visibility of the internet."[128]

Perhaps the biggest change effected by the fair was the establishment of the "Internet Railroad," a global backbone for the internet. In the course of an extensive lobbying campaign that took him around the world seven times in 1995, Malamud managed to secure a significant increase in global connectivity. Before the fair, in some countries the connectivity rate was as low as 64,000 bits per second. As a result of the Internet Railroad, the connectivity around the world increased to 45 million bits per second, an improvement he reported was worth $20 million. To garner donations, Malamud played American and Japanese corporations against each other, preying on the competitive history between the nations over technological prowess. He also preyed on government partisanship in that he publicized Democratic involvement in the fair and thereby gained Republican support from those party officials not wishing to lose out on potential party publicity.[129]

Thus, through overlapping and sometimes competing metaphors, journalists, popular culture producers, policymakers, and users helped construct the internet as both a global space and a virtual American nation. Frontier and highway metaphors in particular produced the internet as American. These particular renderings dovetailed with representations of the internet as a virtual reality and cyberspace in that they suggested the individual could self-actualize. They conflicted, however, in that they imagined the internet as mapable and controllable. In naming its infrastructural contribution the "Internet Railroad," the 1996 World's Fair engaged a rhetoric like that used by news media and policymakers who spoke of an "information superhighway." The opening page, or the entrance to the fair, looked like an amusement park ride, featuring tracks extending in front of the user and leading into tunnels. But the name, "Internet Railroad," also tapped notions of the American West and thereby helping construct the internet as an American frontier. Still, this representation of the United States as the center of this railroad worked with efforts by U.S. policymakers to retain control over domain name assignment and make anything unassigned as foreign presumed to be American.

CorpoNation's Cultural Complexities: Bill Gates Is God, Microsoft Is the Devil

Just as the internet took on characteristics of American nationhood in the 1990s, so did major internet corporations. In the mid-1990s, in keeping with academic notions of globalization, the U.S. government began to see its role as supporter and protector of American corporate interests in the global market and began to pass policies that favored communication corporations. The National Technology Transfer and Advancement Act of 1995, for example, was designed to cultivate relationships between research and development labs in the private and public sector and therefore speed the release of new technology into the corporate world. Perhaps most well-known was the Telecommunications Act of 1996, which was the first major refurbishment of American telecommunication law in half a century. This legislation ultimately relaxed government regulation over consolidation of media corporations, allowing corporations to merge to a greater extent and presumably making it possible for American corporations to better compete in the global market and retain American telecommunications dominance.[130] With this act, the U.S. government relinquished its role as traffic controller. In effect, then, the state reimagined internet space as private real estate instead of public space. At the same time, relationships between government and corporations were so tight that it hardly mattered who was congressional staff and who was a lobbyist because both were heavily involved in crafting policy and, indeed, "some of the law was actually written by the lobbyist for the commu-nication firms it affects."[131]

As the state was increasingly imagined as stepping behind corporations, or corporations in front of the state, the corporation began to increasingly represent the nation itself. These corporations trading on nation are what I call "corpoNations." Operating transnationally, these corporations presented themselves in advertisements and through governmental lobbyists as the new purveyors of American idealism, business practices, culture, and technology to the consuming public. On the one hand, they were global and innovative, pioneers in the new world order of globalization. On the other hand, they were traditional and culturally conservative, holding fast and unwaveringly to American ideals of entrepreneurship, capital, philanthropy, individualism, and creativity.

Corporate embodiment of a national culture is by no means new. Gov-ernments have long had corporate arms, aimed at controlling the economy and guiding it in particular political directions. For example, the East India Company in the late seventeenth and eighteenth centuries served as an eco-nomic prosthetic of the British Empire, colonizing foreign markets much as the British government colonized, well, colonies.[132] Telecommunications cor-porations like British Telecom emerged after such enterprises were removed from state-national affiliation.

CorpoNations are, therefore, a part of a longer history of transnational trade politics. What is new about corpoNations, however, is that they do not necessarily serve the state. Paradoxically, they stand in for the diminished state that those same corporations were imagined by academics as under-cutting. Indeed, the corpoNation was produced by the long history of glo-balization and globalization discourse, in which a new global world order emerged as political, economic and cultural engines were redefined around transnational exchange and organizational models. But the corpoNation was also produced by the conflation of "globalization" with a related but distinct discourse of "neoliberalism" (discussed in more detail in chapter 4), in which humanity would be better served by corporate rather than by state orga-nizations, since corporations facilitate individuality and states encourage homogenization. In merging globalization and neoliberalist value systems, the corpoNation could spin itself through advertisements and campaigns as offering the limitless choices of capitalism in the service of democracy. Enabled by an "inherently democratic new frontier" internet technology and unencumbered by territorially located and technologically inept national governmental "dinosaurs," the corpoNation would efficiently construct a global market that would allow global citizens to choose their products and affiliate themselves with post-state organizations better suited to cultivating new forms of democracy.[133]

CorpoNations helped link the virtual nation to the corporation, becoming cultural carriers and constructors of the nation by capitalizing on the internet's global-yet-also-American identity. The American corpoNation presented itself as exporting American democracy through the virtual nation of the internet. For example, America Online (AOL) not only explicitly capitalized on national identity in its corporation's name, but also provided an America-centric entry-point to the internet.[134] Policy scholar Steven Miller credited AOL's success as one of the "pioneers in commercializing cyberspace" with its "easy-to-use graphic interface."[135] AOL publicized itself as a service provider for people unfamiliar and/or uncomfortable with computers and networking.[136] As "Your Gateway to the Internet," AOL provided a proprietary software called AOL 1.0 for Windows or AOL 2.0 for Mac as early as 1993. This software offered a point-and-click graphical user interface (GUI) when most providers at the time still used command lines.

This software "portal" resembled the Central Park entrance to the internet world's fair or the doorways to cyberspace on the 1995 *Time* magazine cover in that it led users to cyberspace. AOL also claimed in its advertisements to "provide everything a user need[ed] to navigate the Web"—search engines, links, email services, games, shopping pages, chat rooms. Tapping the same utopian rhetoric that imagined individual liberation online, advertisements suggested that "the commercialized World Wide Web—America Online— would be the operative medium of cultural evolution."[137] AOL's browser was the first of its kind and remained the most successful until Yahoo and Netscape gained popularity in 1994. Like Central Park in at the World's Fair, AOL 1.0 was an American gateway to the global space of the internet. But unlike the World's Fair entrance, this portal also steered its clients toward particular links and restricted what clients could access. As internet scholar Tim Wu writes, "AOL was, in those early days, *the platform*, and, in the lingo, operated as a 'walled garden' for its users."[138] If a site did not neatly fit an English AOL keyword, it was difficult to find through the software.[139] In 2000, AOL was sued because the software did not provide universal access to internet sites and search engines; the company ultimately settled out of court for $15 million without admitting guilt.[140]

But corporations did not lay claim to national identity and the status as bearers of national interest without consequence. The American corporation became the stand-in for the United States in the eyes of foreign nations and, therefore, also a target for critiques of invasive American economic policies as well as cultural imperialism or "Americanization." In addition, as with the internet itself and globalization, mid-1990s cultural representations simultaneously deified and demonized American media corporations. Microsoft was at once imagined as an icon of American capitalism and American global economic dominance and as an oppressive, anti-competition and therefore anti-American entity.[141] The conflicting valences extended to the entrepreneurial founder of Microsoft, Bill Gates. In a flood of cultural representations in the mid-1980s and early 1990s, Gates was presented as a visionary computer guru, a veritable computer god. These images blended with those that focused on him as the richest person in the world, as well as the quintessential opportunist American, settling the virtual frontier.[142] A *Nightline* special called "The World According to Gates" treated the computer industry executive as if he were a computer god, like Jobe from *The Lawnmower Man*.[143] On the June 5, 1995 *Time* magazine cover, he was titled "Master of the Universe" and pictured holding a Zeus-like lightning bolt between his fingers. His visions were consistently cited as prescient and discussed using religious terms. When Gates spoke to the audience at a world computer network demo, the scene was described as having the "quality of a religious revival meeting"; Gates and other speakers were like "rock stars before a crowd of thousands."[144] Represented as a work-a-holic, "Driven by the Dream" to work sixteen-hour days, Gates was described as a "visionary leader" and a "computer genius."[145] One *New York Times* article noted that "the main brushstrokes of Mr. Gates' character" are "brilliant, tireless, demanding, unhygienic."[146] He was exceptional, a "Whiz Kid," "Software King," and "Wizard of Business."[147] In these representations, Gates' wealth was often remarked on, but his drive for profit was downplayed. Thus, he was contrasted with other business people like those "who work on Wall Street" and "just want to make a lot of money." Gates drove a Lexus instead of being chauffeured in a Rolls-Royce, and his only "ostentation [was] the occasional $50 bottle of wine to go with trademark cheeseburgers."[148]

In contrast to imaginings of Gates as a humble but powerful god of the computer and internet or opportunist internet explorer, Gates as the powerful head of Microsoft was represented an instrument of brutal capitalism.[149] Most news reports in the mid-1990s described Microsoft as overly aggressive and selfish in its self-preservation business tactics.[150] Much of this focus stemmed from the Federal Trade Commission (FTC) anti-trust investigation that began in 1990. The Department of Justice charged that Microsoft "deliberately created hidden codes in its operating system to hinder competing applications."[151] Microsoft was trying to control access to the internet in ways similar to AOL in that it wanted to serve a gateway function. In 1995 Microsoft consented to changing its business strategies and to not using its control of operating systems to hurt competitors. This suit, which represented an old-fashioned trust-busting approach, was an ineffectual effort by the state to control internet corporations, for although Microsoft agreed to alter its practices, it was sued again shortly thereafter for failing to do so.[152] These critical representations of Microsoft were mapped onto Bill Gates, whose personality was compared to Microsoft's business practices. Gates was featured in a Tom Brokaw special entitled "Tycoon," and he was labeled "The Silicon Bully" by *Business Month Magazine*.[153] Gates was reputed to behave unethically toward his employees, including spying on workers and awarding bonuses based on which employees worked weekends, holidays, and nights.[154] Gates was also represented as sexist and was quoted as saying, "'Let's hire two women because we can pay them half as much as we will have to pay a man.'"[155] The hire of women was apparently designed to help Microsoft score a profitable Air Force contract in the mid-1980s, and one of the women reportedly requested a transfer away from Gates, citing poor treatment.[156] Bill Gates also reportedly interfered in government trade regulation on Microsoft's behalf through his efforts to lobby Bill Clinton to support NAFTA (the North American Free Trade Agreement) in 1993 and to allow Microsoft to supply computers to Mexico and to prevent government involvement in trade with Japan.[157] In this case, Gates' control over trade and the economy was considered so influential that even a state leader would buckle. This is the presumptive power of a corpoNation.

Representations of the internet in news media, popular culture, policy, and academic debates in the 1990s thus reveal the complex ways in which virtual reality, globalization, computing, and the internet were conceptually conflated. Cast as an icon of globalization and, therefore, as a participant in the downfall of the state, the internet was also treated as something in need of state control and controllable by the state, and then as a libratory democratic space. As a result of these related but different metaphors, the internet emerged as paradoxically a global space and a distinctly American one. Imagined as a participant in the breakdown of state power and as a means of empowering corporations on global scales, the internet was cited by a multitude of sources in the U.S. media and cultural sphere as a major player in power shifts associated with globalization. News media coverage, popular culture, and academic debates about globalization abstracted both the internet and the nation, helping to construct both as virtual realities and virtual spaces. Imagined as an American virtual nation, perhaps most overtly in the first online World's Fair, the internet was perceived as both a contributor to the destruction of the state and a preserver of the nation. For policymakers, as a "new frontier" and "information highway," the internet represented democratic access to information (in spite of the reality of the digital divide) and as a mechanism for exporting or spreading "America," or the ideal of American national democratic values. In investing in the "information superhighway," policymakers presented pro-internet policies as helping support the health of democracy at home and abroad. At the same time, notions of the internet as a virtual reality, as chaotic, and as a frontier all suggested that the internet was uncontrollable and thereby helped mask the United States' controlling influences. The state could use corporate power, represented as benevolent and democratic, to become a controlling force in cyberspace while avoiding the perception of the state as oppressor. In this sense, images of the internet emphasized a less powerful *state* while simultaneously reinforcing notions of the *nation* in the form of a globally-swelled, but American-flavored-cyberspace. One way this occurred was through corpoNations such as America Online, or corporations operating transnationally and thereby outside state power, but at the same time retaining national identity as part of their corporate identities. Through the corpoNation, globalization and neoliberalism converged and dovetailed as corporations operated globally and supported the new global world order both welcomed and feared in academic circles while at the same time presenting themselves as carriers of democracy around the world.

4

Self-Colonizing eEurope

The Information Society Merges onto the Information Superhighway

The 2002 award winning German film ½ *Miete*, or ½ *the Rent* follows a computer hacker in his thirties named Peter as he "unplugs"—that is, he makes the conscious decision to live his life off-line.[1] The film's opening shot characterizes this hacker's home life in ways similar to American films like *WarGames* and the *Matrix*. The main character's apartment is disheveled, with empty food containers and dirty clothing strewn about. Near the onset of the film, the hacker emerges from his darkened computer room overjoyed that he finally finished his long-term project, a computer virus. To his horror, Peter discovers that while he was working, his girlfriend has died in the bathtub under ambiguous circumstances: maybe she accidentally overdosed or maybe she committed suicide. In his ensuing panic, he goes to the train station and boards a train without knowing its destination. He lights a cigarette and sits dazed until his cellular telephone rings and frightens him. Instead of answering, Peter flips the phone over, removes the data chip from the back, and burns the chip with his cigarette. In this moment, Peter literally and symbolically destroys his means of digital communication and deliberately unplugs from telecommunication networks. In his words, "I am no longer reachable."[2] In an overwrought, dramatically climactic scene, Peter flings his laptop into the Rhine River.

In American films about the internet in the 1990s or early 2000s, characters did not typically decide to unplug.[3] Instead, as discussed previously, the main characters almost always battled with evil forces over control of the internet, ultimately using the technology as a weapon with which to defeat their foes. In American film, "winning" meant mastery of the internet, not avoidance or rejection. Although American films far out-sell German films in Germany (and elsewhere), and ½ *Miete* was by no means a blockbuster even in Germany, this alternative representation converged with those in the German press. This convergence suggests the internet was "thinkable" in different terms in Germany, where a certain anti-internet sentiment made sense. As German cultural studies have shown, this skepticism of technology stems in part from Germany's legacy of anti-capitalism in which technology became equated with the capitalist domination critiqued by German thinkers. The Frankfurt School in particular argued that technological rationality meant "domination" as "monopoly capitalist culture becomes industrial culture."[4]

Indeed, popular culture and media outlets in the United States and the E.U. member-states presented very different visions of the internet—what it could do and what it was for—and governments in these locations also took varying approaches to its regulation before the year 2000. This comparative chapter looks at these varying national imaginings and, in particular, how they intersected with and were promoted by different policies regulating the technology. An investigation into news media magazines makes the divergent cultural renderings especially visible. For example, in 1994, both *Time* magazine and a German equivalent, *Der Spiegel*, ran cover stories about the internet. *Time*'s cover image pictured the internet as a "Strange New World" through which screens picturing abstract sparks floated. *Der Spiegel* pictured the internet as an educational tool used in the classroom, showing the internet as a screen with the letters "ABC" that was worn as a backpack by a young student.[5] *Time* imagined the internet as an experiential, expansive and bodiless space, while *Der Spiegel* imagined it as a technological tool firmly grounded in human practices.

These different perspectives were reflected in the policy decisions made by the two governments. Unlike policymakers in the United States, who promoted free-market capitalism and aimed to help corporations set up camps on this new virtual frontier, policymakers in Europe in the 1980s and early 1990s regulated the internet using the nationalist and protectivist models used to regulate other media (e.g., the BBC in the United Kingdom and the BRF in Germany).[6] This regulation subsidized national telecommunication corporations with public funds as these corporations expanded service into internet providership. With these subsidies, E.U. member-states hoped to protect domestic jobs in the face of what they viewed as U.S. corporate economic imperialism. Thus, Europeans initially conceptualized and tried to regulate the internet as if it were a public utility, a public space, or an arm of national media organizations. European nation-states focused on providing access to, and protecting the privacy of, all citizens, as well as advocating for global regulations of internet content to further protect their citizenry.

However, this chapter is ultimately about the *failure* of these European policies. It is about a policy-road-tried-but-ultimately-not-taken, or about the failure of European policymakers to put a particularly European stamp on internet regulation. It charts the European Union's eventual adoption of the free-market capitalist approach to the internet developed in the United States. Although in the 1980s and early 1990s, Europeans imagined the internet as fitting into the established regulatory systems for radio and television, this notion became increasingly less viable in the late 1990s. The importance of national beliefs, cultures, values, and historical experiences to the policymaking process diminished in general in the European Union during this period. As a result, deregulatory laws began to emerge that released member-states' national hold on media.[7] The turn of the century brought the E.U.'s eEurope 2005 Project, the nail in the proverbial coffin for statist internet policy in Europe.[8] In short, the European telecommunication market was increasingly liberalized and privatized, meaning that what was once controlled by the state—including broadcasting—increasingly became the domain of private enterprise.

This policy reallocation was produced by and helped generate a discursive shift. What was imagined as a national "public utility" was reconfigured as an inherently global "capitalist space." The adoption of the eEurope 2005 Project—including the endorsement of American-style unsubsidized corporations and hands-off government instead of European-style statist traditions—suggested that the internet functioned as a trans-Atlantic cultural carrier of advanced capitalism. However, this is not a story of limitless U.S. power because, as Ithiel de Sola Pool has argued, to acknowledge U.S. dominance is not necessarily to argue imperialism.[9] Thus, while recognizing American economic and cultural power, this chapter does not argue that an American invader intentionally overpowered the European Union. Instead, Europe was an actor that willingly adopted attractive cultural, political, and economic models in a manner resembling what Reinhold Wagnleitner terms "self-colonization."[10] Policymakers presented the adoption of a U.S. economic internet model as mostly beneficial to Europe and not due to an overt exertion of U.S. power. Further, the European Union attempted to engage U.S. economic tactics in order to make the internet in Europe less statist, but no less European.

Ultimately the European Union's goal—to create a European space online or a public place for its people to interact—did not change in the shift detailed in this chapter. What changed was the path to that goal. The notion of the internet as a virtual nation simultaneously enabled the European Union to imagine itself and make itself a unified entity. In addition, ideas about the internet and how to use it did not flow in only one direction. Discussion of the "digital divide"—or discussion of the gap between people with and without access to computer networking technology—which preoccupied E.U. policymakers in the late 1980s and early 1990s, became a national focus in the United States in the late 1990s.[11] Although U.S. news media did not usually cite European policy or media for bringing this focus to the U.S. agenda, because imaginings of the internet as a tool for economic equality and uplift dominated earlier in European media and policy, the emergence of digital divide debates in the United States suggests the multidirectional and complex nature of globalization.

Protectionist Precedents: Europe before eEurope

While the United States abandoned "universal service policies" in the early 1900s in favor of government-sponsored "natural monopolies," public service broadcasting (PSB) dominated in Europe much later.[12] State-supported national media corporations—like British Telecom in the United Kingdom, France Telecom in France, Deutsche Telekom in Germany—were designed to ensure representations of minority interests and national culture, meaning that for all practical purposes, these corporations were the "voice of the state."[13] Although policies varied among E.U. member-states, these federally supported corporations were (and to some extent, are) powerful in almost all European nations.[14]

Initially, policymakers in the various member-states viewed these corporations as the natural means to enter online spaces, thereby assuming that public corporations would retain their public support and power with regard to the internet. For example, France had a widespread yet primitive internet system called the Minitel that was created in the early 1980s and, at its peak in the mid-1990s, was connected to 14 million homes. The service is all but gone.[15] The system was created by France Telecom, France's national telephone company, and included content as various as train schedules, telephone directories, news, and information. The Minitel terminals—or computer monitors hooked up to telephone lines—were free to telephone subscribers and in the early 1990s boasted 6.5 million terminals, or one for every ten French citizens. In addition, almost a million standard computers were connected to the system.[16] In 1997, the French government began to move away from this system and instead generated a lengthy and complicated plan through which the French government would support France Telecom in the creation of national access to the internet. Although U.S. telecommunications firms—such as AT&T—shared a similar history of state support, this French program was far from the corporate-led policy approach promoted by Al Gore in the United States in the same year.[17] The French plan made the Minitel a primarily governmental project, leaving only "those things the state cannot or does not wish to do" up to private corporations.[18] As late as 1999, the principle source of start-up money for internet corporations was the French Ministry of Economy, Finance, and Industry. This socialist system prompted its minister to say that France was a "capitalist country without capital or capitalists."[19]

To some extent, the European Union assumed that its socialist and protectionist laws could extend to the international legal sphere. In 1993 the European Union sued Microsoft, alleging antitrust abuse. Whereas in the United States the internet was the domain of global business, in the European Union the internet remained the domain of state governments, which collectively sought to discipline Microsoft. This suit demonstrated the European Union's recognition of the differences between U.S. and E.U. member-state regulatory systems. The European Union did not sue the United States to get at what was for all practical purposes a nationally supported corporation, but it did acknowledge that U.S. state support of U.S. corporations worked differently than in Europe. The U.S. government backed Microsoft through indirect and commercial means—by offering the company exclusive government contracts and submitting to its lobbying efforts advocating market liberalization—and thus a suit against the United States was less effective than one directly against Microsoft. The episode demonstrated a paradox in E.U. policy. At the same time as it was edging out competition in its own markets through the state-sponsorship of media corporations, the European Union complained in international courts about Microsoft's efforts to curtail competition.[20]

Although European states retained control of media-access through national corporate institutions in the late 1980s and early 1990s, they could not control content. Sexual content became a primary focus of European public debate about the internet as states dealt with reactions to the technology's use for sex and pornography.[21] Mirroring the early histories in the United States and elsewhere of other communication technologies—print, photography, film—one of the internet's early uses in Europe was for distributing pornography.[22] This is especially the case with the French Minitel, which "first climbed from obscurity to critical mass by becoming the favored distribution mechanism for what are euphemistically described as 'sexual services.'"[23] The "pink Minitel" or "Minitel Rose"—a portion of the system dedicated to dating, erotic conversations, and even prostitution—accounted for 8 percent of all Minitel activity and was so profitable that the state enacted a 33 percent "sin tax" and profited mightily.[24]

Europe was by no means uniform in its reaction to internet technologies and content, and, indeed, conflicts often raged between member-states.
Member-states to some extent constituted their national identities in opposition to perception of E.U. politics and policies.[25] In the case of sexual content,
France was unique as most European nations struggled to suppress sexual
content online. Instead of accepting yet taxing such content, many European
nations resisted "transborder data flows," or content produced in different
countries but available online within national boundaries. Many European
nations attempted to map territorial boundaries onto internet spaces or create filtering devices or "electronic barriers" that would "impose their boundaries onto the new electronic medium."[26] Through this boundary making,
policymakers revealed they imagined the internet as a threat to national sovereignty, to citizens, and to private property. For example, in 1995, Germany
attempted to erect an electronic barrier by ordering the American company
CompuServe to disable German access to particular newsgroups, which the
government claimed contained sexual content that was illegal according to
German decency laws.[27] Authorities claimed CompuServe violated German
law by failing to remove materials, which included over 200 sites that contained materials on pedophilia, bestiality, and initially even some on homosexuality, although the latter were eventually stricken from the list.[28] German authorities raided CompuServe's offices in Munich and two years later
indicted the manger of CompuServe Deutschland.[29] Given that similar content was available elsewhere on the internet, it is likely that CompuServe was
the target of German attention because the company was the largest provider
in Europe; with over 500,000 subscribers, CompuServe claimed it was the
"first global Internet service provider."[30] London's *Financial Times* reported
that this incident marked the first time an internet provider restricted access
to content in response to Germany's legal action.[31]

The German newspaper *Süddeutsche Zeitung* presented the incident as if
German internet users would accidentally discover the content. For example,
one article stated: "When German users find themselves on the information
superhighway, they are confronted with what they can bear the least: Anarchy... Because German users steering through the internet's offerings found
child-pornography, Munich government officials tried to pull the emergency
break—and raided Germany's central internet provider corporation, CompuServe."[32] But the material available on the banned sites was not masked;
sexual content was instead explicitly identified in the wording of the internet addresses. For example, one of the banned sites was "alt.binaries.pictures.
erotica.fetish.feet." Users were not, therefore, as "innocent" in their stum-
bling down the information superhighway as the article suggested.

In this CompuServe example, Germany attempted to enforce its national legal system onto the nation-less territory of the internet. This state action against an internet corporation was an example of what Joel Reidenberg has called Europe's attempt to "preserve important, yet vaporizing, foundations based on territorial principles and sectoral distinctions."[33] The outcome of this conflict, however, also demonstrates that the ultimate control was with the corporate provider and not the hosting nation-state. CompuServe was not required by any national German law to obey the request issued by German government officials. Although the corporation initially obliged, CompuServe eventually repealed the ban and instead offered users a program that allowed them to restrict content of their choosing.[34] The incident caused international conflict after Americans began complaining that German law was restricting their freedom of speech.[35] Because CompuServe's technology did not allow it to choose particular customers, the company had to ban access to 4 million customers in the United States in order to restrict access to its 200,000 German customers.[36] At the time, the U.S. Congress was considering decency laws and holding hearings debating issues of free speech and censorship online—a circumstance that probably encouraged the draconian initial action on the part of CompuServe.[37]

The transnational structure of the internet, therefore, prevented any one nation from necessarily imposing its legal structure onto online spaces. But Germany's efforts to territorialize the internet were also limited by its involvement in the European Union. If Germany or any other member-state wanted to propose a European solution instead of a national one, then that state had to petition through "directives," but this process was very slow.[38] For example, although a directive about data privacy was drafted and proposed in 1990, the final text of the policy was not adopted until 1995, and member-states were not required to execute the directive until 1998.[39] The double bureaucracy of member-state and E.U. regulation made policy implementation far too slow to keep up with changes in internet technology and use in the 1990s.[40]

Statist policies within the European Union—like those in France that created the Minitel and those in Germany that attempted to control internet content—were produced by and were part of a cultural assumption that internet technology was a choice and not an inevitability. As previously argued in this book, U.S. news media celebrated the internet, or what Marshall McLuhan called its "extensions" of the human body; that is, media outlets celebrated how the internet allowed individuals specifically to extend senses such as sight and hearing in order to experience materials from other parts of the world, such as news or cultural products. McLuhan and others saw the potential for media to facilitate new forms of transnational communication and, therefore, to form new kinds of interpersonal connections. While European news media shared this celebratory attitude, European news media and popular culture—especially in Germany—also focused on what McLuhan termed a technology's "amputations."[41] Thus, news media focused not only on what German society might gain, but also on what it might lose as it adopted internet technology. German policymakers feared, for example, that German citizens would be exposed to unwanted and illicit foot fetish content. In another example, an article in the *Süddeutsche Zeitung* opened by suggesting internet commerce would do away with the art of shop-window decoration.[42] In addition to focusing on potential losses, the German paper questioned the usefulness or necessity of the internet in its very title, "Must We All Really Live Online?"[43]

In the film previously mentioned—½ *Miete*, or ½ *the Rent*—the main character, Peter, decides not to live his life off-line.[44] After his girlfriend's death, Peter disengages from communication networks. Throwing his laptop into the river, Peter cleanses himself of his past computer sins, a cleansing highlighted by top-lighting, a cinematic technique employing light shining down from above, as if divinely radiating from heaven. After destroying his computer, Peter stands in judgment of his colleague, a hacker who was trying to purchase his virus for potentially dubious reasons. To this man, Peter says, "Because of guys like us, everything will eventually be destroyed."[45] Flustered by Peter's destructive act toward his computer, the colleague accidentally opens the suitcase he had brought; the bag is filled with dollars—suggesting American economic dominance as well as dominance over online spaces—and the money falls into the water. Peter looks down at his former colleague as he scrambles to collect the "laundered" money and suggests the man also unplug: "Look at yourself! You desperately need a vacation."

Although he is no longer online, Peter remains a hacker of sorts; he begins to "hack" into physical spaces, breaking into people's apartments instead of their computers. Upon his arrival in Cologne, he tries door-handles until he manages to sneak in. He explores a man's apartment, his bookshelves, his files, his bulletin boards, his furniture, and his food. From this point on in the film, Peter begins "lurking," a term for being in a chat room but not participating in the conversation, in real spaces. A reviewer in *Variety* described the film, which was the first to emerge from the "Radical Digital" project at Wim Wenders' Road Movies Factory, as a kind of "Rear Window" for the digital era.[46] Peter sits in public spaces, watching how people interact, tracking their schedules and activities. He notes where people keep their spare keys and breaks into their apartments when he knows they are out. But unlike a cyberspace-hacker—who tries to come and go undetected—this urban-space-hacker leaves gifts, like beer in the refrigerator.

Through this spatial hacking and lurking, Peter rediscovers non–computer-mediated forms of communication, thereby re-territorializing and localizing his interactions. In one home, he moves chess pieces and has an ongoing game with the construction worker who lives there. In another home, he cleans the woman's house, leaving a post-it note in one of her books near a quotation he thinks she would find meaningful. Although initially alarmed to realize someone had been in her apartment, the woman is touched by the quotation marked by the post-it message and decides that the intruder is benevolent; she replies to him by placing a post-it near a quotation in a different book. The two continue this dialogue through the woman's library until he eventually arrives in person at the end of the movie and the two (presumably) begin a romance. Peter, trained in and accustomed to computing, does not directly shift from computer-mediated to direct or oral communication, but instead chooses new mediated screens of invisibility: the chessboard and the book. However, this film suggests that interactions in off-line physical spaces—especially domestic ones—are more meaningful than those online. This film represents the internet as a choice in that a person can conceivably choose not to be online and, in the world of the film, live a more enlightened life. This representation was not lost on German film reviewers. Describing the film envisioning a kind of utopia, one wrote in *Die Welt* that by unplugging, Peter "becomes a human" again.[47]

While clearly one film is not proof of any dominant sentiment, the conspicuous absence of anything similar in American films suggests that this kind of message may not have found the same cultural traction in the United States. As previously mentioned, in no mainstream American film in the 1990s or 2000s that takes up the internet as the major plot element does the character decide to unplug. (While Sarah Connor in *Terminator* disengages from technology at the end, the film does not explicitly take up computer networking technologies but focuses on more embodied, "Frankensteinian" technological fears.) Instead, the main character almost always uses the internet for good, as a weapon with which to defeat the evil forces. In the film *The Net*, for example, Sandra Bullock stars as Angela Bennett, a computer programmer who lives most of her life on computers. She orders her pizzas online before that technology was available. When Bennett stumbles upon a program that allows users to bypass almost any security system, her life gets hacked by an underground conspiracy of hackers; her identity is stolen and replaced with that of "Ruth Marx," a convicted and wanted felon. In opposition to *WarGames,* where hackers are the heroes, in *The Net* hackers are both the heroes and the foes. Whereas in *WarGames,* teenaged hacker David Lightman has to hack into and best an artificially intelligent computer, in *The Net,* adult hacker Angela Bennett must out-hack other hackers. In the final scene, while much has changed about her—she is bathed, tan, and ventures outdoors—she is still on her computer.

I do not intend to argue that *½ Miete* and *The Net* are comparable films. What I do suggest is that the representation of the internet as something that could be escaped or avoided was present (although not necessarily dominant) in Germany in entertainment and news. In contrast, these questions were conspicuously absent from American representations, suggesting that the internet was "thinkable" in different terms in Germany than in the United States. Evidently, German culture incorporated an opposing impulse to the technological determinism present in the United States. Perhaps Germans questioned technology or imagined themselves as dominant over technology—as controlling their destiny—in opposition to Americans, who imagined technology as inevitable and driving history.[48]

This alternative notion of the internet as a choice may stem from the different history the technology had in Europe. In Europe, non-military arms of the state fostered the internet, and so it was not necessarily tied to Cold War anxieties or imagined as a weapon. Instead, perhaps the legacy of oppressive governments in Nazi and communist Europe shaped the ways news and entertainment media producers imagined and framed the technology. In post–World War II Europe, the state was responsible for engendering a "healthy" nationalism, meaning that it was tasked with protecting diverse voices in the public sphere as a means to counter the national fanaticism associated especially with German national identity. Policy scholar Andrew Murray describes this protectionist and state-controlled system as "paternalist" and "functionalist"; it is one in which "state action is considered a means to correct market failures, or in the 'public interest,' managing natural monopolies, public goods, and externalities that may arise (such as in the area of defense, or pollution issues), informational problems, and transactional costs."[49] The internet became part of this project. The internet, therefore, was less a part of Cold War military fears, as it was in the United States, and more a part of anxieties about government surveillance and protecting citizens. This connection offers some explanation as to why anxieties in Germany were more evident than those in France or Britain, given Germany's history of National Socialism and proximity to communism.

Not just a protected public sphere—a space with the potential to inoculate a population against the "wrong" kinds of nationalisms—the internet was also imagined by Europeans as a local rather than a necessarily global space. In 1994, *De Digitale Stad*, or Amsterdam's Digital City, went online, and still exists today.[50] The online city, which was an online presence for the city of Amsterdam, was wildly popular locally. During its inaugural week, Amsterdam suffered a modem-shortage as well as over-loaded telephone lines as the Dutch scrambled to get online. By December 1994, it averaged over 4,000 visitors a day and 120,000 a month.[51] A government initiative and national telecommunication corporation Dutch Telecom founded and funded the digital city.[52] The project rematerialized, centralized, and localized the internet experience for many Dutch. The City was located in a historical and urban marketplace, and it created a language- and location-specific online presence for citizens of the Netherlands and inhabitants of Amsterdam.

The Digital City's technology was cutting edge in that it was the "first real online presence for a city," and it incorporated sound as well as moving images. Yet this online city's servers and public-access computers were headquartered in De Waag, a famous and historic building built to house a market in the 15th century.[53] In this sense, the internet was placed in the context of over five centuries of mercantilism, updating it to cyber-merchantilism but still locating access to the historic spaces of Amsterdam. By 1996, the Digital City website was almost entirely in Dutch.[54] The focal image pictured an impressionistic digital rendering of Amsterdam as if it were shot from an airplane. Within this graphic were two clickable hyperlinks—"Bezoek de Stad als Bewoner" ("Visit the City as an Occupant") and "Bezoek de Stad als Tourist" ("Visit the City as Tourist")—both in Dutch. In addition, other links on the site were to "Laatste Nieuws" ("Latest News"), which contained information on Amsterdam (both its digital and analog incarnations), and "Prijs Informatie" ("Price Information"), where users could find out how to advertise on the site or become a sponsor. The only English on the page was a hyperlink on the left titled simply "English," which led users not only to "official" information from the creators of the Digital City, but also to "unofficial" websites of people from Amsterdam who happened to have English content. The latter were described as tourist guides to the City, or "A selection, to help you find your way. The city consists of squares with information on a theme, and neighbourhoods with homepages."[55] The limited availability of English content is clearly a nationalist decision, given the number of Dutch who speak English.

This Digital City illustrates one way the internet was produced as local in Europe. The website worked culturally to spatialize the internet, delimiting it metaphorically in a way that notions of the internet as a global non-space in the United States did not. A fixed location, a "city," is not a sprawling space like a "new frontier" or an "information superhighway." In its own history, as recorded on the website, governmental supporters and founders of the project described it in local terms, as a "'Test bed,'" where the "first shoots of an electronic community can begin to grow."[56] Imagined as a public sphere that would help produce a more functional state, the Digital City was presented as a communal space that would increase governmental transparency. Services and platforms were designed to "facilitate and renew the democratic processes by creating new channels of communication with the government" through which to "broadcast and collect information," and to house "discussion and opinions."[57] The City's goal—as identified by its founder Marleen Stikker (and the City's "mayor")—was to encourage citizens to scroll through minutes of local government meetings.[58] According to Stikker, the major advantages of digital space were not only allowing greater access to information, but also allowing individuals to participate in their government in new ways.[59] Thus, the Digital City promised universal and open access to all citizens who wanted to be knowledgeable or involved in their government was thereby supposed to contribute to creating better and more efficient policy.

The intense rhetoric of democracy in the Digital City descriptions meant that access was a main priority. Founders hoped that participants would "reflect the overall mixed profile of society" and so made special efforts to ensure a diverse pool of citizens could connect. Beyond creating universal access to this new organ of democracy, Stikker imagined the Digital City as a means to introduce the internet to the Dutch. She wanted the city to "develop a kind of 'data-literacy' among people who up to now were living quite outside it." The user was imagined as "evolving" from a "passive consumer of information into an active provider" of online information.[60] In this, Stikker anticipated "participatory culture" and Web 2.0 lingo used by contemporary theorists such as Henry Jenkins and Clay Shirky.[61] According to this vision, the Digital City would not only serve as a training ground for citizens, community organizations, and businesses on how to use the internet, but also contribute to the development of online technologies. It would help prepare the Dutch for coping with historic shifts of the period, especially globalization.[62]

The Digital City was simultaneously a local (or city) and a nationalist (or state) power play for online spaces. Noting that several digital cities were in the works, Stikker hoped that "due to the early advantage it has gained in both technical matters and content, The Digital City [would] become the 'capital' of a national network of digital cities."[63] Thus, the city would also help foster a European identity through a "national network of digital cities" that could "fulfill a role on a European level through the transfer of know-how and the creation of connections for co-operation across national frontiers."[64] In this vision, Dutch national identity and European continentalism were streamlined into one technological future utopia, a kind of "Dutch virtual nation" with the potential to eventually take on its American counterpart.

In some senses, the democratic rhetoric engaged by founders of the Digital City mirrored that of democratic new frontierism in the United States. These founders, however, imagined the City as a critique of those American metaphors. In their view, the Digital City would deliver to the Dutch what the virtual frontier promised the Americans but failed to provide. For Stikker, the internet was not a new space, but a means of reconfiguring existing space, a means of "changing our current cities and making them more responsive to the people who live in them." Her Digital City was simultaneously material, local, and technological, and not abstract, global, or a virtual reality.[65] Describing the City as made of telephone lines instead of "bricks, concrete and cobblestones," she said it was "just like an ordinary city. Everything you'd come across in ordinary life, we get here too." She noted that through the "Central Station" users could access the internet and thereby "patronize a digital cafe, browse through a digital kiosk, enter the digital house of culture and the arts, or pay a visit to a digital sex-shop, complete with a digital darkroom in the back....We are no moralists." The Digital City was, then, imagined by its leadership as in direct opposition to the internet in the United States. Unlike in those in the virtual frontier, citizens in the Digital City were free. For Stikker, "All those ideas you had heard so often from the United States about the new information society, tele-democracy, electronic citizenship, suddenly became a reality on DDS." Perhaps paradoxically, Stikker, like the German authorities taking on CompuServe later that year, would "not tolerate neo-fascist clubs or child pornography."[66] In the Dutch rendering of the internet, "democracy" meant governmental transparency and not complete unfettered rights to produce and/or consume online content.

Thus, in many places in Europe—especially in France, Germany, and the Netherlands—visions of the internet as global, virtual frontier or as an inevitability did not dominate. Instead, European policymakers, news media, popular culture, and internet users in these places imagined the internet in material and local terms, as a technological choice, or a public service. Although significant variations exist in the ways each European nation-states conceptualized and produced the internet, these various, national-specific cultural and technological histories of the internet worked collectively to produce the "European" internet as physically, culturally, and politically distinct in the late 1980s and early 1990s.[67] In contrast to policymakers in the United States, those in the European Union did not imagine the internet as necessarily driving history, as a rapidly diminishing global virtual frontier. The internet was not necessarily imagined through the American technological determinist lens detailed in previous chapters of this book and documented by historians of American technology. European news media, popular culture, and policymakers imagined the internet as a technological option, as one choice available amongst many, and as an activity grounded in material and regional culture.[68]

Thus, while both the United States and the European Union produced a series of protectionist policies in this period, U.S. policies liberalized government regulations, unfettering media corporations in the hopes of dominating global markets; European policies subsidized national corporations and explicitly local technologies in the hopes of protecting the diversity of voices in the public sphere and protecting domestic jobs in the face of U.S. corporate economic imperialism. In addition, in part because European nation-states competed with one another in media spheres, the enactment of or need to enact inter-European "protectionist" policies to defend against European neighbors emerged. These varying policy approaches reveal a fundamental and historical difference in the ways European and Americans imagine the relationships between the public, industry, and government. Historically, Americans have "turned to private industry as a remedy against perceived caprice and incompetence of government, whereas, in much of Europe, the opposite is true, and it is to government that the population turns for protection against runaway profit motive as driving industrial policy."[69] European socialist policies in the early to mid-1990s regulated the internet as if it were a public utility, prioritizing national corporations, protecting citizens' privacy, and projecting local identity and community onto online spaces. While European protectionist policies and examples of resistance or opposition to new technology are clearly not the same things, the two distinct notions are related in that both involve European fears of American expansionism and global economic dominance.

The Integrationist Turn: Configuring and Connecting eEurope

The story of the European Union, which most historians date at least back to the 1950s, is a story of increasing European or continental power and decreasing national power in the interest of global economic competition. The roots of this integration lie in post-war efforts to rebuild Europe by forming transnational markets and by merging legal structures governing commerce.[70] Although only six countries originally unified in the 1950s, by

1995 the union had extended to nine others.[71] Throughout this history, but especially in the 1990s, Europe shifted its economic policy from the statist models outlined above to more free-market policies. That is to say that beginning in the 1950s but increasingly in the 1990s, E.U. policies superseded those of member-states and became increasingly similar to U.S. policies.[72] With this shift, the meanings and purposes of media in Europe were reimagined. The post–World War II notion that the state should regulate media to ensure a "healthy" nationalism shifted to a notion that media would and should supplant nationalism with "Europeanism." The expectation was that media could be a major part of the cultural web binding E.U. member-states together.

This transition, however, was not always smooth. State control of media organizations, including those regulating the internet, was a major point of contention as nations-states struggled to retain their national identities while simultaneously producing a "European" one. Even as late as 2000, conflict arose—in particular among "dominant actors" like France, Germany, and the United Kingdom—over "integration," or the synchronization of member-states. These powerful nation-states resisted what they perceived as a loss of sovereign power in the face of supra-national E.U. law.[73] Under the principle of "supremacy," E.U. law trumps national laws if there is a conflict between them. This supra-legal system thereby deliberately weakens the nation-state in the interest of establishing continental consistency among legal systems and policies.[74] The European Union's transnational legal system disrupted the notion that national media, national territory, and state government necessarily all worked together to create national identity, or the notion that national territorial space and "politico-communicative space" were mutually productive. This assumption historically underwrote public policy's financial support for national media corporations.[75] In other words, the introduction of a transnational political structure began to dismantle the assumption that states should focus their financial efforts on supporting media designed to reinforce national boundaries. Thus, regulating the internet was not only a question of how to control and manage media, but also a place where tensions within the European Union were worked out.

Although the European Union successfully integrated its markets early in its history, integrating culture proved a more difficult task, a task with both roots and ramifications in cultural and political visions of the internet. European nations may have shared a common history—Roman and Greek roots, Middle Age feudalist economies, Renaissance artistic and intellectual legacies, and involvement in both world wars (but on different sides)— but national identities within each member-state often stressed differences rather than shared elements.[76] In addition, language differences, a hurdle not present in the same way in the United States, slowed or prevented cultural integration.[77] In response, European Union policymakers in the 1990s passed initiatives focused on the production of multilingual websites in one attempt to foster a common culture. Thus, economic and policy infrastructures previously focused on building distinct national cultures through broadcasting shifted toward building a collective European culture. As some scholars have noted, policymakers did not always take into account the issues these policies created, and instead the European focus was "simply extended from one political level to another, without any serious consideration of what might be involved in moving from a national community defined by the boundaries of a single state to an international community defined by integrationist political economics."[78]

Media reform was a major component of the drive to Europeanize, and member-states began to integrate media organizations in the mid-1980s. One of the first main policies was the 1989 Television Without Frontiers Directive (TWF), which stated that "Information is a decisive, perhaps the only decisive factor in European unification" and went on to say, "European unification will only be achieved if Europeans want it. Europeans will only want it if there is such a thing as European identity. A European identity will only develop if Europeans are adequately informed. At present, information via the mass media is controlled at national level." TWF presented national media control as a liability and instead aimed not only to "ensure the free movement of broadcasting services within the internal market," but also to simultaneously "preserve certain public interest objectives, such as cultural diversity, the right of reply, consumer protection and the protection of minors.[79] In this policy image, information was intricately involved in the formation of an eventually distinct European public sphere.[80]

Internet use rose in Europe in the 1990s at the same time as continental European initiatives like TWF emerged.[81] But while television signals were standardized, and therefore easily transmittable and receivable across national boundaries—and, indeed already were transmitted and received across neighboring countries' boundaries even before unification policies were enacted—the internet was a different story. Because the internet developed independently and differently in various European countries beginning in the 1970s, it was not standardized. This posed technological challenges to E.U. media integration, and European nations battled with each other and with the United States over who would set the protocol, or the system computers used to communicate with each other. Development in the United Kingdom was the earliest, most pervasive, and most similar to that in the

United States.[82] The British Post Office and British Telecom controlled connections in the late 1970s in the United Kingdom, which adopted "liberal interconnection policies" much earlier than other European member-states.[83] This meant that a variety of public entities was involved very early in internet development and that the British government was the first to begin liberalizing its telecommunication market.[84]

In contrast to the British, Germans and the French did not take this route. Instead their strong governmental involvement in national research networks—Bildschirmtext ("screen text") in Germany and Minitel in France—slowed the internet's development in those countries and helped reinforce both the assumption and that fact that the early internet was an English-speaking space.[85] This assumption was visible in the content of Germany's main government website which, even as late as 1996, looked like a tourism site aimed at English- and French-language speakers. The site had a plain white background with a photomontage centered in the screen. The montage pictured the Brandenburg Gate—the former dividing line between East and West Berlin and the site of John F. Kennedy's famous "Ich bin ein Berliner" speech—and the office building of the Bundeskanzler, or German Chancellor. The title-text on the site read "Die Bundesregierung Informiert" ("The Federal Government Informs"), and the only other text on the site was in the form of links to "Facts about Germany" and "Allemagne—Faits et Réalités" ("Germany—Facts and Realities"). These links led users to pages that detailed the reconstruction of Berlin after the fall of the Wall, featured "Pictures of the Month," and contained information and images of popular travel sites in Germany.[86] On the entire website, the only information designed explicitly for Germans was on the far left, in a separate window from the main page, which contained a link to press releases. In contrast, the White House website from the same historical moment contained no tourist information or images and instead was simply a searchable database for press releases.[87]

In hopes of integrating these disparate, state-operated and state-subsidized "internets," European policymakers launched the eEurope 2005 Project in December 1999.[88] According to the E.U. initiative document, this project was intended to ensure a "cohesive, not divisive" internet that was "integrating, not fragmenting. An opportunity not a threat." The project was expected to bring "the benefits of the Information Society to the reach of all Europeans" by providing financial incentives to private corporations willing to invest in internet infrastructure that would provide access to more individuals.[89] Arguing that the European Union was losing economic battles with the United States in part because of the internet, the eEurope document noted that

Experience in the United States shows that new technologies can drive growth and create jobs. Internet-related companies alone today account for 2.3 million direct jobs—not counting the considerable indirect employment effects—up from 1.6 million in 1998. The uptake of digital technologies, in the context of flexible labour and capital markets and reduced regulatory impediments to competition, have led to productivity growth and paved the way for the lasting, strong, and non-inflationary economic growth in the United States.[90]

In addition to noting the economic growth produced by internet industries, the eEurope 2005 text also cited higher internet adoption rates as one reason why the United States was gaining ground in online spaces and markets. By 1999, the U.S. internet penetration rate was seven times higher than the European Union's and over eight times that of Japan's.[91] The policy cited "early competition" and American dominance of the telecommunications industry as the reason for its high penetration rate. U.S. corporations were major threats to European media firms in general because U.S. companies provided cheaper and more complete content.

As the eEurope project demonstrates, in the late 1990s European policymakers felt the European Union would have to adopt policies similar to those in the United States in order to compete in media and economic spheres. Policies would no longer subsidize European corporations, but would instead dismantle those protections to promote competition, entrepreneurialism, and innovation. Paradoxically, creating a more liberal market initially required heavy government involvement and rigorous regulation.[92] This regulation would help force member-states to integrate or "harmonize" their media policies, which were characterized in E.U. studies as "a patchwork of inconsistency." This inconsistency distorted and fragmented the market, preventing European corporations from profiting from the "internal market" within Europe and prohibiting the concentration of venture capital required to gain market dominance over emerging technologies.[93] From this perspective, then, it appears that statist policies designed to hamper competition in favor of national media corporations as well as localist projects like the Digital City contributed to Europe's lagging status in internet development. In contrast, the European Union resolved to produce the internet as global (not local) and curb its domestic protectionism in favor of a more capitalist and liberal market policy.

The eEurope Project envisioned an online European space, or a public place in which disparate European citizens could interact. The "e" metaphorically replaced the nation in that "e" not only stood for "electronic," but

also ultimately for Europe in the symbolic trumping of continental identity and governmental structures over national ones. This project called for
member-states to "promote network security and broadband and to promote
eGovernment, eBusiness, eHealth and eLearning" by supporting greater
competition.[94] Although the policy did not generate funds for investment in
computer technology, it did provide a policy framework to redirect existing
expenditures toward investment in connectivity. The project upgraded European telecommunication infrastructure, created financial incentives to adopt
internet technology (especially broadband), removed "regulatory obstacles
to the development of new services," and created government incentives for
corporate investment in information technology. Two years later, an E.U.
study deemed the initiative a success in that penetration rates grew in the
years following, prices for connection decreased, and computer-education
programs increased.[95]

The eEurope Project retained its Europeanness in that its "key objectives"
were presented in egalitarian terms.[96] Universal access and social cohesion
were clearly stated priorities, thereby suggesting that the public utility model
of previous policies continued to influence the eEurope Project. The project hoped this market liberalization would increase internet adoption rates
by creating an "information society," a term that was first coined in 1994
and that framed policy debates about the internet thereafter.[97] Through this
metaphor, the internet was re-imagined as not a national but a continental
public space that could help diverse peoples overcome language, spatial, and
cultural barrier to form a collective identity. Not only a powerful vehicle in
the global marketplace, the internet would be a tool for unifying Europeans
themselves, a distinctly European space "based on its cultural heritage and
linguistic diversity," which Europeans could universally access.[98]

Although policymakers imagined the eEurope project as being in part a
socialist one, they did not acknowledge the problematic nature of using capitalist engines that require inequality to equalize diverse citizens. They did
not problematize the tensions among notions of collective identity, corporate
identity, and national identity. Rather, with this and other forays into neoliberalist statehood throughout the decade, the European Union regulated
"capitalist development in the interest of global capital itself."[99] As Hardt and
Negri note, the assumption behind neoliberalism is that humanity is best
served through corporate and not state organizations, because capitalism
produces individualism and the state produces homogenization or unity.
Neoliberalism positions globalization as "determined by an unregulated capitalism—with free markets and free trade," a notion Hardt and Negri critique
by pointing out that globalization is actually highly regulated. They cite in

particular the annual World Economic Forum in Davos, Switzerland, where the world's oligarchies "plan the destiny of capitalist globalization."[100] The assumption that capital—in itself—held the key to the liberation of Europe's peoples meant that Europe became in some sense Americanized or subject to an American global power. Neoliberalism masks American imperial (not imperialist) power in that it works to produce the United States and its corporations as inherently benevolent forces.[101] This suggests that in efforts to gain ground in opposition to U.S. economic power, E.U. policies paradoxically reinforced U.S. dominance.

Ironically, through initiatives like the eEurope 2005 project, the "communication industry" was presented by E.U. policymakers as "a panacea solution to the long-term loss of jobs in manufacturing industries, as domestic companies move offshore."[102] Like the European Union itself, the creation of a distinctly European space online was imagined as an antidote or a protection against globalization, a "shield against wider global forces."[103] Although academic voices proclaimed the state "dead" in the face of globalization, it was not.[104] As a columnist for the *Süddeutsche Zeitung* wrote in the *New York Times* in 1999:

> Though globocapitalism severely constrains some political choices, the state is not withering away. Indeed, it is flourishing nicely, taking an ever-bigger bite out of gross domestic product. In Europe, the state now grabs a bit more than one-half, up from less than one-quarter 50 years ago. If the state is dwindling, how come it spends and regulates so much?[105]

Moreover, the state did remain important in digitizing Europe. In contrast to in the United States, the European state was still responsible for its citizens' privacy and individual security online. With the eEurope document calling attention to hackings, worms, and viruses like the LoveBug, these threats produced the internet as a source of danger, and focused on the need for security to actively "combat cybercrime," "protect personal data," and ensure privacy through the establishment of a cyber-security task force.[106] The state in the European Union took a more hands-on approach to the internet than the U.S. government, which relied on corporations for online security. In the United States, the eEurope project was covered by *USA Today* as a European power play over online spaces, or an attempt by European leaders to "catch their trans-Atlantic rivals." The article noted that while 10 percent of European households had internet connections, nearly 50 percent of those in the United States did; that the United States dominated content production (95 percent of online content was in English); and that "U.S. companies

dominate the global e-world." The newspaper described the adoption of the
eEurope project as tedious and lengthy—as European policymakers "rumi-
nated endlessly over EU directives"—and contrasted this process to American business efficiency—since "Silicon Valley is not a product of a commission coming together and deciding innovation ought to come about."[107] In
sum, the eEurope Project was no threat to American internet dominance.

If it did not necessarily offer fierce competition (from the American perspective), the project did offer a competing metaphor.[108] Indeed, the "information society" was a deliberate and "direct (European) response to the
U.S. 'information superhighway' project announced by Al Gore in January
1994."[109] A society connotes a unified community with a cultural or physical
center, like a town marketplace. A superhighway connotes mobility and the
possibility of departure from a central location. Europe's conceptualizations
of the internet were a reaction to those in the United States, due in part to
Europe's historically socialist skepticism of American consumerism and in
part to contemporary concerns over American economic and cultural imperialism. Through the metaphor of the "information society" and its corresponding policy strategy, Europe attempted to bolster connectivity through
capitalist expansion, yet simultaneously bring the internet in line with other
kinds of state-controlled media in hopes of keeping American culture outside European borders.

At the same time, European policymakers saw the internet not only as
a weapon for competing with U.S. financial power, but also as a means of
fixing previously unsolvable problems, such as those related to social justice incongruities within and amongst E.U. member-states.[110] In European
visions, the internet provided a new sphere through which previously disadvantaged people might rise in social and economic stature. This egali-
tarianism was positioned in news media as combating what was imagined
as a form of American greed. For example, German newspapers described
the American rush to capitalize on the internet during the "dot.com" boom
as selfishness and wastefulness. A *Süddeutsche Zeitung*'s article titled "The
Goldrush in Cyberspace" opened by describing the founders of Netscape
as "four young men in front of a non-descript office building in California's
Mountain View" who were "washing their cars with champagne." Both the
founders and the firm were described as having brought a "gold-digger mentality" to the internet.[111]

As previous chapters have illustrated, cultural and state practices in the
United States in the early to mid-1990s helped forge links between the internet and nationalist American frontier narratives. Cyberspace was cultivated as—and presumed to be—a new American frontier and an inherently

democratic space, even while it was simultaneously imagined as a global technology and an icon of globalization. As the eEurope 2005 project demonstrates, this American virtual nation, or the notion that the internet embodied "Americanness," was and is transportable abroad. The project overtly identified the internet as a distinctly American space, as a source of U.S. power, and therefore, as a threat to European economic power. This project relinquished assumptions that European policymakers could regulate the internet in traditional statist ways and instead suggested that in order for the European Union to compete economically, it would have to adopt policies like those in the United States. Such policies would focus not on subsidizing national corporations but rather on dismantling state protections to promote competition, entrepreneurialism, and innovation.

However, even though Europe employed similar political approaches to the internet, it retained its alternate value structures. It aimed to use free market capitalism to create its own, distinctly European space online, a transnational public space that could help diverse Europeans overcome language, spatial, and cultural barriers to form a collective identity in the form of one "information society." The eEurope Project presented this society as a universally accessible, but distinctly European space. A tool for domestic community-building, for economic equality and uplift, the internet was considered a new sphere through which previously disadvantaged and disparate people might form a collective identity and, together, rise in social and economic stature. But this effect would occur through free market capitalism. Thus, the adoption of the eEurope 2005 Project suggested that the internet became a trans-Atlantic cultural carrier of capitalism and democracy—and a complicated one.

Complex Cultural Flows and the Digital
Divide Trans-Atlantic Splash-Back

As Lawrence Lessig and Wendy Grossman have noted, while the European Union has a history of adopting internet policies that diverge from those of than the United States, the United States has gone on to adopt some policies resembling E.U. policies.[112] Thus, for example, as producing the internet as a public utility—a policy impulse that focuses on accessibility to the public as a whole—became a goal in Europe in the late 1970s and early 1980s, universal access was not on the forefront of the policy agenda in the United States. Instead, U.S. policymakers focused on colonizing online spaces, fretting about foreign corporations moving into online spaces or markets, and working to ensure American corporations dominated the internet. As a result, U.S. policymakers worried less about whether all American citizens had access, assuming instead (and in keeping with Reagonomics models) that technology would eventually "trickle down" to the citizenry.

But in the late 1990s, this focus on corporate access began to shift, as policymakers became concerned with the "digital divide," or the gap between those with and those without internet access.[113] The concern arose in the wake of a flurry of governmental studies in the late 1990s that detailed the factors—including income, race, education, age, and region—that determined what was called "information disadvantage."[114] Although Census data revealed that computer and internet use increased in the 1990s, it also revealed that it increased in particular groups more than in others.[115] These reports discussed internet access as necessary for cultural citizenship, mirroring terms used in the eEurope initiative to describe the "information society." For example, one report issued in 1999 by the National Telecommunications and Information Administration of the U.S. Department of Commerce and titled "Falling Through the Net: Defining the Digital Divide" concluded: "In the final analysis, no one should be left behind as our nation advances into the 21st century, where having access to computers and the internet may be key to becoming a successful member of society."[116] In addition, the Clinton administration began to discuss computer and networking skills as "basic skills," and as "increasingly important for full participation in America's economic, political and social life."[117] Thus, beginning in the late 1990s, U.S. governmental institutions represented fixing the digital divide as important for U.S. democratic ideals as well as for its economy. This focus in the United States coincided with generalized global focus on computing as governments and corporations braced for the impending turn-of-the-century Y2K disaster.[118]

Because policymakers increasingly discussed the internet as an avenue to citizenship and a potential national disaster in the climate of Y2K, the internet was increasingly discussed in news media as an educational requirement and as a safety concern.[119] School competency (and by extension government competency in running schools) became a focus of digital divide debates. A study by the National Center for Education Statistics showed that in 1998 only 39 percent of classrooms in poor schools had internet connections, as compared to 74 percent in wealthy schools.[120] In the first mention of the "digital divide" in the New York Times, which occurred in 1996, a journalist detailed the stories of two students, John Dixon and Michael Giardina, who lived in Silicon Valley. John, a "freckle-faced fifth grader," attended a school in "one of the region's poorest communities," while Michael was a student attending a "pricey and prestigious" private elementary school. John had to "make do with the school's six-year-old IBM 386 PC," described as "little more than [an] electronic typewriter." He wished the school could afford better technology "so we could look up stuff on the encyclopedia and see pictures." In contrast, Michael had the "latest Apple Power Macintosh" that he could use to "manage his own World Wide Web page."[121]

In response to these reports and to increasing news coverage of internet inequality, Bill Clinton made universal U.S. access to the internet through educational institutions a national goal.[122] In 2000, Clinton, CEOs of U.S. internet provider corporations, members of congress, cabinet secretaries and community leaders conducted a nation-wide tour—called "From Digital Divide to Digital Opportunity"—through which they hoped to "focus national attention on initiatives aimed at overcoming the digital divide."[123] In the same year, the Clinton administration released a "National Call to Action to Close the Digital Divide" in which it announced that over 400 companies and non-profit organizations would "bring digital opportunity to youth, families, and communities across the country." First, this program was designed to "provide 21st century learning tools for every child in every school," or to ensure students were "technologically literate." Second, the program hoped to produce "digital opportunity for every American family and community" by making home internet access "universal," by providing neighborhood access through "community technology centers," and by "empowering all citizens with IT skills." In addition, the initiative created "E-Corps," or the dedication of AmeriCorps members and funds to "high-tech skills" training, and the creation of "NetPrep GYRLS," a program run through YWCAs which was designed to help girls aged fourteen through sixteen with computer networking.[124] These last two programs were in line with the training programs conceptualized but not implemented during the 1980s as first internet policy took shape in that they hoped to teach computing skills and address the inequities present in the internet as a male domain. Through this initiative, the United States positioned itself as the world leader in solving the "newly-discovered" digital divide, although the language of inequality already dominated European internet policy debates at least a decade before.

As this chapter illustrates, the internet's web of signification differed in the United States and in the European Union in the 1990s. In the United States, policymakers, news media, and popular culture producers imagined the internet as an inevitability, as a new frontier that would usher the United States into a new era of global economic dominance. In Europe before the late 1990s, policymakers, news media, and popular culture producers envisioned the internet as a technological choice and as a public utility that the state should provide through its support of national telecommunication corporations. Despite these differences, political imaginings of the internet in the two locations increasingly dovetailed. While European policymakers increasingly imagined the internet as a free market and a means for global economic power, American policymakers increasingly imagined the internet as a requirement for competent democratic citizenship. As Europe "Americanized" its internet policies—increasing competition by dispensing with state support for national telecommunication corporations—the United States "Europeanized" its internet policies—increasing state-support for bridging the digital divide.

Tweeting into the Future

Affecting Citizens and Networking Revolution

Egyptians took to the streets in 2011 in a revolution that would overthrow a regime that had controlled the country for three decades. In the midst of the unrest in Egypt, the *New York Times* website featured an image: a woman holding a scorecard that read "Facebook: 2, Dictators: 0" (presumably, mocking the deposed dictators in Tunisia and Egypt). The revolution became known (both in and outside Egypt) as the "Facebook Revolution" as news organizations such as *Fox News, CNN,* and the *New York Times* reported that Egyptian Facebook users laid the online social networking groundwork essential to the political activists.[1] In particular, news media cited the Facebook page entitled "We Are All Khaled Said," which quickly garnered 130,000 fans after it was created to honor a businessman who was beaten to death in 2009.[2] Said was killed after he reportedly posted a cell phone recording of corrupt police dividing the goods seized in a drug bust. The page became the largest dissident page in Egypt and a main location where the initial January 25 protests were planned.[3] The protests touched off dramatic and violent clashes among state military, citizen and mercenary thugs, and protestors throughout Cairo, but primarily in Tahrir Square. President Mubarak's ultimate resignation on February 11 was met with widespread national celebrations.

Clearly, internet-based media were important in the story that unfolded in Egypt. The number of people with Facebook pages in Egypt increased more than 400 percent between 2008 and 2010, a significant increase even though that still meant less than 4 percent of Egyptians were online.[4] Yet, the "Facebook Revolution" label is also clearly problematic. A revolution on Facebook might not reflect a revolution on the ground. For example, in Iran in 2009, messages about state violence against protesters flooded out over the internet and news media. A cell phone video recording Nega Agha Soltan's death became such a profound focus of Twitter posts and reposts that the protests became the "Twitter Revolution." Shortly thereafter, a former staffer at the National Security Council called for Twitter to be nominated for a Nobel Peace Prize.[5] But, as Evgeny Morozov illustrates, assessing who was in-country and who was not was complicated as Tweeters outside of Iran changed their time zones to hide the identities of in-country compatriots.[6] Because of the internet's anonymity, an online presence does not necessarily mean in-country sentiment.[7]

Malcolm Gladwell famously argued against the hyperbolic rhetoric about media revolution in "Small Change: The Revolution Will Not Be Tweeted," in the *New Yorker*. Using the civil rights movement as his model in this article, Gladwell observed that strong ties are necessary for significant change. Social networking, he argued, encourages weak ties. Clicking your support of a fan site is not the same as protesting at a lunch counter. For Gladwell, the technological determinist rhetoric distracted from the real causes that determined revolution: "Where activists were once defined by their causes, they are now defined by their tools."[8] Gladwell's piece appeared after the Iranian revolution failed to produce regime change, but three months before Ben Ali was ousted out of Tunisia and before Egyptian regime change. When pushed to recant in the wake of developments in Egypt, Gladwell stuck to his guns, arguing that Facebook did not cause the revolutions. People did. "People protested and brought down governments before Facebook was invented. They did it before the Internet came along." For Gladwell, "People with a grievance will always find ways to communicate with each other. How they choose to do it is less interesting, in the end, than why they were driven to do it in the first place."[9] Indeed, the online movement that ultimately helped overthrow Mubarak had legitimate grievances, and opposition movements to Mubarak were in place offline well before Facebook existed.

But if social media were not the whole story, why did they become dominant in narratives for understanding revolutions in the Middle East? Why the "hyper-enthusiasm" in particular in American news media about the role of new media? To answer this question, this chapter looks to the history of social networking. The history of blogs offers insight into how what Marwan Kraidy terms "hypermedia space"—a "fluid communicative environment" made up of "mobile telephony, tweets, email, social networks, text messaging, digital cameras, online videos, electronic newspapers, and satellite television"—became instrumentally linked with productive and democratic citizenship, especially among youths.[10] This chapter charts the mediated and political narratives about blogs and social networking that circulated during in the first decade of the twenty-first century, when the networking technologies became popular. As Lisa Gitelman has argued, the "novelty years, transitional states, and identity crises" of a new medium are especially useful in determining a technology's shape. The novelty years of the blog were instrumental in shaping visions of the social media networks that followed.

As this chapter illustrates, news media initially represented blogs as "unmediated" and authentic proxies to individual users. This representation dovetailed with those cultivated in particular by users and academics who imagined the internet's new blogs as able to fill the vacuum left by skepticism about commercialized news media and mass culture: if the blog could supplant newsroom standards of objectivity with radically authentic subjectivity, then bloggers themselves could be an antidote to dysfunctional and corrupt news media and its corporate culture. Envisioned by users, news media, and academics as offering authentic participation, blogs also became for these cultural agents vehicles for individuals to push back against corporate media interests and reclaim power through democratic means. As blogs gave way to microblogging and other social media, companies like Twitter capitalized on these visions of blogging and mapped visions of political legitimacy and authenticity onto a new (but related) technological practice. Ultimately, all of these shifts together worked to reconfigure new media political participation as idealized and revitalized democratic civic engagement and was part of a larger policy shift toward governmental "transparency."

In this context, the Facebook Revolution frame made sense. The frame capitalized on visions of the internet as authentic, as democratic, and as a space where transparent and benevolent nationhood happened. It functioned as a strain of discourse that reassured Americans (but clearly not all) that the revolution would promote "the right kind" of democracy, one that would support capitalism and U.S. national interests. It metaphorically extended the American virtual nation abroad through the corpoNation. But the frame also highlighted the ways Egyptians at home and abroad participated in diasporic nation-building, in the ways international news coverage tapped visions of and options about the protests from a variety of sources. It noted the messiness that is nation in the face of a transnational medium and acknowledged that the internet is not cleanly only nation or only transnation, but both.

The Rise of Blogs: Auteur Bloggers and the Internet's First Scalp

In 1999, when approximately fifty blogs existed, a *Chicago Tribune* article titled "She has Seen the Future and It Is—Weblogs" compared reading a blog to "breaking into a psychiatrist's office and rifling through the files until you come upon an especially juicy set of notes from a client session."[11] Another reporter described what he called an "odd intimacy" to blogs, writing that it was as if they were "addressed to the reader across the breakfast table."[12] As in these examples, early news media representations of "web-logs" presented the websites as intensely personal, as windows into the minds and souls of blogging individuals.[13] As American users, journalists, and academics tried to make sense of blogging, they began to imagine the blog as authentic, uncommodified, and strangely "unmediated" proxies of the user's self.[14] As Jeffrey Sconce notes, popular imaginings of electronic media have long offered the "possibility of analogous exchanges, electricity mediating the transfer and substitution of consciousness and information between the body and host of electronic media technologies." This vision, he adds, has been "central in describing both the wonders and horrors of an emerging cyberculture."[15] In the case of the blog, the rhetoric suggested (or fantasized) the blog would be the ultimate democratic medium, if it remained authentic and uncommodified.

Indeed, the very roots of the blog lie in explicitly anti-capitalist impulses. The term "weblog" is generally attributed to Jorn Barger in 1997.[16] Barger, a self-taught James Joyce expert, spent much of 2005 reportedly roaming the streets of San Francisco as a homeless man holding a sign reading "Coined the term 'weblog,' never made a dime."[17] Other than this attempt to capitalize on his "coinage" with literal coinage, Barger did not attempt to market his idea or the first weblog ("Robot Wisdom"). His interests lay in connecting people and the information they valued rather than in personal monetary gain.[18] Thus, the roots of the blog more closely resemble anti-capitalist, utopian rhetoric associated with the internet of the 1980s—specifically the hacker ethic—than capitalist rhetoric engaged by computer entrepreneurs of the 1990s as they built their bubble.[19]

But, as with other technological innovations, the number of blogs did not take off until corporations intervened. After Pyra Labs released its "Blogger" software in 1999, for example, the number of blogs increased substantially.[20] This software made blogging easier in that users no longer needed to have knowledge of html or other programming languages to blog. While making it easier and more widespread, this technology also made blogging less technologically transparent as blogging became less like computer programming and more like word processing. By 2001, Pyra had registered 80,000 users and struggled to cope with the 400 to 500 new users that tried to register every day.[21] By 2005, the number of blogs increased to 40,000 a day and by 2007, Technorati, a website tracking blogs, estimated 70 million existed.[22] By 2011, over 161 million blogs existed.[23]

As participation in blogs increased, so did efforts to explain the techno-logical phenomenon. By 2000, the *Milwaukee Journal Sentinel* already regu-larly published a "Hall of Fame Weblogs" called "Weblogs, Weblogs Every-where: We Tell You Where to Find Them."[24] 'Blog' was the "most looked-up word of 2004," according to *Reuters*, as the public struggled to learn what they were and who produced them.[25] In its first article on the subject in 2001, *U.S. News & World Report* described the blog as "a frequently updated Web page consisting of brief, dated entries, with new ones pushing the old to the bottom of the page."[26] The high level of searches, the webmaps of the blogo-sphere, and especially the instruction manuals for reading blogs like that in *U.S. News* illustrate that the writing and reading of blogs was not a natural phenomenon, but instead learned. Through explicative labor such as this, news media helped set the common sense assumptions about blogs by help-ing standardize and normalize reading practices. Thus, early representations in news media of the technological phenomenon had exceptional influence in setting the cultural expectations, or the frames, used to think about and to consume blogs.

These early news reports and blogosphere maps characterized bloggers as anti-corporate rebels and internet technology itself as an art form, a mech-anism for presenting the essential self (realistic or fantastic) to the world. For example, in "She Has Seen the Future and It Is—Weblogs," Julia Keller described "webloggers" as a "self-selected group of mostly young (under 30), relentlessly verbal, fiendishly well-read, usually subversive folks who relish tying together the shoelaces of the stiffly homogenized corporate world."[27] Imagined as an escapee from destructive corporate influences, the blogger was figured as an educated, presumably white, energetic rebel engaging the internet as his or her personal vehicle for protest. News media often cited the structure of the internet—as an essentially interpersonal medium (a prob-lematic assumption in itself)—as enabling this rebellious spirit. For example, one journalist described blogs as having the "complete opposite structure of conventional media, which is top-down, boring and inherently arrogant."[28] Similarly, Jon Katz, author of *Geeks*, argued in a 2000 interview with the *San Diego Union-Tribune* that blogs "embody personalized media on the Net," where "enterprising geeks" can unseat the corporate powers of news produc-tion and instead create "interesting new sites that set out to define news in different ways, to be interesting, coherent and more civil."[29]

Just as a film was imagined as reflecting the personality of auteur directors in the 1970s, the internet weblog was imagined twenty years later as capable of reflecting auteur bloggers. Presented in romantic and emotional terms, a blog was "like an independent film on an endless loop" or a "memoir of the future," and, as such, it could be "highly personalized and exhilaratingly eccentric, with more than a touch of the rebel and the poet."[30] In focusing on the potentials for intimacy, such reports presumed a shared feeling between reader and writer, a feeling that affectively bound the two. Envisioning the blog as an intensely personal and obsessive pursuit, journalists sometimes paradoxically celebrated the universal accessibility of blogs, as well as their potential as artistic products. Blogs could be "part diary, part consumer's guide for television, movies and music, and part transcript of an all-night phone call with a best friend. Anybody's best friend."[31] Such news coverage that framed blogs as universally accessible and authentic interpolated readers to both sense and trust the emotional realism available on blogs. In contrast, the period was characterized by widespread public distrust of mass media and concerns about mass media bias. As survey data overwhelmingly showed, a majority of Americans in the early 2000s viewed media as biased toward special interests, government, and advertisers. (This concern outpaced concerns over bias along liberal/conservative or Democratic/Republican valences.[32])

Academic critiques of mass media positioned the blogger rebel as an antidote to defunct media organizations.[33] For example, media scholar Dan Burstein argued that media industries ignored the voices of the public in order to "make *their* voices heard" in what was an age-old critique of the gatekeeping power of media, or of media as controllers of public knowledge and access.[34] Burstein proclaimed the blog as the key to the future of democracy in that although "professionals still have control over the biggest, most powerful, most visible mainstream media," through the technological developments of blogging "'everyone' now has a meaningful shot at being heard."[35] Although he acknowledged that what he called the "crazies and irresponsible people" also gain access to the microphone, Burstein ultimately pronounced blogs as enabling what he called "the ordinary citizenry" to "re-engag[e] in the lost art of the public conversation."[36] Thus, for academics and bloggers alike, blogs represented the mobilization of an emerging knowledge society, a society in which Keller's rebel auteurs would be able to break through corporate media monopolies to reach the public with their authentic artistic realism. Notions such as this in academic debates worked along with pervasive distrust of mass media in the public and with representations of blogs in news media as "unmediated" and authentic to culturally produce the blog and the blogger as purveyor of truth and as democratic citizen-hero.

The representations of bloggers as revolutionary were neither universal nor seamless. On the contrary, like most representations in the cultural sphere, these, too, were contested. In a 2002 article asking "Will the Blogs

Kill Old Media?" journalist Steven Levy noted that new technologies are often imagined as revolutionary when they emerge, but more often than not eventually serve the established power hierarchy.[37] Taking a broader historical view of the emergence of blogs than many other reporters, Levy humorously wrote that some bloggers in 2002 were "even predicting that the Blogosphere is on a trajectory to eclipse the death-star-like dome of Big Media" and that "by 2007, more readers will get news from blogs than from *The New York Times*."[38] In direct opposition to most academics and new media outlets, Levy wrote, "Blogs are a terrific addition to the media universe. But they posed no threat to the established order." As evidence, Levy snarkily cited utopian prophesies about the internet that suggested "Big Media were sitting ducks for upstart competitors with cool Web sites." While he recognized that the internet made the media sphere more participatory, the technology "couldn't drive readers to your door... and the majority of news-surfers visit only the top few sites."[39] For Levy, while blogs contained revolutionary potential, they would not likely threaten media corporate power.

Bloggers themselves, however, often imagined their collective role as checking corporate media. As the metaphorical vigilante console cowboys on the digital frontier, they would create a healthy public sphere. For example, on July 21, 2002, the *New York Times* front-page story "Flaws in the U.S. Air War Left Hundreds of Civilians Dead" became the target of blogger critique. Bloggers alleged that the article reported inaccurate data about casualties in Afghanistan. But the old-new media circuit went further, as the bloggers' critique itself became a target of news media. *U.S. News & World Report* ran a story called "Flogged by Bloggers" that stated, "bloggers descended on the article like ants on a picnic," playing "'gotcha' with the established media."[40] Speed and ease of linking online sources were on the side of the bloggers in the figurative battle over information between corporate and non-corporate forces. While the elite ombudsmen of the past required time to craft their coverage critiques, one article noted that bloggers "work quickly, while the stories they target are fresh" and work together to empower the citizen, linking to each others' sources "so readers can judge for themselves."[41] News media and academics imagined bloggers as strong and resilient revolutionaries, able to fend off attempts by "established media" to "shrug off complaints of bias as the ravings of right-wing fanatics." One journalist advised his readers to "keep an eye on bloggers" because the "main arena for media criticism is not going to be books, columns, or panel discussions, and it certainly won't be journalism schools. It will be the Internet. Web diarists are calling the print media's bluff."[42]

Early coverage focused not only on blogs as checks on the truth of media messages, but also as watchdogs on government. The notion that blogs should and could watch government dates as far back as the blog itself. Perhaps the ultimate proto-blogger celebrity was Matthew Drudge, creator of the drudgereport.com, and the individual responsible for breaking the Monika Lewinski scandal. In the wake of Drudge's revelation, Kenneth Starr's investigation into Bill Clinton's relationship with intern Monika Lewinski was released online in 1998, and became so popular that it caused computer systems to fail. Nearly every major news organization covered the release in terms of increasing government transparency and a more functional democracy in light of enterprising individuals online.[43] While the *Post* released the document directly, instead of linking to Drudge, the release would not have occurred without Drudge's participation. "Lewinskygate" occurred before the coinage of "weblog," yet both it and Matthew Drudge appear in academic histories of blogging. This might seem strange because drudgereport.com was more an information aggregator, a personalized collection of hyperlinks to other places, than a coherent diary narrative. It was surprisingly un-bloglike in its disassociation from Matt Drudge's personality. Yet, Drudge has influenced notions of blogging in that he is cited as one of the bloggers who made a difference in politics.

Blogs checked the media and policy agendas at the same time as they forced items onto these agendas. In December of 2002, Senate Republican leader Trent Lott of Mississippi spoke at Strom Thurmond's one-hundredth birthday party: "I want to say this about my state: When Strom Thurmond ran for president, we voted for him. We're proud of it. And if the rest of the country had followed our lead, we wouldn't have had all these problems over all these years either."[44] In saying that Strom Thurmond should have won the presidency in 1948 as the segregationist candidate, Trent Lott asserted white supremacy and suggested the civil rights movement had been bad for the country. Despite its sensational nature, news media were slow to pick up this story and instead the story was pushed onto the media agenda by bloggers. Due in large part to media attention begun by bloggers, Lott was ultimately forced to publically apologize for his "poor choice of words" and resign as Republican majority leader.[45] This power shift then became the subject of news media reports that stated: "in our high-tech and increasingly decentralized America, the swelling furor over Lott's words was first sparked not by other politicians or mainstream media, but on weblogs."[46] As political reporter Michael Barone noted, blogs revealed Lott's "affectionate nostalgia for segregation"—a nostalgia that "offends not just blacks but the large majority of Americans, who renounce that past."[47] A *New York Post* reporter famously called Lott's resignation the "internet's first scalp," a metaphor that not only strangely racialized bloggers as invading Native Americans (in a news event already imbued with racialized rhetoric), but also suggested that a single warrior or terrorist can brutalize an individual in a significant way using internet technologies.[48] This rhetoric re-embodies the internet in the wake of 1990s disembodiment rhetoric detailed in previous chapters.

Although news media and academics imagined blogging as containing extraordinary potentials for liberation not shared by other media technologies, this idealized liberation was neither seamless nor given. Understood as proxies of the self, or as authentic mirrors of their producers, blogs triggered anxieties rooted in mythology about the potential ills of self-obsession. Steven Levy wrote, for example, that blogs would succeed as democratic icons only if they retained their "authenticity" by remaining anti-corporate and if they resisted the seductions of narcissism. Even as early as the late 1990s, reporters and bloggers voiced fears of corporate influence, observing that even " as Weblogs increase in popularity, danger looms: They may be co-opted by corporate entities," which "would be a shame, because corporate sponsorship might muffle the feisty voice of Weblogs."[49] The assumption was that as blogs became more popular, corporate entities would colonize, copy, or pollute them and would thereby strip blogs of their authenticity. The cybercitizen blogger hero was only that if he or she (and at the time mostly he) remained anti-corporate.

Visions of blogs as projections of the self not only brought anxieties about commercialization to the surface, but they also drew out percolating anxieties about the internet and privacy. As Levy wrote in *Newsweek*, the format of blogging "seduces participants into sharing personal thoughts and opinions," but because of open access online, these "intimate thoughts suddenly come to the attention of unwanted readers."[50] As an example of this phenomenon, Levy recounted a story of a high school student whose mother read about his youthful indiscretions from his blog. Levy reported that, "Real life, he's learned, sometimes intrudes on the Blog-o-sphere. One day there may not be a difference."[51] Levy imagines the internet and blogs as seamless pathways to the blogger's interiority, or a window into the unseen and private instead of a projection of the self into the public sphere.

Kill Your Blog, Tweet Your Politics

Although by November 2008, *Wired* magazine had already declared the blog dead, the rhetoric of the blog lived on in social networking technologies. In the article titled "Kill Your Blog: Still Posting Like It's 2004? Well,

Knock It Off. There are Chirpier Ways to Get Your Word Out," a *Wired* reporter wrote: "Twitter … is to 2008 what the blogosphere was to 2004." He cited "cut-rate journalists and under-ground marketing campaigns" as having "drown[ed] out the authentic voices of amateur wordsmiths."[52] Clearly, Twitter (or microblogging) was not blogging, but *Wired* imagined Twitter as the next generation, as an example of progress and productive newness that incorporated and built on the best of the past. Twitter added a new kind of authenticity that stemmed not only from the individual, but also from the collective, the individual's social network. Thus, the new potential sphere for authentic democratic expression was Twitter, and the user migration was in full force.

In its promotional materials, Twitter seemed to implicitly mediate the potential for corporate co-option, as well as anxieties that media consumers would become self-obsessed or increasingly interact only with like-minded individuals in media bubbles. "Insulating media enclave[s] of information and opinion," such media bubbles diminish opportunities for encountering diverse sources or, most importantly, belief systems counter to those already-held by the media consumer.[53] Political scientists Daniel W. Drezner, and Henry Farrell, for example, argue the blogosphere may have a "corrosive effect on the body politic" in that it may produce what Robert Putnam calls "cyberapartheid" and "cyberbalkanization" or what Cass Sunstein describes as a giant echo chamber that enables individuals to "wall themselves off from others."[54] The idea that the blogosphere was the space of self-centered people in an enclosed world increasingly infiltrated by corporate interests gained ground, and these were nails in the blog's cybercoffin.

Twitter, however, claimed its platform was designed to be explicitly value-neutral, to focus on the authentic life and on the mundane. Tweets would answer the question, "What are you doing right now?" Tweets would be daily diaries or logs, reflections of one's daily practices or moods, not unlike the psychologist office notion of the blog. However, the instructional video on Twitter's "help" site in 2008 featured only explicitly political examples and screen-captures. "JoePublic09" was the imagined user. His tweets were "What time is the rally?" and "Crucial vote today." "Joe" was a "Human Rights Attorney" in D.C. who tweeted voter reminders to get his followers to the polls. He tweeted about political rallies, about Obama, and about the failing economy of the mid-2000s. Using this example, the Twitter site explained the site's potential to "reach billions of users instantly," "issue public safety alerts, real-time news developments, inform constituents, solicit feedback." For its promotional material, Twitter did not choose "JaneHomemaker09," an evangelical school board member and mother of four tweeting about making tuna sandwiches for her kids. Twitter used a leftie political activist living inside the beltway. Thus, while on the one hand Twitter described its purpose as mundane, as not explicitly corporate, or political, on the other, it promoted its explicitly (leftist) political potentials.

At the same time, the company added a zing of political activism by embedding itself in successful political blogs—like Wonkette—and by bragging about its political uses. Twitter publicized how then-presidential candidate Barak Obama announced his vice-presidential candidate over Twitter. News media coverage of the 2008 presidential campaign assisted Twitter in this project by focusing on Obama's use of the site and other new media and social networking websites to promote a candidate, contact supporters, distribute materials, organize rallies. Dubbed the "Triple O"—"Obama's Online Operation"—this strategy was described by the *Washington Post* as "the envy of strategists in both parties, redefining the role that an online team can play within a campaign."[55]

Indeed, the traditional horserace or strategy-focused coverage of electoral politics long discussed by media scholars had a new sphere of contest.[56] Who had more Facebook friends? Whose YouTube channel had more views? Political leaders fretted about their party's online presence and, Republicans in particular, about the "enthusiasm gap" as measured by social media participation.[57] In the early 2000s, this online battle was fought over the coveted "Millenial" voters (born after 1980)—the most plugged-in generation, over 90 percent of whom used the internet by 2010 (as compared to 70 percent of the general adult population and as low as 40 percent of more "reliable" voter, older populations).[58] Coverage of new media in the campaign almost exclusively showed Obama as a web-master, leveraging online fundraising, contacting more and younger constituents through social networks, and collecting more or better information about those constituents through the internet.[59] This type of coverage continued into the Obama administration as Obama appointed a number of new media corporate heads, including Twitter CEO Dick Costolo and chief executives of Google and AOL, to central advisory positions.[60]

Alongside praise for Obama's multi-platform campaigning, criticism of John McCain's reported inability to use computers appeared in news reports.[61] For example, in a *St. Petersburg Times* article by Andy Borowitz, McCain became an object of satire:

> In a daring bid to wrench attention from his Democratic rival in the 2008 presidential race, Sen. John McCain today embarked on a historic first-ever visit to the Internet. Given that the Arizona Republican had never

logged onto the Internet before, advisers acknowledged that his first visit to the World Wide Web was fraught with risk. But with his Democratic rival Barack Obama making headlines with his tour of the Middle East and Europe, the McCain campaign felt that they needed to "come up with something equally bold for John to do," according to one adviser.[62]

The joke worked in its historical moment because McCain's discomfort and lack of experience with computer technology were so widely publicized. In the 2009 campaign, social networking and multi-platform internet skills became part of a public performance and criteria by which to judge presidential candidates—signs of how "in touch" and forward-thinking they were.

This campaign strategy was part and parcel of larger movements toward participatory culture and government transparency. Referred to as "open source politics" by Micah Sifry, this strategy mandates a level of "interactivity" that is "aimed at showing that the candidate is 'listening to the public' in the same way that a photo-op supposedly shows that a candidate cares about some issue."[63] But open source politics rhetoric also mandates a new, sit-forward citizen, a citizen engaged in what scholars have recently called "participatory culture."[64] In the early 2000s, blogs (and later on, social media networks) became the sites of online collectives, the spaces that produced collaborative public spheres. This technological shift dovetailed with an expansion and politicization of narratives about blogs. In particular, the DailyKos, begun by Iraq War veteran Markos Moulitsas in 2002, allowed users to contribute "diaries" to the front page. As Sifry observes, this blog served as a "huge collaboration engine" and was a "thriving and intimate network of many little villages."[65] As politicians, internet users, scholars, and journalists increasingly imagined the internet—the blogosphere and social media networks in particular—as a political space, the role of the citizen "greatly expanded" to be "not just ... a passive consumer of political information and occasional voter, but ... an active player, monitoring what government and politicians are doing."[66] Not only bloggers, but also all internet users (or, as Jay Rosen pithily called them, "the people formerly known as the audience") were reimagined as potential participants in the political process in that they could both consume and produce media messages.[67] By 2010, the Pew Center for Internet and American Life estimated that 82 percent of American internet users (or 61 percent of the population) "looked for information or completed a transaction on a government website" and that 23 percent of users made up what researchers called the "government participatory class," individuals who "participate in the online debate around government policies or issues, with much of this discussion occurring outside of official government channels."[68] In a sense the early role (and responsibility) of the blogger as check on the mass media merged with more general internet use.

The individualistic and democratic imagery of early blogs also shaped internet policies of the period. In the years following the emergence and popularization of blogs, the U.S. government held a number of hearings and passed a number of policies designed to promote "productive" (meaning democratic or capitalistic) use of the internet and to protect citizens already online.[69] Earlier policies (of the 1990s) had focused on U.S. citizens as demographic groups and worked to correct the "digital divide," or the underrepresentation of certain racial or economic minority groups online.[70] However, policies of the early 2000s conceptualized internet users as discrete individuals, as U.S. citizens in need of state protection or as citizens of the internet (cybercitizens) deserving of state aggression. In other words, domestic policies worked to protect individual American users from scams, theft, and to some extent corporate invasion, while foreign policy initiatives worked to dismantle restrictions over online spaces and, particularly in China, liberate individual users.[71] In the wake of 9/11, political and military operatives fretted over individual users and designed policies aimed to dismantle suspected terrorists' cybercitizenship in the name of protecting democracy.[72] By conflating personal liberty, democracy, and online spaces in some instances and not others, U.S. domestic and foreign internet policies worked in tandem with popular culture and news media to produce American citizen-users as producers of the ultimate democracy at home, and the American nation-state as protector of both the internet and democracy around the world.

In addition, in the wake of the Iraq War and 9/11, news media and policymakers began to focus on governmental "transparency" as a new goal, and new media as the vehicle for reaching that goal. In 2006, Congress passed the Federal Funding Transparency and Accountability Act, which required "full disclosure of entities receiving federal funding" and mandated that this disclosure be effected through "the existence and operation of a single searchable website, accessible to the public at no cost to access."[73] This policy assumed the internet could provide transparency to government funding. And, as it turned out, the internet also provided transparency to the policymaking process leading up to this policy. The bill, sponsored by Senators Obama and Coburn, "had been stymied by a so-called 'secret hold' placed on it by an unknown senator." The Sunlight Foundation, "the first Washington-based nonprofit dedicated to using technology and the internet to open up government," crowdsourced (asked the online collective) information to discover the senators holding up the bill; after being exposed, Senators Ted Stevens and Robert Byrd reversed their actions and the bill passed in Congress.[74] In a sense, the policy push to produce transparency through the internet and the unmediated authenticity and radical subjectivity attributed by academics, bloggers, and journalists to the blogosphere merged with a focus on government accountability. As technology scholar and blogger David Weinberger wrote, "Transparency is the new objectivity ...Transparency brings us to reliability the way objectivity used to."[75]

"Tweeting" is not the same as the blogging that preceded it, but Twitter cloaked itself in blogging's authenticity through its focus on the mundane. At the same time, it simultaneously engaged the legacy of the politically active citizen blogger. Considerable slippage occurred in news media, academic debates, policy images, and corporate cultural locations between microblogging and blogging, between news coverage of the 2008 presidential campaign and Twitter marketing strategies, and in particular between visions of broken objectivity and internet technological fixes, aimed to create transparency or radical subjectivity (or both). These slippages worked to merge notions of online individual authenticity with collective politics and helped to reimagine the internet as the ultimate democratic space, a place in which individuals might interact in authentic ways, form collective bonds and authentic grassroots political organizations to reshape government, and interact with politicians poised and ready to hear them.

National/Global Affective Citizenship

In imagining blogs and early social networking as able to affectively address media consumers, to bind them together in a loose ideological sense, and to interpolate consumers as political subjects with the potential for authentic governmental and media reform, early news coverage highlighted the blog's potentials to form what Lauren Berlant terms an intimate public. In her work on "national sentimentality," Berlant argues that the U.S. public sphere is an "affective space of attachment and identification" that is produced in part by mass culture and media.[76] Media organizations engage affect in order to create markets for their products, but the affect also helps interpolate (in the Althusserian sense) individuals in the public as national subjects, as citizens, and as consumers. This intimate public helps form the individual and individual action in that it "provides anchors for realistic, critical assessment of the way things are and provides material that foments enduring, resisting, overcoming, and enjoying" being an individual within and in opposition to a public.[77]

But the intimate public is not a product of false consciousness or mind control. It engages power in that it helps individuals form a common sense about the world, but participation is fueled by "desire for reciprocity with the world," meaning the individual retains agency in Berlant's model. In her focus on agency, Berlant does not intend to downplay the intimate public's power. She focuses on the ways this public helps produce the future through its power to "respond to material interests," as well as "magnetize optimism about living and being connected to strangers in a kind of nebulous *communitas*."[78] This intimate public may marshal subjects in service of the nation or commerce as well as resistance to one or both. Berlant calls intimate publics "juxtapolitical" because they are "incoherent" like the individuals who instantiate them, and yet they "thrive in proximity to the political, occasionally crossing over in political alliance, even more occasionally doing some politics, but more often not, acting as a critical chorus that sees the expression of emotional response and conceptual recalibration as achievement enough."[79]

A deep and diverse wealth of academic work continues to study and debate what the internet does or does not do to its users, how it affects communities, empathy, and the national body politic. Nicholas Carr, Jaron Lanier, Steven Johnson, and others argue complex relationships exist between internet technology and users and collectives. Carr, for example, argues that the very structure of the internet itself alters the neurological makeup of the human brain, thereby decreasing the capacity for deep or critical thinking and empathy. The internet, in this vision, is a participant in the formation of on- and off-line behaviors and affect and not necessarily a mirror for a static, off-line truth.[80] As issues such as cyber-bullying rose and fell on the public agenda, debates raged amongst journalists, policymakers, parents, and users that merged anxieties about appropriate youth technology use with visions of the internet as a place of affective belonging and collectivity. These debates often positioned the health of the future public on the health of online interactions and health of affective collectivity. These academic debates as well as news media representations and internet user practices worked to culturally reconfigure social networking sites as legitimate American political spheres and places where citizens may (and leaders must) perform political affect and belonging. These debates positioned the internet as the place where personal, corporate, and national futures would happen. But it also (re)made the internet into a potential personal and social liability. Thus, social networks became a place where America happened and where it would happen for better or worse, and a location through which a variety of citizenships and performances of citizenship might emerge.

To complicate matters, in the early 2000s the internet was increasingly populated by non-Americans. During the rise of Twitter and the exhausting build-up of the 2008 presidential campaigns, China became the world leader not only in cell phone use, but also in internet use.[81] While this still meant that only 17 percent of China's population was online (as compared to 71 percent of the U.S. population), the news folded into long-established anxieties about the U.S. losing the "technology race" with other countries, in particular Japan, China, South Korea, and India. Policymakers and journalists attributed the surge in Chinese users not only to China's economic strength, but also to its national sponsorship of cheap technology and its subsidies that made broadband access as cheap as $10 a month.[82] This nationalization of internet access followed on the heels of reports two years earlier about the ways American corporations helped China spread access (that is, a restricted access that complied with its state's ideological political positions). In particular, these reports indicted Microsoft for blocking words like "democracy" and "freedom," Google for its limited search results in its Chinese version, and Yahoo for its data leaks about users to Chinese officials (which resulted in a journalist's imprisonment).[83]

These and other activities on the part of American corporations have led researchers Goldsmith and Wu to pithily note that "the Great Wall of China was built with American bricks."[84] Google had become the "internet's switch," in China and abroad, and the "custodian of the Master Switch" of informational exchange.[85] As Siva Vaidhyanathan writes, Google's power over the internet and over global culture arises in part because of consumer choices, meaning "we now allow Google to determine what is important, relevant, and true on the web and in the world. We trust and believe that Google acts in our best interests."[86] But Google is also "American," and part of the trust in it stems from its status as a corpoNation, or a nation-imbued corporate stand-in for the state. From this notion flows the assumption that Google has users' and America's best interest at heart. In the case of China, however, Google's status as a corpoNation contributed to a sense of betrayal. Not only was America losing the great race to populate the internet, but also its corporations were aiding the competition. If the internet was becoming a legitimate and authentic public sphere for American citizens to connect, to be activists, and to solve the problems caused by corporate media, it was also becoming a place where American corporations were helping rival nations oppress their people.

This online population shift occurred in a historical moment marked by diminishing U.S. power as internet arbiter. International agents participated increasingly in the Internet Corporation for Assigned Names and Numbers

(ICANN), which assigns domain names instead of the U.S. government. In addition, signs pointed to the diminishing power of the English language online. In the late 1990s, Arabic speakers could access Arabic websites, although not easily due to alphabet differences and because the writing moves from right to left. In an article titled "Stake Me to Your Breeder: Brian Whitaker Tests the Toils of Surfing in Arabic," a *Guardian* journalist noted that although Arabic was the world's sixth most prevalent language in 1998, "in computer terms, it lags far behind" and that the "World Wide Web is certainly not as worldwide as it ought to be."[87] However, while more languages became available in online spaces, the underlying structure remained English-based and Western-oriented.[88] As philosopher David Golumbia noted, ""like Hollywood films and U.S. television, the computer exerts a powerful attractive pull toward English that is perceived by many non-English-speakers as 'modern opportunity.'"[89] Arabic language domain names emerged in late 2009, and the first internet addresses to use non-Latin characters allowed non-English speakers new access.[90] Billed by the *Guardian* as "a significant moment for the internationalization of the world wide web—half of whose users do not use a Latin script as their primary language," the technological development and ICANN policy change meant that Arabic speakers no longer had to have their websites "hosted under Latin addresses."[91] This challenged, although did not dismantle, the English bias online.

On the one hand, the 2000s was a moment characterized by remapping physical and often national boundaries onto the internet. Users in the Middle East increasingly went online more easily and used more Arabic-language sites. The internet began to mirror the oppressive shape of governments, as in China. This mapping of nation onto the internet challenged late 1990s globalization rhetoric, in which scholars expected that the nation would fade away and citizens would become netizens. But on the other hand, as more diverse peoples got online, news media, academic work, and policy debates increasingly imagined the internet as neither national or transnational, but both. The internet began to seem "less inherently American," less homogenized and homogenizing. Scholars began to imagine alternative visions of power online. If users and nations might not become Americanized (directed power) or self-colonized participants in the American virtual nation (soft power), the internet could be a simultaneously national and transnational hybrid space, a proxy for a multitude of virtual nations and a place where those nations and their citizens bleed into one another in complicated and diasporic ways.

Indeed, in 2010 during what would become known as the "Arab Spring," journalists and policymakers portrayed the internet as a technology that might help new Tunisian and Egyptian nations happen in and through national and transnational ways.[92] These visions were, of course, inconsistent, diverse, and contested as a number of agents around the world tried to make sense of changes in the region. During the Arab Spring, news media, corporate visions, and policymaker statements battled over what the internet meant for Middle Eastern citizenships, with debates focusing in particular on whether the internet extended a version of American citizenship into non-U.S. territories; whether it facilitated non-American citizenships in those places, or whether it created diasporic global citizenships. Deeply at issue in this debate were the potential roles of the American virtual nation and the corpoNation, and especially Facebook's role in what would become known as the "Facebook Revolution."

Friending the Revolution

The idea of the Facebook Revolution appeared within a larger conversation and a larger set of anxieties. Given the enormously complicated history between the United States and Middle East, U.S. policymakers, news media, and academics looked on unrest in Egypt with some concern.[93] What would this new nation become? The Facebook Revolution notion, as a strain of discourse, functioned to reassure. While the narrative obviously did not alleviate all anxieties, it relieved some. The presence or even dominance of a strategy of representation within a discursive world does not mean that strategy is successful. This particular strain of discourse contained the Muslim uprising within American technological determinism and American exceptionalism.[94] It credited the United States, as inventor of the internet and home of Facebook, with liberating the Middle East. However, according to the Facebook Revolution construct, the United States did not exert directed power through invasion (or even Obama's "leading from behind" soft-power leadership strategies[95]); rather, American corporate powers simply provided the Egyptian people with the technologies of self-liberation and self-determination. This presented a paradox delicious to U.S. news media and policymakers: A country in which an oppressive leader (Mubarak) attempted to protect his police state by shutting down the internet was liberated by the internet. U.S. news media and policymakers such as President Obama imagined Mubarak's act as a significant disavowal of personal freedom. In addition, calling for Mubarak to reinstate internet connections was a major strategy of the Obama administration for dealing with the complicated conflict, a means for Obama to critique Mubarak but not directly support the protesters. Of course, in the months surrounding the Middle East revolutions, the Obama administration and congressional leaders were in the midst of debates about whether the United States should have a similar "internet kill switch."[96] The consensus amongst policymakers was that such a switch would be employed only in the protection of domestic democracy and not to stymie dissent. In any case, in a moment in which curtailing internet access abroad meant ruthless power plays and inauthentic authority, the rights of American citizens to organize in public spaces also had to apply to digital spaces.

The internet played a complicated role in the Middle East, both in terms of the role that connectivity played in the revolution itself and in terms of how its functions were interpreted. Because of connectivity, the Facebook Revolution was not about Egyptian or American politics; it was about transnational politics. It was not only a national event; it was also a transnational phenomenon. Facebook facilitated an intimate public in that it allowed Egyptians both inside and outside Egypt to connect and to feel connected, to participate and to feel like they were participating. It allowed, for that matter, nationals from a multitude of countries a level of involvement, as well as becoming a window into the revolution viewable by journalists and politicians around the world. This gave observers access to revolution leaders, clues where the protests were moving, and insight into what the revolutionaries were facing and how they were faring. Facebook allowed connections online that could in theory be invisible to security forces of Mubarak's police state, except that in order to involve a broad population in Egypt the pages had to risk including informants, thereby risking becoming subject to the government surveillance they were trying to dismantle.

In the Arab Spring, Facebook was a site of media convergence, a platform for multimedia informational exchanges. Facebook users could repost blog posts, post their own pictures and videos, comment from hand-held devices on other posts, and update where the protests were moving and counter-revolutionaries hiding. As Clay Shirky writes, "the chance that someone with a camera will come across an event of global significance is rapidly becoming the chance that such an event has any witnesses at all."[97] Facebook's air of authentic citizen journalism and multiplatform media content made for good copy. With little cost to the network, CNN produced sexy packages composed of "on the scene" participant coverage performing authenticity through shaky camerawork and poor resolution. Video and images were simultaneously heartbreaking, soul-crushing, and empowering to watch.

In a historical moment when media organizations expend increasingly fewer resources on foreign correspondence and foreign coverage, the insight offered into the revolutions in the Middle East through the internet's multiplatform connectivity was clearly important to the success of the revolution and to the revolution's reception around the world. But it was also problematic. Mediated experience is, well, mediated. Although media forms often aspire to mask their mediation—Hollywood style aspires for an audience that forgets it is watching a film—mediated experience is always indirect. Mediated experience differs from direct experience. Watching a concert on video is not attending a concert. Watching YouTube clips of a protest is a different experience of that protest. Yet, YouTube, Facebook, blogs, and so on collectively offer the illusion of understanding. In writing about this "irony of technology," Susan Douglas notes that "communications technologies can often have the exact *opposite* consequences of what we think and hope they might be." Indeed, she argues that "the great irony of our time is that just when a globe-encircling grid of communications systems indeed makes it possible for Americans to see and learn more than ever about the rest of the world, Americans have been more isolated and less informed."[98] Because journalists could "view" a protest from their desks, for example, media organizations could use the internet as justification for closing foreign offices, which they did at an astounding rate as the internet expended in the 1990s. As Morozov noted about the "Twitter Revolution" in 2009 in Iran, journalists imagined they knew what was happening in-country because they were watching Twitter feeds.

As "driver" of the revolution in the "Facebook Revolution" frame, Facebook became a democratic hero that incorporated Muslim revolutionaries into an American narrative of self-determination. Converging with ideas about the blogosphere, the Facebook Revolution frame imagined the internet as a space of democracy and authenticity, and one that empowered Egyptian citizens against their corrupt government and defunct media. The narrative participated in the discourse that constructed social media and the blogosphere as inherently political and potentially revolutionary. The narrative had affective appeal. As Melani McAlister observes, there was something beautiful and magical in thinking that the same medium that connected Americans to friends and family was the same medium that connected individuals abroad and allowed them to improve their lives.[99] The Facebook experience was familiar to Americans, and the narrative appealed to journalists in part because they thought it tricked the American public into caring about a foreign news event.[100] It allowed Americans to imagine the internet as neither the source of oppression and surveillance nor the destroyer of social fabric, but instead as empowering, deeply personal, and authentically democratic. But the narrative also imagined fundamental American participation, assuaging American fears that the United States had lost control over the technology as well as both global politics and economics. If, as this chapter argues, social networking rode in part on the cultural representations of blogging that imagined the internet as a technology capable of unmediation, of serving as an authentic proxy to the self, and as a legitimate political space, then Facebook represented idealized democratic communication with the potential to be the purveyor of American-style, self-determined democracy.

As a corpoNation, Facebook offered a way of being that was at once individual, authentic, political, and corporate. New media helped rehabilitate Facebook from its stigma as a location for pictures of drunken frat parties and reintegrated American corporate power into the landscape of American democracy and freedom. The latter was especially important in the wake of the scandals about American internet corporations in China. (Recuperation began, of course, shortly before the social media revolution mania when Google pulled out of China in the wake of hacking activities and domestic critiques that it was not upholding its corporate motto to "not be evil.") The Facebook Revolution frame helped mitigate fears that American corporate powers acted in opposition to the internet's "real" meaning—democracy— and thereby betrayed both America and the technology itself. Indeed, news media highlighted that one of the primary Facebook group organizers was also a Google employee.[101] In addition, the trope reinforced the residual notion from early coverage of blogs that—unlike radio and television—the internet provided individualistic and democratic participation even after the technology was commodified. Binding democracy, capitalism, individualism, and technology into a new corpoNation package indicated future democratic health. As Tim Wu writes, Google (and Apple) "are determining how Americans and the rest of the world will share information ... the future of Apple and Google will form the future of America and the world."[102] The logic here is that the internet, through American ambassador corpoNations, will not only help citizens overthrow oppressive regimes, but also simultaneously organize radicalism and dissent in the interest of American foreign policy and foreign markets. As the state and corporations come to be conflated (as with neoliberalism), so are economic and democratic interests.

This common sense curtailed alternative options for what the internet might mean by conflating diverse notions of the internet, democracy, and capitalism and by sprinkling the conflation with inevitability. But, as the previous chapter illustrated, neither the internet nor its meanings were inevitable. The Facebook Revolution could have been understood differently, as evidenced by the variety of frames that floated through non-American news media, such as "January 25 Revolution," or the "White Revolution." But in the United States and to a large extent in Egypt, the "Facebook Revolution" frame dominated the news media agenda until the "Arab Spring" frame superseded it.

This American technological determinism-inflected frame downplayed many historical legacies and characteristics of the revolution. As many media scholars and cultural critics in news media have noted, the Facebook Revolution trope obscured Egyptian agency. In mediating "changing of the guard" fears of youth rebellion domestically and Muslim youth terrorist fears abroad by reincorporating the internet as a legitimate performance of citizenship, this narrative also diminished activities off line as well as activities by non-youths. As media scholar Marwan Kraidy notes, the "new media" narrative obscures the role of "old media," and thus the less glamorous stories of off-line organization, of people watching TV and talking to their neighbors, are lost.[103] If anything, the "Facebook Revolution" should have been called the "Al Jazeera Revolution," as the television network had much higher penetration rates and served as the main informational source for both those living in the Middle East and diaspora actors.[104] But in the United States, the revolution could not be televised, it had to be Facebooked. Only the new possess revolutionary potentials. Focus on Facebook also drowned out discussions of the serious problems in Egypt that caused the unrest, such as problematic economic and education systems. In other words, as Sifry observes, in terms of revolutions, "the degree of internet penetration, social network usage, and mobile phone ownership may not matter as much as more basic factors like demographics, unemployment rates, and education levels."[105]

The frame may have obscured the identities of actors involved in the revolution. In the wake of the initial protests, pro-Israel policymakers and activists, as well as Fox News and NPR journalists worried that the Muslim Brotherhood was behind the revolution.[106] Indeed, if the revolution had been framed as the "Muslim Brotherhood Revolution" instead of the "Facebook Revolution," the American popular reaction would have clearly differed. The extent to which the Muslim Brotherhood actively encouraged the Facebook Revolution frame remains unclear, but the LA Times reported that the organization was actively "muting its religious message," suggesting Muslim Brotherhood leaders understood the potential advantages to downplaying the Brotherhood's involvement.[107] The Facebook narrative certainly had the potential to mask the organization's involvement by sidetracking attention onto the groups on Facebook that professed more secular, economic, apolitical, and grass roots rationale for revolution. The frame made the revolution feel universal, secular, populist, or all these qualities together.

The frame also redirected attention away from sometimes direct U.S. governmental involvement in new media revolutionary impulses. The State Department took direct action in facilitating new media revolutionary potentials abroad. It created a Facebook group called "Alliance of Youth Movements," which was a coalition of groups from a dozen countries who use Facebook for political organizing. In December of 2008, the State Department also brought an international collection of activists (including one from Egypt's April 6 group) as well as Facebook executives and representatives from Google to New York City for a three-day conference.[108] During the "Twitter Revolution" in Iran, the State Department asked Twitter to delay upgrades to help protestors. These direct actions on the part of the U.S. government were deflected as public attention focused on activity on (or spurred on by) Facebook and away from government and religious involvement both inside and outside Egypt.

And, once again, the "Facebook Revolution" frame was by no means smooth, universal, or uncontested. In his interview with Gigi Ibrahim, an Egyptian activist, comedian Jon Stewart mocked notions of American involvement in the Egyptian revolution at the same time as he acknowledged American soft power. When asked how she became involved with the movement, Ibrahim reported that she had taken a class at the American University in Cairo called "Social Mobilization under an Authoritarian Regime," through which she became aware of opposition movements in place for decades. Acknowledging American influence in stirring opposition to Mubarak, Stewart replied, so "we were there fermenting revolution." Stewart—after noting the silliness of the "Facebook Revolution" title by saying "those were not tweets on the square"—said, "We're a freedom loving people. We love freedom and we like to spread it." Ibrahim called the United States "an overbearing father" to which Stewart replied "but the father that you, years later, look back at and say 'I'm glad.'" In this statement Stewart tapped a long domestic history of "benevolent supremacy" and "American exceptionalism," or the ways Americans have historically imagined the United States as uniquely and righteously positioned as a "Good Samaritan" with the "idealistic responsibility of feeding the world and organizing the peace."[109] Stewart, however, also acknowledged anxieties about waning American power when he continued: "We spread freedom, unless it's people we think might not like us … and we're worried you might not like us." Ultimately, however, Stewart poked fun at American egotism in naming the revolution a "Facebook Revolution" by asking, "or are we not the center of your universe and you're just looking to express your own democratic voices and it really might not have that much to do with us which, by the way, would be harder for us to take?"[110]

Stewart's hypothetical and clearly satirical question raised an important critique of the Facebook Revolution frame in noting that the frame gives more credit to an American social networking site than to the activists who used it. The future of Egypt remains an open question as I write this in 2011. The Iran "Twitter Revolution" in 2009 resulted in little long-term change. The Arab Spring revolutions may not last, which will change the end of this story.

In conclusion, imagined in news media, academic scholarship, and policy debates as the ultimate democratic medium—as authentic and unmediated—blogs and bloggers were also envisioned as able to fill the vacuum left by skepticism about commercialized news media and mass culture: if the blog could supplant inept newsroom standards of objectivity with radically authentic subjectivity, then bloggers themselves could be an antidote to dysfunctional and corrupt news media and its corporate culture. This cultural construction of blogs and the internet itself served a number of interests, in particular that of bloggers, policymakers, and cultural critics. Bloggers could imagine and represent themselves as "console cowboys" on the digital frontier, building on residual representations from 1980s hackers and reinforcing notions of democratic individualism through resistance to both government and corporate power. Politicians could point to the individual as the basic American social and political organizing unit and as evidence of a healthy or potentially healthier democracy. Imagined as a cure for the ills of corporate interference in the public sphere, blogs provided users, policymakers, and academics with a vehicle to express anti-corporate and anti-government sentiment that emerged in the wake of the millennium, during and after the "dot.com" bubble burst, and during the Bush administration's era of governmental expansion in the wake of 9/11.

As blogs gave way to microblogging and to a multitude of social networking sites, cultural imaginings began to bleed between quite diverse online activities. Corporate visions of, for example, Twitter actively worked to map visions of political legitimacy and unmediated authenticity from blogging onto its microblogging site. Thus, the cultural legacy of blogs worked to reconfigure new media spaces as ideally suited to democratic civic engagement, as spaces where leaders must address those they purport to lead, as legitimate spaces for the performance of "unmediated" affective belonging and citizenship, and as spaces in which individuals could congregate to speak back to and discipline governmental and media powers. For journalists, policymakers, and internet users, the internet became a place where nation happened.

Finally, in the wake of revolutions in the Middle East, journalists, policymakers, and users in the United States and abroad imagined Facebook as a potential revolution-driver, a place where revolution may take place, and a place where it may be "observed" (accurately and in real-time around the world simultaneously). Appearing in the context of larger anxieties about the United States and the Middle East, the "Facebook Revolution" frame worked to assuage American anxieties by crediting the United States and its company Facebook for participation. In both deserved and undeserved ways, the frame imagined American national-corporate powers as uniting Egyptian people through internet technologies, guiding them toward self-liberation and self-determination. The technological determinist flavor obscured the bodies and bodily risk required for revolution. The frame's American exceptionalist flavor obscured involvement by the U.S. government and (possible) Muslim Brotherhood involvement.

By imagining Facebook as a way of being at once individual, authentic, political, and corporate, the frame reinvigorated visions of the internet (dating back to the 1980s but also present in the wake of the blog's popularization) as authentic, as democratic, and as a space where nation could and should happen. This helped rehabilitate corpoNations in the wake of the scandals by re-nationalizing them. But the frame also complicated those visions of the internet as national by highlighting its transnationalism, by presenting the internet as at once a multimedia platform through which activists shared a variety of media products and organized offline protests, a space in which national and transnational activism took place in diasporic ways, and a location where journalists, leaders, and counter-revolutionaries might observe online and offline activities for better or worse.

CONCLUSION

As Jeffrey Sconce snarkily notes, historical writing tends to end where it began, because "cyclical returns in history imply the existence of immutable forces, power brought to light and made predictable by the insight of the author's historical analysis. 'History repeats itself' goes the well-known aphorism."[1] While this book ends in some senses where it began, it does so to illustrate the ways history *fails* to neatly repeat itself. The visions of the internet detailed in the previous chapters do not recycle efficiently like a historical Ferris wheel, nor do they whiz along on a linear rollercoaster into the sunset. The carnival that is history and culture is much messier. Still, discourses elaborated in the previous chapters merge, re-emerge, submerge, mix, and shift as things change, as new historical events happen, as users imagine and re-imagine networking, as corporations and start-ups develop and sell new technologies, as policymakers advocate for different government action.

The internet's cultural history (like its technological shape) does not determine its future. But knowing the history of discourses that have shaped the perception of the internet's meanings, problems, and possibilities lends insight into ongoing developments and debates. For example, in 2011, governments around the world fretted about WikiLeaks. The website, created in 2006 most likely by Julian Assange, defined its mission as "bringing important news and information to the public" by allowing sources to anonymously leak information and thereby publicizing "suppressed and censored injustices."[2] The site's most famous leaks to date involved documentation of civilian causalities in Iraq and Afghanistan, as well as classified diplomatic cables from U.S. embassies around the world.[3] But the site also leaked information as diverse as documentation of publically unremarked government-corporate alliances, Sarah Palin's hacked emails, and Scientology's secret Bibles. Was Assange a hacker, a terrorist, or a concerned global citizen invested in governmental and corporate transparency? As journalists, academics, and politicians in the halls of Congress debated the various leaks, a number of discourses discussed in the previous chapters reemerged and reconfigured.

First, coverage of WikiLeaks was reminiscent of the "teenaged technology" discourse from the 1980s, which cast internet users as rebellious teenagers with the potential to destroy the world. News media coverage of and books about WikiLeaks presented Assange as mildly adolescent, as a petite, irresponsible, moody, and difficult-to-work-with rebel who struggled to keep track of his clothes, passport, and schedule. To U.S. policymakers, Assange was a volatile yet powerful former hacker who lacked self-control, and his working outside governance and morality made him potentially menacing on a global scale.[4] Thus, visions of Assange in news media and policy debates shared some qualities with the fictional David Lightman, the teen hacker who accidentally almost blew up the world in *WarGames*. But they are clearly different. Out were the days of the Cold War parental state; in were the days of the post-9/11 days of the "state of exception."

Second, Assange's personal story—as a homeless, country-hopping bandit avoiding legal retribution for both his informational leaks and his personal infractions (two rape accusations)—was mapped onto WikiLeaks itself. In news media, WikiLeaks was an uncontrollable entity with distributed servers, nameless employees, and anonymous sources scattered around the world.[5] WikiLeaks, a transnational "pariah" and the "world's most dangerous website," was run by Julian Assange, a social pariah, who would "boast about how many children he had fathered in various parts of the world."[6] Just as Bill Gates and Microsoft were linked, personifying computer technology through the biography of one of its innovators, so was WikiLeaks a window into the troubled life of Assange, and vice versa.

Third, imagined as a deterritorialized menace, the supposed power of WikiLeaks stemmed in part from its perceived post-nationalism. Much was made of the ways WikiLeaks capitalized on the internet's decentralized and anonymous structure. Assange did not need to meet or contact leakers as he could use an anonymous, digital drop box to collect leaks. Just as it would be difficult to imagine the internet as a virtual reality or an experience if it remained only text-based, so it would be difficult for WikiLeaks to exist without the structure of the internet, which facilitates anonymity and transnational interactions. Yet the internet is neither entirely deterritorialized nor anonymous; rather, it does rely on nationally embedded structures and tracking systems to function. This means that nationally located corporate organizations, or what Goldsmith and Wu call "intermediaries," such as PayPal, the Swiss Bank Postfinance, and Bank of America could put a halt to Wikileak's economic engines.⁷ Moreover, its most famous leaker, Private Bradley Manning, was exposed and jailed for leaking diplomatic cables in part because of Assange's failure to follow through with all capabilities for ensuring anonymity and in part because the internet's U.S. military origins mean that activities online are trackable.

Fourth, in forcing important issues onto the news media agenda—by leaking information about U.S. war atrocities to the *New York Times* and *Der Spiegel*—WikiLeaks emblematized early news media fantasies of the best of what the blogosphere could offer. WikiLeaks could, in this vision, force and enforce governmental and corporate "transparency," particularly in the military spheres it explicitly targeted. Even the name "WikiLeaks" itself played on notions of participatory culture, borrowing the "wiki" from other collaborative publishing sites. Despite what this name might suggest, however, the site was editorially controlled and did not allow unvetted leaking, or uncontrolled participation. Its structure was more blog than wiki, but the site cloaked itself in the "authenticity" of participatory culture, presenting itself as a collective and transnational whistleblower protecting democracy by increasing government and corporate transparency. At the same time, WikiLeaks further complicated visions of early blogs as authentic and non-hierarchized vehicles of transparency by relying on established news organizations to facilitate and publicize the leaks. In a battle of attention scarcity, WikiLeaks could not gain significant public awareness without also using organizations like the *New York Times*, the *Guardian*, and *Der Spiegel*.

Finally, some credited WikiLeaks with sparking 2010 revolutions in the Middle East. According to this logic, by releasing cables from the U.S. ambassador to Tunisia which described the nation as "a political kleptocracy (one was even titled, 'Corruption in Tunisia: What's Yours is Mine')," WikiLeaks exposed Tunisian governmental transgressions to the detriment of the status quo.⁸ In some ways, WikiLeaks profited in the same way that Facebook did, in that both enjoyed a public relations bump from the Middle East uprisings. The revolutions, however, also brought the divergent natures of the two organizations into relief and, in a way, highlighted varying visions of what the internet was and should be. Furthermore, visions of WikiLeaks and Facebook as symbols of the internet's rising political power highlighted generational rifts. Assange was a nominee for *Time Magazine's* Person of the Year in 2010, but was beaten out by Facebook's Mark Zuckerberg. Assange's goals were reminiscent of an early 1980s hacker ethic that imagined information as "wanting" to be free, that embraced ruthless transparency as both inevitable and good, and that valued political change (not financial reward) as the most delicious fruit of online labors. Zuckerberg, also a former hacker, embodied an entirely different ethic based on the idea that individuals should to be free to share information, photos, likes/dislikes, social connections, and dating statuses. The fruits of Zuckerberg's labor were excessive income windfalls and an extensive, U.S.-based, global corporate empire. In a *Saturday Night Live* comedy sketch, "Julian Assange" (played by comedian Bill Hader) quipped, "I give you private information on corporations for free, and I'm a villain. Mark Zuckerberg gives your private information to corporations for money, and he's man of the year."[9] In both the WikiLeaks and the Facebook visions of internet possibilities, information should be "free," but for different purposes and with different effects. The battle between Assange and Zuckerberg for "Person of the Year" was a contest between two new media entrepreneurs, but it was also a contest between visions. These visions tapped historical-but-still-present hacker liberationist ideals that both overlapped and challenged neoliberal, corporate ideals.

This nod to a complicated (and at the time of this writing, ongoing) story is not meant as a thorough interrogation of the discourses surrounding WikiLeaks. Rather, this gesture is meant to illustrate how the previous chapters will help explain the future as it unfolds and as new events require others to add to, update, critique, and continue the work started here. Indeed, WikiLeaks has been a news event through which the world's policymakers, news media, as well as political activists of all stripes have debated many of the issues raised in this book. Those debates also included threads of inquiry such as privacy, free speech, and security which this project could address only briefly. My hope is that future studies of the internet will not only look forward to its potentials, but also back to its histories—technological, political, social, economic, and cultural—to contextualize and reflect on what ideas are taken for granted in future moments. The internet is not a fait accompli; it is always becoming and always changing. Nonetheless, narratives from its past development play out in its future conceptualizations, shapes, and regulations. Without interrogating those narratives and understanding how they inform present visions, we risk deciding our future with the internet based on incomplete and biased visions of the technology. In the new, there is always residual old. Those vestiges of the past are key to understanding the nows and planning the whens.

This book changes the questions we have asked about the internet. Instead of asking "What does it to do us?" and "How do we use it better?" this book has asked "What do we think?" "Why do we think that?" and "What are the consequences of those assumptions?" This book demands attention to the discourses that have animated the internet and will do so in the future. It requires that we think about how those discourses defining and redefining our relationship to internet technology replicate or intersect with broader discourses important to our collective lives, such as democracy, neoliberalism, citizenship, and nation (or nationalism). This project requires that we examine the messiness behind the formation of "common sense" and, in particular, the way political common senses do not emerge from universal truths nor in light of inevitable technological progress but are instead constructed by numerous agents through complex cultural coordinated conjunctures.

As this book has shown, between the 1980s and the late 2000s the internet became a major player in the global economy and one of the most transformative technologies in both American and world history. Users had new ways to relate to one another, to share their lives, spend their time, shop, work, learn, organize, and take political or social action. At the same time, the internet became an important topic in the public sphere, capturing the attention of millions as they struggled to figure out what the technology was, what it could and should do, and what it might become. The foregoing chapters describe the varying, yet overlapping ways news media, popular culture, academics, and policymakers in the United States, Europe, and Middle East (and to a more limited extent elsewhere) made sense of the internet.

Collectively, these chapters illustrate that the internet was (and is) at once a technology with changing capabilities and practices and a discursive object, or a cultural location. A number of agents—including journalists, advertisers, users, hardware and software designers, policymakers—participated in the formation of a number of ways of thinking about the internet and our experiences with it. These common senses were porous, conflicting, contested, and variable. They reflected desires and anxieties about the present, about the future, and about related issues such as the health of democracy, the utility of capitalism, the status of globalization, and American global dominance. This explains how the internet was represented in popular culture, news media, and in policy debates as simultaneously a scary military weapon and a creative toy for teenagers in the 1980s; as an information superhighway, a virtual reality, a marketplace, a workplace, a commodity, and an engine of capitalism in the early 1990s; as an icon of globalization, an engine of capitalism, an inevitability, and a public utility in late 1990s; and as a strangely unmediated proxy of its users and a simultaneously national and transnational political sphere in the 2000s. These visions of the internet have had productive power, and, if not always in simple or direct ways, they shaped the technology's future. These discourses have constituted reality, knowledge, policy, and technology. They have produced and masked deep assumptions about internet technology that have been manifested in policy decisions in the material infrastructures of the internet, which in turn have also shaped common understandings, even as they have gone, until recently, largely unnoticed by existing literature about the internet.[10]

This book adds to the wave of new studies that remedy this oversight by offering three new perspectives on the internet. First, while this book tells the cultural and political history of the internet, it does not only offer a historical account. Indeed, the central approach and focus are new. Studying the history of the internet's meanings—the history of mediated and political narratives *about* the technology and not merely its technological history, its content, or narratives produced by inventors—punctures what have become regular presumptions about the internet, its governance, and growth. By problematizing the technologically determinist histories that place technology itself as the primary (or sole) driver of history, policy, culture, and social structures, this book demonstrates that the internet—as a technology and set of cultural meanings—transformed in accordance with larger changes in culture and policy as much as with the intrinsic capabilities of technology itself. The internet's technological "essence" makes it neither a technological progress train to a utopian future nor a neo-fascist vehicle to universal oppression. This study makes a case for the importance of a cultural history of the internet by demonstrating in very concrete terms how representations of the internet both relied on and helped formulate larger cultural assumptions about the nation, the state, democracy, public space, consumption, and capitalism. As such, this story differs from those told in technological and policy histories, in news media and popular culture, and in cyberculture scholarship.

Second, investigating this particular history helps reshape the way we understand the development of public policies. In contrast to most work on internet policy, which presents culture as either outside of or an obstacle to the policymaking process, these chapters demonstrate explicitly and specifically the ways culture determines policy. Cultural values and not an objective reality outside of culture set policy agendas, shape policy debates, and help determine policy outcomes. At the same time, policy itself is not outside discourse. Policy is a cultural actor. Policies validate and legitimize particular cultural voices and representations over others, amplifying them in the cultural sphere.

Third, this book contributes a systematic, comparative perspective to the study of the internet and internet policy by contrasting cultural and political representations in the United States, Europe, and (to a much lesser extent) Egypt. This critical perspective demonstrates how representations of the internet produced by a number of agents for diverse purposes were (and are) intricately linked with national identity even as they grapple with a "global" technology. Indeed, the internet has served as a cultural location in which national debates—about mass media, globalization, democracy, public space, consumption, capitalism, and America's place in the world—take place. For example, in the 1990s, both American and European policymakers imagined citizens as going transnational online and yet both hoped the experience could be re-nationalizing. In the United States, policymakers envisioned an "American virtual nation," a new frontier created by nation-inflected corporations, or corpoNations. In the European Union, policymakers initially envisioned an extended local European utility, an internet space sponsored by the state. E.U. policymakers ultimately adopted a strategy similar to the U.S. vision that would engage the U.S. corpoNation, yet still hoped to nationalize the internet. In the 2000s, news media and politicians linked the internet with American domestic democratic health online by naming the revolution in Egypt the "Facebook Revolution." Thus, the Arab Spring, the period in which Egyptians (and others) protested and ultimately incited regime change, imagined an essentially American internet (an American virtual nation) and American corporate sponsorship in the self-liberation of an oppressed people. But the narrative also imagined the internet as a location of hybrid diasporic activism, in which Egyptian voices could participate in the making of a liberating online space able to transport that liberation sentiment in effective ways.

Not only do these comparative examples point out alternative visions of the internet available abroad, but they also reveal the hidden national flavors in domestic visions and the ways the internet operates simultaneously and alternately as national and transnational. Yet most internet scholars as well as contemporary journalists and policymakers view the internet as self-evidently American, democratic, and capitalist. They envision internet adoption as inevitable, and the free market and corporate forces as its natural regulators. This book illustrates how voices—both in the United States and abroad—helped to *construct* the internet in these ways in part through cultural representations and policy initiatives. By acknowledging the United States' dominant and formative power in the internet's history while simultaneously recognizing the technology's internationality, the influence of international actors, and the varying models for the internet offered by other countries and cultures, this book innovatively illustrates how transnational engagement shaped the internet. Internet studies that do not ask comparative questions at best create an incomplete picture of how the dynamics of power operate and at worst recreate and reinforce uninterrogated American exceptionalism.

Only by examining a layered history—the intricate ways that people formulated and produced views about the internet using news media and popular culture content, political leadership, and their own interactions with technology—can we get to the messy processes that are culture and history. By looking at the complex interplay between culture and politics (and politics as culture), we better understand the conflicting and indirect ways culture and policy hybridized transnationally. We see how cultural constructions of the internet and the policy directions ultimately loosened U.S. government regulations that not only helped shape the internet's technological development, political regulation, and everyday character, but also created the internet as a capitalist tool rather than a common good. While these understandings helped shape the internet's development and regulation, the shape and character of their development was far from inevitable. The internet could have been both understood and regulated differently.

This book is at once a historical/theoretical intervention and a practical call for change. I hope to disrupt uncritical debates about the internet's development and instead prompt individuals, academics, users, and policymakers to recognize the internet not only as a technology, but also as a cultural and political formation. This recognition, I hope, will liberate us from the bounded understandings we now carry in our heads about what can be done with and by the internet. As images of new technologies appear, we should think critically about their historical legacies and political implications. As new policies emerge, we should examine the cultural roots and unacknowledged assumptions that participated in the policymaking process. This will unbind us from our uninterrogated assumptions and opening new possibilities for future common senses.

In sum, the internet's history has been forged on cinema screens and in congressional debates as well as on computer screens and in laboratories. The internet's meanings have been multiple and have been made by teen-hackers as well as corporate moguls, by nationalist policymakers and transnational activists. This book has told the history of the not-inevitable players who have staked claims for the internet's future, envisioned alternatives for interacting online, and ultimately helped define the meanings and uses of a communications technology that has become central to daily life for millions around the globe. If the stories in this book are any indication and if nothing changes, the extensive history of mapping cultural and political concerns onto technology will continue. Popular visions of technology tangentially related to technologies themselves will continue to mediate relations among nations, corporate and governmental institutions, and technology users. These popular visions, while often hugely important in decision-making processes and justifications, will continue to go largely unacknowledged in collective histo-ries and may obscure the "roads not traveled." By revisiting these visions, this book advocates for a return to some of these conversations and justifications, for the unearthing of forgotten alternatives, for a more transparent incorpo-ration of popular culture into policymaking and politics. I hope that through these stories, the internet has become unpredictable again.

Lexis-Nexus Newspaper Coverage Search Data
Newpapers: USA Today, New York Times, Washington Post, Los Angeles Times
Location: headline, lede, highlight, body
Terms: (computer highway or computer superhighway or information highway or
    information superhighway), internet, cyberspace, world wide web, (computer and
    modem)

year	superhighway	internet	cyberspace	world wide web	modem	total
1980	0	0	0	0	3	3
1981	0	0	0	0	7	7
1982	0	0	0	0	13	13
1983	1	2	0	0	49	52
1984	3	3	1	0	53	60
1985	2	5	1	0	80	88
1986	0	1	0	0	88	89
1987	2	3	0	0	83	88
1988	1	10	2	0	114	127
1989	6	15	1	0	166	188
1990	6	34	6	0	165	211
1991	7	19	9	0	150	185
1992	9	24	15	1	214	263
1993	271	205	69	3	322	870
1994	849	982	348	87	467	2733
1995	516	3273	814	1113	562	6278
1996	260	5329	839	1940	536	8904
1997	131	6396	692	1540	451	9210
1998	89	8989	657	1483	454	11672
1999	69	18480	837	1270	533	21189

NOTES

INTRODUCTION

1. Dave Barry, "Lost in Cyberspace: In Which the Famous Funnyman Ventures onto the Information Highway and Finds a World so Wacky Even He Couldn't Make It Up," *Newsweek,* October 14, 1996, 85; Barry, *Dave Barry in Cyberspace.*
2. Gitelman, *Always Already New,* 1. Also see de la Peña, *Body Electric.*
3. For more on the cultural history of computing, see Friedman, *Electric Dreams*; Edwards, *Closed World.*
4. "Machine of the Year: The Computer Moves In," *Time,* January 3, 1983.
5. U.S. Census Bureau, "Computer Use in the United States: October 1984 (P23-155)," Table 1, 1988: http://www.census.gov/population/socdemo/computer/p23-155/tab01.pdf (accessed September 24, 2007).
6. Norris, *Digital Divide.*
7. U.S. Census Bureau, "Computer Use, 1984"; U.S. Census Bureau, "Internet Activities of Adults by Type of Home Internet Connection: 2010 (1158):" http://www.census.gov/compendia/statab/cats/information_communications/internet_publishing_and_broadcasting_and_internet_usage.html (accessed May 19, 2011).
8. Castells, *The Internet Galaxy,* 15. For more, see Rodman, "The Net Effect."
9. Bob Khan, a scientist at the DOD coined the term in 1974. Gauntlett, "Introduction to the New Edition."
10. See newspaper coverage content analysis data in the appendix.
11. Turner, *From Counterculture to Cyberculture.*
12. "Timeline, 1985," Computer History Museum: http://www.computerhistory.org/timeline/?category=net (accessed June 5, 2008).
13. Castells, *Internet Galaxy,* 17.
14. Ibid.

15. Edwards, *Closed World.*
16. Gitelman, *Always Already New,* 5–6.
17. Castells, *Internet Galaxy,* 33.
18. Gitelman, *Always Already New.*
19. McCarthy, *Ambient Television,* 227.
20. Gitelman is especially critical of the tendency to essentialize the technology in literature on the internet; Gitelman, *Always Already New.* Rabinovitz and Geil note the ahistorical, teleological, and/or technological determinist terms plaguing cultural studies of the internet; Rabinovitz and Geil, *Memory Bytes.* Jameson makes a similar argument about periodization; Jameson, *Postmodernism.* Vaidhyanathan argues this same plague exists in public and/or policy (as well as academic) debates; Vaidhyanathan, *Anarchist.*
21. Rabinovitz and Geil, *Memory Bytes,* 3.
22. Gitelman, *Always Already New,* 2.
23. Ibid., 5.
24. Penley and Ross, *Technoculture,* xiv.
25. Silver and Massanari, *Critical Cyberculture Studies,* 5. Also see Park, "Critical Forum"; Jones, "internet@academia.com."
26. Latour, *We Have Never Been Modern*; de la Peña, *Body Electric.*
27. Williams calls for putting "intention" back into media studies. Williams, *Television,* 40.
28. Sconce, "Tulip Theory," 189; Davis, *Techgnosis,* 9.
29. Gitelman, *Always Already New*; de la Peña, *Body Electric*; Marvin, *Old Technologies.*
30. Spigel, *Make Room for TV,* 4.
31. McAlister, *Epic Encounters,* 8. Edwards defines "discourse" as a "self-elaborating 'heterogeneous ensemble' that combines techniques and technologies, metaphors, language, practices, and fragments of other discourses around a support or supports" and produces "both power and knowledge," or "facts, logic, and the authority that reinforces it." Edwards, *Closed World,* 40.
32. Bourdieu, *Outline of a Theory.*
33. Ibid.
34. McAlister, *Epic Encounters,* 9, citing Bourdieu, *Field of Cultural Production,* 57.
35. *Net Effect* was published as I finished final edits on my manuscript. Streeter, *The Net Effect.* Also see Wu, *The Master Switch*; Gitelman, *Always Already New*; Goldsmith and Wu, *Who Controls the Internet?*; Poster, *Information Please*; and Friedman, *Electric Dreams.*

36. Latour, *We Have Never Been Modern*, 64.
37. Sconce hopes new media will be "where 'theory' does not derive from a study of the 'object'; rather the object of new media studies derives (so far) more from theoretical conjecture than demonstrable impact." Sconce, "Tulip Theory," 187.
38. Latour, *We Have Never Been Modern*, 64. Max Weber strikes a balance similar to Latour in his argument that while ideas have power and agency to affect change and drive history, material also contributes to (but does not determine) this equation. Weber, *The Protestant Ethic.*
39. Technology has always been "hybridized," simultaneously worldly and an object of discourse. Latour, *We Have Never Been Modern*, 55.
40. Lessig argues that the internet's architecture (code) enacts regulatory power over its users and advocates inclusion of technology into studies of policy. Lessig, *Code.*
41. "The 'content' of any medium blinds us to the character of that medium," McLuhan, *Understanding Media*, 9, cited in Gitelman, *Always Already New*, 5–6.
42. ARPANET debuted at a conference in Washington, D.C., in 1972, at which Vint Cerf, one of ARPANET's original designers, created the International Networking Group (INWG). This group aimed to create an "international network of networks," which they accomplished by 1974 when a satellite network system linked computers in Britain, France, Germany, Italy, Norway, and the United States. See Moschovitis, et al., *History of the Internet*, 76–80.
43. Castells, "Communication."
44. McAlister notes this in her study of foreign policy. McAlister, *Epic Encounters.*
45. Ibid., xviii.
46. Wood, "Stuart Hall's Cultural Studies."
47. For research on framing, see Iyengar, *Is Anyone Responsible?*; Entman, "Framing"; Gitlin, *Whole World*; Page and Shapiro, *Rational Public*; and Baumgartner and Jones, *Agendas.*
48. Entman, "Framing," 52.
49. News media perpetuate "cultural mythologies" about technology. Sconce, *Haunted Media*, 2.
50. Ibid., 2.
51. Ibid., 184.
52. Bourdieu, *Outline of a Theory*; Friedman, *Electric Dreams.*
53. Stone, *Policy Paradox*, 122.
54. Gitelman, *Always Already New*, 5–6.

55. Deleuze and Guattari call a "rhizome" a nonhierarchical and noncentered network structure. Using this term means I read cultural production as if it grows like moss (decentralized) instead of a tree (centralized). Deleuze and Guattari, *Thousand Plateaus*.

56. Spigel writes that although the "dialogue between mass culture and the public is never direct, these media discourses did help to construct ways of seeing television." Representations "begin to reveal the discursive conventions that were formed for thinking about a new medium during the period of its installation" even though they "cannot definitively demonstrate how people actually used television in their own homes." Spigel, *Make Room for TV*, 186–87.

57. Gitelman, *Always Already New*, 5–6. Similarly, de la Peña argues that technology are adopted or discarded based on how well they fit into historically-specific cultural ideals. De la Peña, *Body Electric*. Marvin argues that new technology reaffirms established cultural hierarchies and power structures and is strategic. This study does not intend to argue the level of intentionality argued by Marvin, but does engage her argument that technologies are not essentialized entities but are instead involved in and affected by power. Marvin, *Old Technologies*.

58. Sconce, *Haunted Media*, 9.

59. Lilley, "On Neoliberalism."

60. Poiger offered a useful model for the comparative transnational elements in this study. Poiger, *Jazz, Rock, and Rebels*.

61. Wagnleitner, *Coca-Colonization*.

CHAPTER 1

1. The film was the first realistic mainstream representation of the internet. The film grossed $79,568,000 and made $6,227,804 opening weekend. It also received several Oscar nominations (1984): Best Cinematography, Best Sound, Best Writing, Screenplay Written Directly for the Screen. The phrase "*WarGames* scenario" comes from David Alpern and Mary Lord, "Preventing 'WarGames,'" *Newsweek*, September 5, 1983, 48.

1. *NBC Nightly News with John Chancellor,* "WarGames," July 13, 1983, Vanderbilt News Archives.

2. U.S. Congress House Subcommittee on Transportation, Aviation, and Materials of the Committee on Science and Technology, *Hearing on H. 701, Computer and Communications Security and Privacy*, 98th Cong., September 26, October 17, 24, 1983; U.S Congress House. Subcommittee on Transportation, Aviation, and Materials, Committee on Science and

Technology, *Computer and Communication Security and Privacy Report*, April 1980, H. 702. These resulted in the Counterfeit Access Device and Computer Fraud and Abuse Act of 1984. U.S. Public Law 98-473, 98th Cong., October 12, 1984.

3. Proposed policy initiatives included: the Federal Computer Systems Protection Act of 1983, S. 1733, sponsored by Senator Paul Trible (August 3, 1983), read twice and referred to Senate Judiciary Committee and the Subcommittee on Criminal Law (August 9, 1983); the Computer Crime Prevention Act of 1984, S. 2270, sponsored by Senator William Cohen (February 8, 1984), read twice and referred to Senate Judiciary Committee and the Subcommittee on Criminal Law (February 13, 1984); a Bill to Penalize Unauthorized Direct Access to Individual Medical Records through a Telecommunications Device, H.R. 4954, sponsored by Representative Ron Wyden, referred to House Committee on Energy and Commerce, Subcommittee on Health and the Environment, House Committee on the Judiciary and the Subcommittee on Civil and Constitutional Rights (March 1, 1984); the Counterfeit Access Device and Computer Fraud and Abuse Act of 1984. H.R. 5112, sponsored by Representative William Hughes, (March 13, 1984), referred to House Committee on the Judiciary and the Subcommittee on Crime (May 8, 1984); the Computer Fraud and Abuse Act of 1984, S. 2864, sponsored by Senator Arlen Specter, (July 25, 1984), read twice and referred to the Committee on Judiciary and Subcommittee on Criminal Law (July 30, 1984); the Federal Computer Systems Protection Act of 1984, S. 2940, sponsored by Senator Strom Thurmond (August 9, 1984), read twice and referred to the Committee on Judiciary and Subcommittee on Criminal Law (August 17, 1984).

4. Federal Criminal Code Amendment, H.R. 4301, sponsored by Representative Lawrence Coughlin (November 3, 1983), which was revised in the enacted law, would have set potential fines at up to $100,000 or imprisonment for up to ten years or both. Computer Crime Prevention Act of 1984, S. 2270, sponsored by Senator William Cohen (February 8, 1984), read twice and referred to Senate Judiciary Committee and the Subcommittee on Criminal Law (February 13, 1984). This policy would have made all unauthorized computer infiltration automatic felonies, would have set the punishment for such infractions at "not more than three times the amount of the gain derived from the offense or $50,000, whichever is higher, or imprisonment for not more than five years, or both."

5. Federal Computer Systems Protection Act of 1984, S. 2940, sponsored by Senator Strom Thurmond (August 9, 1984), read twice and referred

to the Committee on Judiciary and Subcommittee on Criminal Law
(August 17, 1984).

6. U.S. Public Law 98-473, 98th Cong., October 12, 1984. Counterfeit Access
   Device and Computer Fraud and Abuse Act of 1984.

7. This act was first amended in 1986 and was then called the "U.S.
   Computer Fraud and Abuse Act of 1986." Determining "intent" in
   accordance with the 1984 act became a problem during the 1991 case
   of *United States v. Morris*, the Cornell graduate student responsible for
   the first internet worm. In deliberation, the courts recognized the dif-
   ficulty in determining intentionality in computer access. Amendments
   continued into the early 2000s, but the original 1984 and 1986 versions
   continue to set the main precedents for contemporary computer crime
   prosecutions. For more on the international influence of U.S. telecommunication policies, see de Sola Pool, *Technologies Without Boundaries*,
   214–215.

8. *WarGames* followed the less popular film *Tron*, which also represented
   computer networking as a video game.

9. McAlister, *Epic Encounters*, 8.

10. Michael Malone, "The Big Fight for Computer Sales," *New York
    Times*, August 1, 1982, C4; Robert Metz, "Market Place; I.B.M. Threat
    To Apple," *New York Times*, September 2, 1981, D6; Michael Schrage,
    "IBM'S PCjr. Wins Analysts' Favor," *Washington Post*, November 3, 1983,
    B1; Thomas W. Lippman, "Personal Computers: An Explosion in the
    American Marketplace," *Washington Post*, January 9, 1983, G2; William
    Marbach, Ayako Doi, and Richard Sandza, "Computers in a Briefcase"
    Newsweek, August 30, 1982, 70; Thomas Watterson, "What Happens
    when IBM Tastes Small-computer Market," *Christian Science Moni-
    tor*, September 15, 1981, 20; Andrew Pollack, "Technology: Compatible
    Computers," *New York Times*, March 3, 1983, D2; William Marbach and
    Peter McAlevey, "A $100 Home Computer," *Newsweek*, May 3, 1982, 63;
    Robert Metz, "Market Place; What Price Technology?" *New York Times*,
    January 28, 1981, D3; Andrew Pollack, "Next, a Computer on Every
    Desk," *New York Times*, August 23, 1981, C3; Michael Schrage, "Showing
    Off: Home Computer Makers Target the Masses," *Washington Post*, June
    12, 1983, F1.

11. "'War Games' Film Cited in Computer Bank Intrusion," *New York
    Times*, November 6, 1983, A75; Edmund Gravely, "Basic Hacking, from
    Data Base to Port," *New York Times*, October 16, 1983, C15; "Philip Hilts,
    "Computer 'Break-In' Method Poses Big Crime Risk," *Washington Post*,

March 4, 1982, A13; "Russia's Secret Weapon: U.S. Technology," *U.S. News & World Report*, March 17, 1980, 51; David Alpern, David Martin, Elaine Shannon, Richard Sandza, and Ron LaBrecque, "The KGB's Spies in America," *Newsweek*, November 23, 1981, 50; Orr Kelly, "Drive to Keep Secrets Out of Russian Hands," *U.S. News & World Report*, February 8, 1982, 39; "Russians in Our Back Yard to Stay?" *U.S. News & World Report*, October 15, 1979, 23; Tom Morganthau, David Martin, and Elaine Shannon, "Spying on U.S. Business," *Newsweek*, November 12, 1979, 43; Stuart Mieher, "Crime Can be Computerized, too," *Washington Post*, September 21, 1981, 29; Jonathan Harsch, "Computer Crime: Grappling with a 'High Tech' Problem," *Christian Science Monitor*, November 4, 1981, 5; Jonathan Harsch, "U.S., Soviets Already Fought World War III—by Computer," *Christian Science Monitor*, March 18, 1981, 7; Allan Mayer, "The Computer Bandits," *Newsweek*, August 9, 1976, 58; Orr Kelly, "Eavesdropping on the World's Secrets," *U.S. News & World Report*, June 26, 1978, 45; Orr Kelly, "If Terrorists Go after U.S. Nuclear Bombs..." *U.S. News & World Report*, March 12, 1979, 43; "The 'Nagging Feeling' of Undetected Fraud," *U.S. News & World Report*, December 19, 1977, 42.

12. William Broad, "Computer Security Worries Military Experts," *New York Times*, September 25, 1983, A1; Robert Dudney, "Billions Down the Pentagon Drain," *U.S. News & World Report*, April 27, 1981, 25; David Burnham, "Computer Security Raises Questions," *New York Times*, August 13, 1983, A7; Judith Cummings, "Coast Computer Buff Seized in Intrusion into Military-Civilian Data," *New York Times*, November 3, 1983, A26; Robert Dudney, "How Russia Steals U.S. Defense Secrets," *U.S. News & World Report*, May 25, 1981, 39; Orr Kelly, "Eavesdropping on the World's Secrets," *U.S. News & World Report*, June 26, 1978, 45; Robert Martin, "How Strong Is Russia?" *U.S. News & World Report*, February 11, 1980, 17; Gordon Wilkin, "Military Bases: Shields against Recession; High Tech—Military Style," *U.S. News & World Report*, September 27, 1982, 67.

13. Edwards, *Closed World*.

14. Michael Mallowe and David Friend, "Russia's High Tech Heist: The U.S. Mounts a Belated Effort to Halt the Theft of Electronic Secrets," *Life* 6 (April 1983): 29–36.

15. *ABC Evening News with Rick Inderfurth*, "WarGames," July 8, 1983, Vanderbilt News Archives.

16. *NBC Nightly News with John Chancellor*, "WarGames," July 13, 1983, Vanderbilt News Archives.

17. *ABC Evening News with Rick Inderfurth*, "WarGames," July 8, 1983, Vanderbilt News Archives.
18. *CBS Evening News with Dan Rather*, "WarGames Scenario," August 11, 1983, Vanderbilt News Archives.
19. "Cracking Computers," *Life 7* (January 1984): 50.
20. *ABC Evening News with Peter Jennings*, "WarGames Sentinel," August 11, 1983, Vanderbilt News Archives; *NBC Nightly News with Tom Brokaw*, "WarGames," August 11, 1983, Vanderbilt News Archives.
21. *NBC Nightly News with Roger Mudd*, "WarGames," August 18, 1983, Vanderbilt News Archives.
22. *NBC Nightly News with John Chancellor*, "WarGames," July 13, 1983, Vanderbilt News Archives.
23. *NBC Nightly News with Roger Mudd*, "WarGames," August 18, 1983, Vanderbilt News Archives.
24. Moschovitis, et al., *History of the Internet*, 123.
25. Vegh, "Hacking for Democracy."
26. *NBC Nightly News with Roger Mudd*, "WarGames," August 18, 1983, Vanderbilt News Archives.
27. *CBS Evening News with Bill Kurtis*, "Computer Codes," August 23, 1983, Vanderbilt News Archives.
28. For more on Reagan's "Star Wars," see Schaller, *Right Turn*.
29. *CBS Evening News with Peter Jennings*, "NASA Computer Break-In," July 17, 1984, Vanderbilt News Archives.
30. Entman, "Framing," 52.
31. Pan and Kosicki, "Framing Analysis," 70.
32. Graber, *Mass Media*, 8.
33. Entman, "Framing," 52.
34. Baumgartner and Jones, *Agendas*, 25.
35. Ibid.
36. Graber, *Mass Media*, 5, 8.
37. Visions of hacking as "accidental and innocent" shifted to "deliberate and criminal" after high-profile international and domestic hacks in 1986. Moschovitis, et al. ,*History of the Internet*, 121–24.
38. Jed Horne, "Your Plug-In Pal: Can Any Home in American Afford to be Without a Computer?" *Life 4* (October 1981): 56.
39. Otto Friedrich, "The Computer Moves In," *Time*, January 3, 1983, 23.
40. Moschovitis, et al., *History of the Internet*.
41. Gitelman, *Always Already New*, 114.
42. Ibid., 20.

43. "Tips on Buying," *New York Times*, June 4, 1981, C8; Don Nunes, "Why Buying Instead of Leasing a Computer Can Save Money," *Washington Post*, September 20, 1982, 7; "Computer Retailing; Little Trustbusters," *The Economist*, November 26, 1983, 72; "Thinking of Buying a Home Computer?" *New York Times*, August 25, 1983, C9; Sari Horwitz, "Tips on How to Deal with a Death in the Computer Maker Family," *Washington Post*, February 18, 1985, 27; Debra Hatten, "Buying a Computer—Pin Down your Need," *Christian Science Monitor*, July 23, 1985, 21; William Marbach and Penelope Wang, "Adam Hits the Brier Patch," *Newsweek*, January 14, 1985, 61; "Selling Computers; Nooks and Crannies," *The Economist*, September 4, 1982, 72.

44. Philip Elmer-DeWitt, "Forty Days and Forty Nights," *Time*, April 16, 1984, 60.

45. Eric Berg, "AT&T and Coleco in Video Game Venture," *New York Times*, September 8, 1983, 1D; Erik Sandberg-Diment, "Personal Computers; Hello, Outside World," *New York Times*, February 15, 1983, C5; Peter Lewis, "Peripherals: Those Cable Specialists," *New York Times*, October 23, 1984, C7; Andrew Pollack, "Technology Moving Data from A to B," *New York Times*, September 22, 1983, D2.

46. Michael Moritz, "The Wizard Inside the Machine," *Time*, April 16, 1984, 56–63.

47. Although he does not discuss it in these terms, framing internet use as involving magic helped deify hackers and create what internet scholar Ted Friedman calls "Hacker Mystique," the notion that hackers were specially empowered in the unknown and unknowable realm of the internet. Friedman, *Electric Dreams*, 173.

48. Otto Friedrich, "Glork! A Glossary for Gweeps: Even Users Should Grok this Cuspy Sampler of Computerese," *Time*, January 3, 1983, 29.

49. Anderson, *Imagined Communities*.

50. Otto Friedrich, "Glork! A Glossary for Gweeps: Even Users Should Grok this Cuspy Sampler of Computerese," *Time*, January 3, 1983, 29.

51. Ibid.

52. "Learning a New Language—Computerese," *Business Week*, December 20, 1982, 89; "As She is Spoke," *The Economist*, October 27, 1984, 88; Erik Sandberg-Diment, "Personal Computers: Hacking the English Language to Bits and Bytes," *New York Times*, September 13, 1983, C4; Marshall Ingwerson, "The 'Elves'; Young Superexperts of the Computer World," *Christian Science Monitor*, December 5, 1980, B22; Erik Sandberg-Diment, "Personal Computers: Primers in Old Fashioned

Printers," *New York Times*, November 16, 1982, C6; Sharon Begley and Robb Allan, "Can Ada Run the Pentagon?" *Newsweek*, January 10, 1983, 71; Richard Severo, "Computer Scholars Live for More than Graphics, Chips and Pixels," *New York Times*, July 2, 1983, A23; James Barron, "When Neighborliness Turns High Tech," *New York Times*, September 22, 1983, C1; "Man, Meet Machine," *The Economist*, October 27, 1984, 87; Greg Johnson, "Surviving the Computer Invasion," *Industry Week*, January 24, 1983, 42; Clara Germani, "Training Firms Help Executives Surmount 'Computerphobia,'" *Christian Science Monitor*, April 19, 1983, 6.

53. Don Nunes, "Computer Lingo, Those Joysticks and Software, In One Easy Lesson," *Washington Post*, February 21, 1983, WB7.

54. Marvin, *Old Technologies*, 4.

55. Ibid., 7.

56. Johnson. *Everything Bad*, 46.

57. Friedman, *Electric Dreams*, 173.

58. Otto Friedrich, "The Computer Moves In," *Time*, January 3, 1983, 15.

59. Moschovitis, et al., *History of the Internet*, 111. The *WarGames* movie itself resulted in at least one licensed video game: *WarGames* (for ColecoVision, Commodore 64 and VIC-20, Atari 8-bit; Thorn Emi Video, 1983).

60. Moschovitis, et al., *History of the Internet*, 111.

61. Once MUDs (Multi-User Dungeons) and other largely text-based chat-room interactive games became popular in the late 1980s and early 1990s, more games were played online.

62. Mark Schrage, "Atari to Tap 'Smart Phone' Market," *Washington Post*, March 17, 1983, E1.

63. Mark Potts, "Atari Add-on Turns Games to Computers," *Washington Post*, February 10, 1983, B1.

64. The first cover focused on shifts from industrial to post-industrial economic structures. "The Computer Society," *Time*, February 20, 1978. The second focused on Steven Jobs of Apple Computer and his entrepreneurial business models. "Striking It Rich: American's Risk Takers: Steven Jobs of Apple Computers," *Time*, February 15, 1982. The third is detailed in this paragraph. "Computer Generation: A New Breed of Whiz Kids," *Time*, May 3, 1982.

65. John Meyers, "A Letter from the Publisher" *Time*, May 3, 1982, 3.

66. Otto Friedrich, "The Computer Moves In," *Time*, January 3, 1983, 23.

67. Jed Horne, "Your Plug-In Pal: Can Any Home in America Afford to be Without a Computer?" *Life 4* (October 1981): 54.

68. Otto Friedrich, "Glork! A Glossary for Gweeps: Even Users Should Grok this Cuspy Sampler of Computerese," *Time,* January 3, 1983, 29.

69. Frederic Golden, "Computers: Here Come the MicroKids," *Time,* May 3, 1982, 52.

70. Roger Rosenblatt, "The Mind in the Machine," *Time,* May 3, 1982, 58.

71. Philip Elmer-DeWitt, "Mixing Suntans with Software," *Time,* August 22, 1983, 61.

72. Frederic Golden, "Pranksters, Pirates and Pen Pals," *Time,* May 3, 1982, 54; Jed Horne, "Your Plug-In Pal: Can Any Home in American Afford to be Without a Computer?" *Life 4* (October 1981): 54.

73. Daniel Cuff, "Business People: Ex-Microsoft President to No. 2 Job at Metheus," *New York Times,* June 23, 1983, D2; "A 25-Year Tandy Veteran Takes over at Microsoft," *Business Week,* July 11, 1983, 74F; William Marbach, Hope Lampert, Kim Foltz, Jennet Conant, and George Raine, "The Giant Takes Command," *Newsweek,* July 11, 1983, 56; "A Software Whiz Kid Goes Retail," *Business Week,* May 9, 1983, 111.

74. Michael Moritz, "A Hard-Core Technoid," *Time,* April 16, 1984, 62.

75. Levy, *Hackers*; Friedman, *Electric Dreams.*

76. Gates promoted and produced "closed source code," which would prevent accessing and changing source code without authorization; Moschovitis, et al., *History of the Internet,* 88–89.

77. Wu also writes about Jobs being "self-styled" as a "bona fide countercultural." Wu, *Master Switch,* 274.

78. Alexander Taylor, "The Seeds of Success," *Time,* February 15, 1982, 11.

79. Jay Cocks, "The Updated Book of Jobs," *Time,* January 3, 1983, 26.

80. Ibid., 26.

81. "Some Tips on Entering the Computer Field," *New York Times,* March 27, 1983, 12; Lucia Mouat, "For Two 11-Year-Old Girls, Computer Camp is Something to Byte Into," *Christian Science Monitor,* July 18, 1983, 8; Joyce Purnick, "Computers Draw 1,100 to Classes," *New York Times,* August 15, 1983, B3; "Computers: No More a 'Women's World' than Any Other," *New York Times,* September 6, 1982, A16; "Careers," *New York Times,* April 20, 1983, D19; Gregory M. Lamb, "From Out-of-Work Teacher to Computer Programmer," *Christian Science Monitor,* May 9, 1983, 7; James Wheeler, "Pleasures of Programming," *Washington Post,* October 2, 1983, 9; Elizabeth M. Fowler, "Careers; A Job Lift from Data Processing," *New York Times,* August 20, 1985, D19; Elizabeth M. Fowler, "Careers; Software Engineers In Demand," *New York Times,* May 5, 1982, D21; Jon Hamilton, "80s Graduate: Coming of Age in Brave New (Computer) World," *New York Times,* January 8, 1984, L58;

Elizabeth M. Fowler, "Careers; Achieving Computer Literacy," *New York Times*, March 30, 1983, D21; Dennis Williams and Dianne McDonald, "The Great Computer Frenzy," *Newsweek*, December 27, 1982, 68; Tom Nicholson, George Hackett, and David Friendly, "The Hottest Games in Town," *Newsweek*, August 16, 1982, 55; Otis Port, "Superfast Computers: You Ain't Seen Nothin' Yet," *Business Week*, August 26, 1985, 91.

82. Michael Moritz, "The Wizard Inside the Machine," *Time*, April 16, 1984, 59.
83. Medovoi, *Rebels*; Berlant, *Queen of America*.
84. *WarGames* dir. John Badham (1983, Los Angeles: Metro-Goldwyn-Mayer), Script, 20.
85. Ibid.
86. Ibid., 36--39.
87. "*WarGames* Trivia," Internet Movie Database: http://imdb.com/title/tt0086567/trivia (accessed May 24, 2007).
88. *WarGames* dir. John Badham (1983, Los Angeles: Metro-Goldwyn-Mayer), Script 36–39.
89. McAlister, *Epic*, 8.
90. Berlant, *Queen of America*, 25–28.
91. Medovoi, *Rebels*.
92. As several works have noted, the internet was (and is) dominated by Western, upper- and middle- class white males. See Turkle, *Life on the Screen*; Norris, *Digital Divide*. Chapter 4 looks at the historical moment in which this becomes identified as a problem.
93. Friedman, *Electric Dreams*, 173.
94. Levy, *Hackers*.
95. Levy, in Turner, *Counterculture*, 132–135.
96. Sobchack, "Reading *Mondo*," 15.
97. Ibid., 18.
98. Ibid., 25.
99. Ibid., 18.
100. Hebdidge. *Subculture*.
101. Moschovitis, et al., *History of the Internet*, 27.
102. Light, "When Computers Were Women."
103. Philip Elmer-DeWitt, "Forty Days and Forty Nights," *Time*, April 16, 1984, 57.
104. The actual bug "is still under tape along with the records of the experiment at the U.S. Naval Surface Weapons Center in Dahlgren, VA." Michael Moritz, "The Wizard Inside the Machine," *Time*, April 16, 1984, 58.

105. Michael Moritz, "A Hard-Core Technoid," *Time*, April 16, 1984, 63.
106. Philip Elmer-DeWitt, "Forty Days and Forty Nights," *Time*, April 16, 1984, 60.
107. Michael Moritz, "The Wizard Inside the Machine," *Time*, April 16, 1984, 59.
108. Jed Horne, "Your Plug-In Pal: Can Any Home in America Afford to be Without a Computer?" *Life* 4 (October 1981): 58.
109. "Video Game V.I.P.S," *Life* 6 (January 1983): 72.
110. Cohen, *Folk Devils*, 9.
111. Hall, "Changing Shape," 42.
112. Ibid.
113. Sutter, "Nothing New." For more, see Critcher, *Critical Readings*; Chauncey, "Post-war."
114. Hall, "Changing Shape," 42.
115. McLuhan, *Understanding Media*; Philip Elmer-DeWitt, "Plugging into the Networks," *Time*, September 19, 1983, 87; Jed Horne, "Your Plug-In Pal: Can Any Home in America Afford to be Without a Computer?" *Life* 4 (October 1981)," 58.
116. Philip Elmer-DeWitt, "Plugging into the Networks," *Time*, September 19, 1983, 87.
117. Ibid.
118. Donna Haupt, "Hello, Mr. Chips: The Computerized Class of '87," *Life* 7 (May 1984): 99–104.
119. Ibid., 99.
120. Ibid., 100.
121. Medovoi discusses the politics of teenaged rebellion in similar terms. Medovoi, *Rebels*.
122. Direct connections among *WarGames*, the hearings, and the law were made by 1980s news media and mentioned in terms of free speech regulation, as demonstrated by Robert Berry, "Free Speech in Cyberspace: The First Amendment and the Computer Hacker Controversies of 1990," Master's thesis, the School of Journalism and Mass Communication at the University of North Carolina, Chapel Hill, 1991.
123. Policy may direct capital (human or otherwise) toward something that benefits the policymaker; it may also solve a problem, thereby selling a policymaker to his or her constituents; and it may (also or instead) provide a symbolic solution or symbolic attention to a real or non-existent problem in order to suggest to voters that policymakers are proactively addressing their needs. Politicians may act on or change their political goals under the real, perceived, or cited pressure

mobilized by a particular film. Members of Congress may also display symbolic attention, meaning they discuss issues in and through the media, but no policy changes. For more on these cultural uses in the policy sphere, see Edelman, *Constructing the Political Spectacle*; Downs, *Political Theory*.

124. U.S. Congress, House Subcommittee on Transportation, Aviation, and Materials, Committee on Science and Technology, *Hearing on H. 701, Computer and Communications Security and Privacy*, 98th Cong., September 26, October 17, 24, 1983.

125. Ibid., 1.

126. Ibid.

127. Ibid., 5.

128. Ibid., 94–95.

129. Ibid.

130. Ibid., 5.

131. Kingdon, *Agendas*, 88.

132. Ibid.

133. Ibid., 26.

134. Ibid.

135. Ibid., 2.

136. Ibid., 14.

137. Ibid.

138. Ibid., 2.

139. Ibid., 5.

140. Ibid.

141. Ibid., 26.

142. Ibid., 29.

143. Ibid., 5.

144. Ibid., 3.

145. U.S. Congress House Subcommittee on Transportation, Aviation, and Materials, Committee on Science and Technology, *Computer and Communication Security and Privacy Report*, April 1980, H. 702, 24.

146. House, *Hearing on H. 701*, 5.

147. Ibid., 94–95.

148. Ibid.

CHAPTER 2

1. Friedman has also written about this advertising campaign. Friedman, *Electric Dreams*.

2. IBM advertisement, *Life* 8 (January 1985), 74–75.

3. Because of the Chaplin campaign, IBM "went from zero to . . . over 40% of the personal computer market." Papson, "IBM Tramp."
4. John Greenwald, "Softening a Starchy Image," *Time*, July 11, 1983, 54.
5. Friedman, *Electric Dreams*; Edwards, *The Closed World*.
6. Stoll, *Cuckoo Egg*.
7. "The Internet Survey," *Economist*, July 1, 1990, 9.
8. These were the first widely popular home computers. Most computer historians name the Scelbi 8H and the Altair 8800 as the first commercially available computers. The *Guinness Book of World Records* recognized the C64 in 1996 as "the greatest selling single computer model of all time." "Timeline, 1982," Computer History Museum: http://www.computerhistory.org/timeline/?category=cmptr. (accessed June 5, 2008). Apple's Macintosh was the first commercially viable computer with a mouse and the first to use a graphic user interface (GUI). "Timeline, 1984," Computer History Museum. In 1983, IBM had sold 800,000 PCjrs, making it the most popular home computer in the world at the time. Friedman, *Electric Dreams*, 181–204.
9. "Chat rooms" (sites onto which individuals could post messages and read other messages) and the "Computer Bulletin Board System" (CBBS, or chat rooms for people with specific interests and hobbies) emerged in the late 1970s. Moschovitis, et al., *History of the Internet*, 68.
10. Ibid.
11. For more on the term "internet," see Gauntlett, "Introduction to the New Edition."
12. For a history of the "computer as human" discourse, see Friedman, *Electric Dreams*.
13. Haraway, "A Cyborg Manifesto"; de la Peña, *Body Electric*; Broderick, *Reading by Starlight*; and Luckhurst, *Science Fiction*.
14. Broderick, *Reading by Starlight*, 155; Luckhurst, *Science Fiction*, 17; Volti, *Society and Technological Change*.
15. Friedman, *Electric Dreams*, 173. The first "computer" was technically a (usually female) person outfitted with a calculator to compute artillery gun firing tables. Moschovitis, et al., *History of the Internet*.
16. "The Computer in Society" Issue, *Time*, April 2, 1965.
17. Roger Rosenblatt, "The Mind in the Machine," *Time*, May 3, 1982, 58.
18. Hofstadter and Dennett, *The Mind's I*.
19. Kurzweil, *Singularity*.
20. The film stressed the replicants' exterior human appearance and internal humanity, desire to know lineage and fear of mortality. *Blade Runner*; *Terminator*.

21. U.S.P.S. advertisement, *Time,* July 11, 1983, 2; IBM advertisement, *Time,* May 3, 1982, 31; IBM advertisement, *Time,* February 15, 1982, 50; IBM advertisement, *Life* 7 (June 1984): 92–93; Timex Sinclair 1000 advertisement, *Life* 6 (January 1983): 129; Toshiba advertisement, *Time,* January 18, 1982, 57; Commodore 128 advertisement, *Life* 8 (September 1985): 75.

22. James Fallows, "Personal Preferences: Computers," *The Atlantic* 253 (May, 1984): 98; "Man, Meet Machine," *The Economist,* October 27, 1984, 87; "The Trendiness of Desktop Publishing; Paste and Scissors Go Electronic: Biting into Apple," *The Economist,* January 24, 1987, 76; Paul Karon, "Making Humans Masters of Their Machines: Computer Ergonomics," *PC Week* 4 (September 1, 1987): 57; Franklynn Peterson and Judi K.Turkel, "How to Judge Whether a Computer Will Be Friendly," *San Diego Union-Tribune,* March 30, 1987, A18; T. R. Reid, "Apple's New Hypercard is Simple, Approachable and Friendly," *Washington Post,* August 31, 1987, F13; Mark Monday, "Computers Becoming 'Friendly' to Handicapped Users; Program at Southwestern College Aims to Train the Disabled for Real-world Work," *San Diego Union-Tribune,* August 27, 1987, B6; Michael Schrage, "Computers and Paper Can Coexist as Happily as TV and Radio," *Washington Post,* February 20, 1984, 15; Myron Berger, "Easier Computing," *New York Times,* September 21, 1986, G52; Lucretia Steiger, "This Computer Is 'User Friendly' about Fashion," *San Diego Union-Tribune,* November 18, 1984, D4; T. R. Reid, "Hitchhiker's Guide to Some Fun Interactive Computer Games," *Washington Post,* September 30, 1985, 9.

23. William Marbach, Gerald Lubenow, and Frank Gibney, "Invasion of the Computers," *Newsweek,* December 28, 1981, 57.

24. IBM advertisement, *Time,* May 3, 1982, 31; IBM advertisement, *Time,* February 15, 1982, 50; IBM advertisement, *Life* 7 (June 1984): 14–15; IBM advertisement, *Life* 7 (June 1984): 92–93.

25. U.S.P.S. advertisement, *Time,* July 11, 1983, 2.

26. IBM advertisement, *Time,* May 3, 1982, 31.

27. McLuhan, *Understanding Media.*

28. Deleuze and Guattari, *A Thousand Plateaus,* 88.

29. Haraway, "A Cyborg Manifesto."

30. Cohen, "Masoch / Lancelotism."

31. Latour, *We Have Never Been Modern.*

32. James Fallows, "Personal Preferences: Computers," *The Atlantic* 253 (May, 1984): 98; Paul Karon, "Making Humans Masters of Their Machines: Computer Ergonomics," *PC Week* 4 (September 1, 1987): 57; T. R. Reid, "Apple's New Hypercard Is Simple, Approachable and

Friendly," *Washington Post*, August 31, 1987, F13; Mark Monday, "Computers Becoming `Friendly' to Handicapped Users; Program at Southwestern College Aims to Train the Disabled for Real-world Work," *San Diego Union-Tribune*, August 27, 1987, B6; Myron Berger, "Easier Computing," *New York Times*, September 21, 1986, G52; Lucretia Steiger, "This Computer Is 'User Friendly' about Fashion," *San Diego Union-Tribune*, November 18, 1984, D4.

33. Philip Faflick, "The Hottest-Selling Hardware," *Time*, January 3, 1983, 28.

34. IBM advertisement, *Time*, February 15, 1982, 50.

35. Moschovitis, et al., *History of the Internet*, 100.

36. IBM advertisement, *Life 7* (June 1984): 92-93.

37. McAlister, *Epic Encounters*, 8.

38. Curt Suplee, "1984; Orwell's Vision," *Washington Post*, September 4, 1983, K1; John Corry, "1984 Revisited," *New York Times,* June 7, 1983, C17; David Gelman, "Slouching Toward 1984," *Newsweek*, February 21, 1983, 53; Joseph McLellan, "Big Brother Would Need Valium to Handle 1984; Orwell's Visions of Power and Technology Didn't Allow for Our World's Complexity—Or Bob Dylan," *Washington Post*, January 1, 1984, H1; Jonathan Yardley, "1984: Academically Abused," *Washington Post*, October 22, 1984, C2; Mike Feinsilber, "The Orwellian Year: Is Big Brother Watching?" *The Associated Press*, December 22, 1983; Edwin M. Yoder, "Big Brother Never Had a Chance," *Washington Post*, December 8, 1983, A19; Walter Goodman, "The Vision of Both Orwell and Kafka Is as Sharp as Ever," *New York Times*, December 30, 1983, B3; Abigail Trafford, "Orwell's *1984*—Coming True?" *U.S. News & World Report*, December 26, 1983, 86.

39. Jed Horne, "Your Plug-In Pal: Can Any Home in American Afford to be Without a Computer?" *Life 4* (October 1981): 58.

40. Ibid.

41. Woods claimed she accidentally hit a foot pedal while reaching for a phone call. Photographs demonstrating how the accident could happen were submitted as legal evidence. "Nixon Interviews," *New York Times,* September 2, 1977, 9.

42. Gitelman, *Always Already New*, 93, citing Mumford, *The Pentagon of Power.*

43. De la Peña, *Body Electric*, 217.

44. De Sola Pool, *Technologies Without Boundaries*, 10.

45. As a result, for the first time since the 1940s, most Americans said that instead of a "better life," they expected to pass on to their children

"mounting debts and a declining living standard," Schaller, *Right Turn*, 1.

46. Ibid.

47. Chevan and Stokes, "Growth."

48. Gitelman, *Always Already New*, 93.

49. *CBS Evening News with Dan Rather*, "AT&T Strike," August 12, 1983, Vanderbilt News Archives.

50. William Serrin, "Can U.S. Labor Program Itself for the Future?" *New York Times*, November 15, 1981, D3; Seth King, "Jobless Rate is up to 10.1% in Month, Worst in 42 Years," *New York Times*, October 9, 1982, A1; Pat Patterson, "Corporations in Crisis: Coming to Grips with the Information Age," *Industry Week*, March 5, 1984, 57; Ed Townsend, "Two Ways to View America's 9 Percent Jobless Rate," *Christian Science Monitor*, April 19, 1982, 5; William Serrin, "Part-Time Work New Labor Trend," *New York Times*, July 9, 1986, A1; "A Changing Work Force Poses Challenges," *Business Week*, December 14, 1981, 116; William Serrin, "Subcontracting a Key Issue for Labor," *New York Times*, November 26, 1986, B8.

51. David Gelman, "Slouching Toward 1984," *Newsweek*, February 21, 1983, 53; Mike Feinsilber, "The Orwellian Year: Is Big Brother Watching?" *The Associated Press*, December 22, 1983; Walter Goodman, "The Vision of Both Orwell and Kafka Is as Sharp as Ever," *New York Times*, December 30, 1983, B3; Abigail Trafford, "Orwell's *1984*—Coming True?" *U.S. News & World Report*, December 26, 1983, 86.

52. *ABC Evening News with Peter Jennings*, "Computer Monitoring," May 29, 1984, Vanderbilt News Archives.

53. Turkle, *Life on the Screen*.

54. Friedman, *Electric Dreams*, 109.

55. Caroline McCarthy, "Remembering the '1984' Super Bowl Mac Ad," *CNet*, January 23, 2009: http://news.cnet.com/8301-13577 3-10148380-36.html (accessed July 28, 2012).

56. *Metropolis*; *Blade Runner*; *Terminator*; and, later, the Borg in *Star Trek: The Next Generation*.

57. Friedman, *Electric Dreams*, 111.

58. Ibid., 181–204.

59. Gitelman, *Always Already New*, 15.

60. Turkle made a similar argument, Turkle, *Life on the Screen*, 33.

61. *Modern Times*; Friedman, *Electric Dreams*, 106.

62. Roberts and Wallis, *Introducing Film*, 131.

63. Chaplin juxtaposed images of sheep with images of workers heading to the factories, commenting on the depersonalization of workers and frantic pace of factory life in the industrial era. *Modern Times.*
64. Papson, "The IBM Tramp."
65. IBM advertisement, *Life* 7 (June 1984): 14–15.
66. IBM advertisement, *Life* 7 (February 1984): 70-71.
67. Papson, "The IBM Tramp."
68. Ibid.
69. Friedman, *Electric Dreams.*
70. John Greenwald, "Softening a Starchy Image," *Time,* July 11, 1983, 54.
71. IBM advertisement, *Life* 7 (February 1984): 70–71; IBM advertisement, *Life* 8 (January 1985), 74–75; IBM advertisement, *Life* 7 (June 1984): 14–15; IBM advertisement, *Life* 7 (June 1984): 92–93; IBM advertisement, *Time,* May 3, 1982, 31.
72. Wise, "Community," 126; Williams, *Television*; Volti, *Society and Technological Change*; Adas, *Machines.*
73. Latour, *We Have Never Been Modern,* 69–78.
74. Joel Dinerstein made this observation in his comments while attending the Technology Caucus Roundtable at the annual American Studies Association (ASA) meeting in Philadelphia, October 11–14, 2007.
75. Barthes, *Mythologies.*
76. Papson, "The IBM Tramp."
77. Manuel Schiffres, "Talking by Computer Is a New Way of Life," *U.S. News & World Report,* August 27, 1984, 59; Michael Schrage, "Sending Software Via Phone, Cable May Be Wave of Future," *Washington Post,* May 14, 1984, 1; "Computer Tapping: A La Modem," *The Economist,* October 25, 1986, 100; Eric N. Berg, "Practical Traveler: Tips for Taking a Computer Along," *New York Times,* June 23, 1985, J3; Kathleen Sullivan, "Long-term Research Key to Quest for Next Generation," *Computerworld,* October 22, 1984, 30; Erik Sandberg-Dimet, "Modem Installation: Child's Play, Almost," *New York Times,* May 8, 1984, C4; Elmer-DeWitt, "Forty Days and Forty Nights," *Time,* April 16, 1984, 63; Peter Lewis, "A Lonely Road for a Modem Maker: Hayes Is Ignoring Industry Standards at the High-speed End of the Market," *New York Times,* April 10, 1988, C12; Manuel Schiffres, "Stretching Frontiers Of Home Computers," *U.S. News & World Report,* March 11, 1985, 69; Jed Horne, "Your Plug-In Pal: Can Any Home in American Afford to Be Without a Computer?" *Life* 4 (October 1981): 58.
78. Elmer-DeWitt, "Forty Days and Forty Nights," *Time,* April 16, 1984, 63.

79. Robert Fishman, *Bourgeois Utopias: The Rise and Fall of Suburbia* (New York: Basic Books, 1987).

80. Peter Lewis, "A Lonely Road for a Modem Maker: Hayes Is Ignoring Industry Standards at the High-speed End of the Market," *New York Times,* April 10, 1988, C12.

81. Jed Horne, "Your Plug-In Pal: Can Any Home in American Afford to Be Without a Computer?" *Life* 4 (October 1981): 58.

82. The computer was becoming part of the requirements for ideal democratic individualism. Marx, *Machine in the Garden.*

83. Northern Telecommunication advertisement, *Life* 4 (November 1981): 84–85.

84. Toshiba advertisement, *Time,* January 18, 1982, 57.

85. AT&T advertisement, *Life* 8 (May 1985): 117.

86. Ross, "Hacking Away," 259.

87. Ibid.

88. Ibid.

89. Vaidhyanathan, *Anarchist,* xiii.

90. Gitelman, *Always Already New.*

91. Douglas, "The Turn Within," 623.

92. Bourdieu, *Outline of a Theory of Practice*; Friedman, *Electric Dreams.*

93. Bourdieu, *Outline of a Theory of Practice.*

94. Schaller, *Right Turn,* v.

95. Moschovitis, et al., *History of the Internet*; Tom Ashbrook, "Mavericks of the Megabyte: Do Hackers Hurt or Help?" *The Boston Globe,* November 22, 1988, 65; John Markoff, "Cyberpunks Seek Thrills in Computerized Mischief," *New York Times,* November 26, 1988, 1; Evelyn Richards and R. Jeffrey Smith, "Computer Detective Followed Trail to Hacker Spy Suspect; Work Called Key to West German's Arrest," *Washington Post,* March 4, 1989, A1; Dana Nichols, "Phone Industry Fights Rise in Long-Distance 'Hacking,'" *San Diego Union-Tribune,* July 3, 1987, A1; Michael Specter, "Hackers' Easy Ride: MIT Students Fear that in Wake of 'Virus,' Files Will Be Closed, Creativity Stifled," *Washington Post,* November 11, 1988, A1; John Markoff, "Hackers: Founts of Creativity Often Blind to Consequences," *The Oregonian,* November 10, 1988, G03; Al Fasoldt, "Hackers? Crackers? Worms? Polly Wants an Explanation," *The Post-Standard,* November 27, 1988, 28; Robert McCartney, "Computer Hackers Face Spy Charges; W. Germany Indicts 3 Accused of Selling Data to Soviet KGB Agent," *Washington Post,* August 17, 1989, A32; Tom Fermazin, "How to Head off Hackers," *Network World,* April 10, 1989, 71; "Feds Whack Hacker Ring," *Computerworld,* June 5, 1989, 1;

"Insider Crimes Threaten Corporate Well-being," *Computerworld*, June 3, 1987, 25; Sid Moody, "Computer Technology Faces Increased Risks," *The Oregonian*, February 8, 1989, C11; Mark Clayton, "Hackers Expand Their Illegal Skills to Voice Mail," *Christian Science Monitor*, December 27, 1988, 14; John Burgess, "Hackers Find New Way to Tap Long-Distance Phone Lines; Illegal Users Ring Up Big Bills for Companies by Gaining Access to Message Systems," *Washington Post*, October 6, 1988, F1; Robert McFadden, "Phone Codes: Newest Scam on the Street," *New York Times*, May 12, 1987, A1; John Markoff, "Living With the Computer Whiz Kids," *New York Times*, November 8, 1988, A16; A. Horton, "Hackers Beating the System for Fun … or Something Else? Computer Crime Fears Growing," *Herald*, February 3, 1987; "Computer Hackers Gain Access to NASA System," *San Diego Union-Tribune*, September 16, 1987, A-1.

96. Schaller, *Right Turn*, 13.
97. Ibid., 127.
98. The *New York Times, LA Times, Washington Post,* and *USA Today* cumulatively printed 3 stories in 1980, 88 in 1985, and 211 in 1990. See "Lexis-Nexis Graph" in chapter 3.
99. Peter McKillop, "Sayonara, America," *Newsweek*, August 19, 1991, 32; Peter Dworkin and Manuel Schiffres, "Silicon Chips: U.S. Gets Set for a Comeback," *U.S. News & World Report*, November 25, 1985, 80; Mark Whitaker, "Why Japan Won't Slow Down," *Newsweek,* May 15, 1989, 56; Robert Christopher, "Don't Blame the Japanese," *New York Times*, October 19, 1986, F76; David Sanger, "How Japan Does What It's Doing to Keep Its Economy in Top Gear," *New York Times,* November 27, 1988, A1; David Sanger, "A High-Tech Lead in Danger," *New York Times*, December 18, 1988, A2; Theodore White, "The Danger from Japan," *New York Times*, July 28, 1985, F19; Margaret Shapiro and Fred Hiatt, "Tokyo's Vast Economic Might Still Growing around World," *Washington Post*, February 13, 1990, A1; Hobart Rowen and Jodie T. Allen, "Brave New World, Inc.; To Superfirms, Borders Are Just a Nuisance," *Washington Post*, March 19, 1989, C1; Paul Blustein, "Japan's Corporate Connections Create Challenge for U.S. Businesses," *Washington Post,* October 6, 1991, A1; John Burgess, "Japan Trades to Win Its Way; A Rich and Anxious Nation," *Washington Post*, August 12, 1985, A1; Joel Kotkin and Yoriko Kishimoto, "Let's Quit Whining and Get to Work! Forget Those Gloom-Mongering Prophesies—America's Economy Is the Envy of the World," *Washington Post*, January 17, 1988, C1; James Fallows, "The Japanese Difference," *Washington Post*, February 5, 1989, D1.

100. Schaller, *Right Turn*, 1 and 176-8.

101. Michael Schrage, "The Lure of the New Technologies: Companies Radically Reshaping Old Business Values, Traditions," *Washington Post*, January 13, 1985, E1.

102. Jack Anderson, "Germany Is West's Worst Security Risk," *Washington Post*, January 28, 1985, B32.

103. Stoll, *The Cuckoo Egg*.

104. Michael Schrage, "The Lure of the New Technologies: Companies Radically Reshaping Old Business Values, Traditions," *Washington Post*, January 13, 1985, E1.

105. ARPANET first linked to computer science departments at universities in the 1960s. Moschovitis, et al., *History of the Internet*, 38.

106. Schaller, *Right Turn*, 176.

107. Stuart Auerbach, "U.S.-Japan Trade Strains Persist: Harmony of Reagan-Nakasone Meeting Belies Deep Frustration, Both Sides Agree Obstacles to Balanced Trade Remain, Japanese Say Nation Doesn't Resist Imports," *Washington Post*, January 6, 1985, K1; Michael Schrage, "The Lure of the New Technologies: Companies Radically Reshaping Old Business Values, Traditions," *Washington Post*, January 13, 1985, E1.

108. Michael Schrage, "The Lure of the New Technologies: Companies Radically Reshaping Old Business Values, Traditions," *Washington Post*, January 13, 1985, E1.

109. Schaller, *Right Turn*, 177; Crichton, *Rising Sun*; Prestowitz, *Trading Places*; Choate, *Agents of Influence*; Paperback Best Sellers, *New York Times*, September 26, 1993, G32.

110. Schaller, *Right Turn*, 177; Crichton, *Rising Sun*.

111. Michael Shapiro, "Is 'Rising Sun' a Detective Story or Jeremiad?" *New York Times*, July 25, 1993, B9.

112. Ibid..

113. Stuart Auerbach, "Reagan Strategy Targets 4 Market Areas in Japan: Sectors Form Basis of Joint Effort," *Washington Post*, January 6, 1985, K4.

114. Schaller, *Right Turn*, 178.

115. The Omnibus Trade and Competitiveness Act of 1988 was passed by overwhelming majorities of both the Senate and House of Representatives. U.S. Public Law 100-418. August 23, 1988. Hearings included: Senate Subcommittee on International Trade, Committee on Finance, *Hearing on S. 361, Telecommunications Trade*, June 26, 1984; Senate Subcommittee on International Trade, Committee on Finance, *Hearings on S. 361, Export of U.S. Telecommunications Products*, May 3, 1985;

Senate Subcommittee on Communications, Committee on Commerce, Science, and Transportation, *Hearings on S. 261, International Telecommunications*, February 28, 1987; House Subcommittee on International Finance, Trade, and Monetary Policy, Committee on Banking, Finance, and Urban Affairs, *Hearings on H. 241,U.S.-Japan Economic Relations*, June 9, 1987; Senate Subcommittee on Governmental Affairs, *Hearings on S. 401, Government's Role in Economic Competitiveness*, June 8–9, 1987.

Selected publications include: U.S. Congress, Senate, *Promoting Expansion of International Trade in Telecommunications Equipment and Services*, November 26, 1985, S 363.; U.S. Congress, House, *Telecommunications Trade Act of 1986*, February 6, 1986, H 363.; U.S. Congress, House, *Technology Education Act of 1986*, August 11, 1986, H 343.; U.S. Congress, Senate, *Education for a Competitive America Act*, June 16, 1987, S 543; U.S. Congress, Senate, *Technology Competitiveness Act of 1987*, June 22, 1987, S 263.

116. Omnibus Trade and Competitiveness Act of 1988.

117. Ibid.

118. Ibid.

119. Andrew Pollack, "The Daunting Power of I.B.M.: It Keeps Growing Stronger as Rivals Struggle and Some Voice Concern," *New York Times*, January 20, 1985, F1.

120. T. R. Reid, "'Security Experts' Should Have Read Up on the White House Computer," *Washington Post*, March 2, 1987, W21.

121. Evelyn Richards, "U.S. Plan to Restrict Encryption Software Exports Draws Protests," *Washington Post*, November 14, 1991, B11; John A. Adam, "Secrets and Ciphers," *Washington Post*, January 24, 1988, C3; Michael Schrage, "Md. Supercomputer to Help NSA Encrypt, Crack Codes; Underscores Importance of Computing to Defense," *Washington Post*, December 3, 1984, 3; Kevin McManus, "They're All Ears," *Washington Post*, March 8, 1991, N9; Lawrence J. Magid, "Turning Computer Dreams into Realities," *Washington Post*, February 26, 1990, F19; David Sanger, "Change in Data Coding of Computers Expected," *New York Times*, April 15, 1986, D1; Peter Lewis, "Building a Moat with Software," *New York Times*, September 3, 1989, C7; John Markoff, "U.S. Export Ban Hurting Makers of New Devices to Code Messages," *New York Times*, November 19, 1990, A1; Erik Sandberg-Diment, "A Speedy Way to Encode Material," *New York Times*, August 23, 1987, C12; Gina Kolata, "Tied Up in Knots, Cryptographers Test Their Limits," *New York Times*, October 13, 1991, D4; John Markoff, "Move

on Unscrambling of Messages Is Assailed," *New York Times*, April 17, 1991, A16.

122. Vin McLellan, "Data Network to Use Code to Insure Privacy," *New York Times*, March 21, 1989, D5.

123. Deleuze and Guattari, *A Thousand Plateaus*, 88.

CHAPTER 3

1. "1996 Internet World's Fair:" http://park.org (accessed December 5, 2007).

2. Katie Hafner, "Internet: The Man with Ideas: The Robert Moses of Cyberspace Plans a 1996 World's Fair," *Newsweek*, July 24, 1995, 61. Malamud, *A World's Fair*, 173.

3. The prefair connectivity rate was as low as 64,000 bits per second in some countries, but the Internet Railroad increased connectivity around the world to 45 million bits per second. By no means was everyone connected. Malamud, *A World's Fair*, 9.

4. "Sites from People, Small Companies," 1996 Internet World's Fair Archive: http://park.org/ (accessed December 5, 2007).

5. Miyoshi, "A Borderless World?"; Sassen, *Losing Control?* See Vaidhyanathan, *Anarchist*; Friedman, *Lexus*; Micklethwait and Wooldridge, *A Future Perfect.*

6. As globalization's "beginning," "driver," and as "always already there," the internet was an abstraction of space and time. Hardt and Negri, *Empire.*

7. Vaidhyanathan, *Anarchist.*

8. Campbell and Carlson, "Panopticon.com"; Turkle, *Life on the Screen.*

9. High Performance Computing and Communication Act of 1991, U.S. Public Law 102-194, 102nd Cong., December 9, 1991; High Performance Computing and High Speed Networking Applications Act of 1993, H.R.1757, 103rd Cong., September 14, 1993; National Competitiveness Act of 1993, S.4.1, 103rd Cong., March 16, 1994; National Communications Competition and Information Infrastructure Act of 1994, H.R.3636. 104th Cong., June 28, 1994..

10. Harvey, "Privacy," 234–45.

11. Golding, "Worldwide Wedge," 804.

12. By 1964, laboratories in Great Britain were keeping pace with those at MIT and RAND Corporations in internet technology development; Moschovitis, et al., *History of the Internet.*

13. Ibid., 76–80.

14. Digital divide scholars note discrepancies between Western and Eastern access. Norris, *Digital Divide.*

15. Queen Elizabeth II of England sent her first email in 1976. Moschovitis, et al., *History of the Internet*, 76.

16. John Markoff, "The Executive Computer; A Web of Networks, an Abundance of Services," *New York Times*, February 28, 1993, C8; John Markoff, "A Free and Simple Computer Link," *New York Times*, December 8, 1993, D1; Mary Lu Carnevale, "World Wide Web," *Wall Street Journal*, November 15, 1993, R7; Bob Metcalfe, "On Surfing the Internet and Other Kids' Stuff," *InfoWorld*, November 1, 1993 67; Ed Krol, "Internet's Web Is Doing Just Fine, Thank You," *Network World*, April 19, 1993, 31; Robert O'Harrow Jr., "Computer-Friendly Homes Increasing; Electronic Bulletin Boards Provide Many Residents with Comfort, Communication," *Washington Post*, December 27, 1992, B1; "Internet Wires the Planet for Computer Users," *St. Petersburg Times*, May 23, 1993, I1; David Landis, "World Wide Web Helps Untangle Internet's Labyrinth," *USA Today*, August 3, 1994, D10.

17. The Web popularized Hypertext Transfer Protocol (HTTP), Hypertext Markup Language (HTML), and Universal Resource Locator (URL); Castells, *The Internet Galaxy*, 15.

18. Ibid., 10.

19. Turner, *From Counterculture to Cyberculture*, 213.

20. Additional graphs and data in chapter 3 and appendix.

21. "Y2K" indicates the anticipated computer meltdowns as 1999 turned to 2000 because many computer programs were written using two-digit year codes (99 for 1999). For more, see Powell et al., *Communications Y2K*. "Dot.com bubble" indicates financial speculation that occurred between 1995 and 2000 on the value of internet growth and growth of related corporations. For more, see Cassidy, *Dot.con*.

22. The few broadcast television evening news reports about the internet in the 1980s were almost exclusively about domestic issues (e.g., banking, security, hacking). Beginning in 1994, a variety of stories began to appear on various international topics. For example, in 1996 stories appeared about China's online censorship.

23. "Internet Wires the Planet for Computer Users," *St. Petersburg Times*, May 23, 1993, I1; David Landis, "World Wide Web Helps Untangle Internet's Labyrinth," *USA Today*, August 3, 1994, D10; Vic Sussman and Kenan Pollack, "Gold Rush in Cyberspace," *U.S. News & World Report*, November 13, 1995, 72; John Markoff, "The Executive Computer; A Web of Networks, an Abundance of Services," *New York Times*, February 28, 1993, C8; John Markoff, "A Free and Simple Computer Link," *New York Times*, December 8, 1993, D1; Mary Lu

Carnevale, "World Wide Web," *Wall Street Journal,* November 15, 1993, R7; Bob Metcalfe, "On Surfing the Internet and Other Kids' Stuff," *InfoWorld,* November 1, 1993 67; Ed Krol, "Internet's Web Is Doing Just Fine, Thank You," *Network World,* April 19, 1993, 31; Robert O'Harrow Jr., "Computer-Friendly Homes Increasing; Electronic Bulletin Boards Provide Many Residents with Comfort, Communication," *Washington Post,* December 27, 1992, B1.

24. Steven Levy, "The Internet Crash Scare: Yes, The Net Is Overloaded and Slow, But Even a Global Gigalapse Won't Stop the Revolution," *Newsweek,* September 16, 1996, 96.

25. Moschovitis, et al., *History of the Internet,* 153.

26. Levy, "The Internet Crash Scare," 96.

27. John Simons, "Waiting to Download. Only Market Forces Can Unclog the Internet," *U.S. News & World Report,* December 30, 1996, 60.

28. Articles, for example, noted the competition by reporting provider membership; in 1995, 4 million people used America Online, 3.7 million CompuServe, and 2.2 million Prodigy. Jack Egan, "1996 Tech Guide: Online Goes Big Time," *U.S. News & World Report,* November 20, 1995, 104; John Markoff, "A New Information Mass Market," *New York Times,* September 3, 1993, D1; David Bank," Dial MCI to Hop on Net: Commercial Rush Will Transform Internet into Mass-Market Medium," *San Jose Mercury News,* November 22, 1994 1F; Laurent Belsie, "Powerful Internet Should Skyrocket as Firms Go On-Line," *Christian Science Monitor,* March 16, 1994, 8; John Markoff, "Murdoch Move Part of Scramble by Media Giants into New Market," *The Oregonian,* September 7, 1993, B9; Paul Wiseman, "The Internet Snares More Businesses," *USA Today,* July 7, 1994, B1; Peter H. Lewis, "The Executive Computer; A Growing Internet Is Trying to Take Care of Business," *New York Times,* December 12, 1993, C7; Edmund Andrews, "MCI to Offer One-Stop Shopping on the Internet," *New York Times,* November 21, 1994, D2; Steve Alexander, "Capitalism via Internet; Computer Network Attracting Attention as Another Means to do Business," *Star Tribune,* June 14, 1994, 1D; "Putting It All in the Pipeline," *Newsweek,* November 7, 1994, 62; Katie Hafner, "Making Sense of the Internet," *Newsweek,* October 24, 1994, 46.

29. Moschovitis, et al., *History of the Internet,* 299.

30. A rhizome is a nonhierarchical and noncentered network structure. Deleuze and Guattari, *A Thousand Plateaus.*

31. McAlister, *Epic Encounters,* 277–78.

32. Hardt and Negri, *Empire,* 280–81.

33. Ibid., 8–9.
34. Ibid., 299.
35. Turner, *From Counterculture to Cyberculture*, 1; Vaidhyanathan also wrote about this assumption. Vaidhyanathan, *Anarchist*,151.
36. Reich, *The Work of Nations*, 3–8; cited in Hardt and Negri, *Empire,* 151.
37. Hardt and Negri, *Empire*, 5.
38. George H.W. Bush, "Address to the Nation on the Invasion of Iraq," January 16, 1991: http://www.millercenter.virginia.edu/scripps/digitalarchive/speeches/spe_1991_0116_bush (accessed August 26, 2007).
39. See Harvey, *Condition of Postmodernity*; Herman and McChesney, *Global Media*; Jameson and Miyoshi, *Cultures of Globalization*; Kaplan and Donald Pease, *Cultures of United States Imperialism*; Lowe and Lloyd, *The Politics of Culture;* Robbins, *Feeling Global;* Thussu, *Electronic Empires*; Wilson and Dissanayake, *Global/Local*.
40. Miyoshi, "A Borderless World?" 97.
41. Wang et al., *New Communications Landscape*, 8.
42. Sassen, *Losing Control?*
43. Miyoshi, "A Borderless World?" 93.
44. Golding and Harris, *Beyond Cultural Imperialism;* Herman and McChesney, *The Global Media*; Kavoori, "Discursive Texts"; Thussu, *Electronic Empires;* Wilson and Dissanayake, *Global/Local*.
45. Hetata, "Dollarization"; Wang et al., *New Communications Landscape*; Bhabha, *Nation and Narration*. This notion still persists in more contemporary academic work: Castells, *Rise of the Network Society*; Ebo, *Cyberimperialism*; Stald and Tufte, *Global Encounters*; Miller and Slater, *The Internet*.
46. Gitelman, *Always Already New*, 132–38.
47. Turner, *From Counterculture to Cyberculture*, 1, quoting Negroponte, *Being Digital*, 182.
48. McLuhan, *Understanding Media;* McLuhan and Powers, *The Global Village*.
49. McLuhan and Powers, *The Global Village*.
50. Rabinovitz and Geil, *Memory Bytes*, 3.
51. Goldsmith and Wu, *Who Controls the Internet?*, 14.
52. Ibid., 25–27.
53. Gitelman critiques this notion as naïve. Gitelman, *Always Already New*, 16.
54. In April 1995 a truck bomb blew up in a downtown federal building in Oklahoma City. For more, see Joseph Treaster, "Terror in Oklahoma City: The Bomb: The Tools of a Terrorist: Everywhere for Anyone,"

New York Times, April 20, 1995, B8; Keith Schneider, "Terror in Okla-
homa: The Internet: Talk on Bombs Surges On Computer Network,"
New York Times, April 27, 1995, A22; Rory O'Connor and Dan Gillmor,
"Bomb's Shock Wave Hits Online Freedom: Anti-Terrorism Backlash
Carries Threats to Secrecy, Outspokenness of Internet Culture," *San
Jose Mercury News,* May 7, 1995, 1A; Charles M. Sennott, "Bomb's
Ingredients Seen as Common," *The Boston Globe,* April 21, 1995, 30;
Rory O'Connor, "Online Speech Limits Sought: Feinstein Lobbies to
Ban Hatemail, Bomb Recipes," *San Jose Mercury News,* May 12, 1995,
1A; Paul Andrews, "Net Falters in Coverage of Bomb Aftermath," *The
Seattle Times,* April 30, 1995, C1; Dennis Romero, "Terrorist Threat
Lurking on Info Highway," *Chicago Sun-Times,* April 24, 1995, 21;
Serge F. Kovaleski, "Oklahoma Bombing Conspiracy Theories Ripple
Across the Nation," *Washington Post,* July 09, 1995, A3; Vic Sussman,
"Hate, Murder and Mayhem on the Net," *U.S. News & World Report,*
May 22, 1995, 62; Steven V. Roberts, Ted Gest, Kenneth T. Walsh, and
James Popkin, "After the Heartbreak," *U.S. News & World Report,* May
8, 1995, 26; "Militias Armed and Angry," *The Economist,* April 29, 1995,
28.

55. Vic Sussman, "Hate, Murder and Mayhem on the Net: Many Are
    Shocked by What's Online, but Others Say It's Nothing New: Try Your
    Local Bookstore," *U.S. News & World Report,* May 22, 1995, 62.

56. Simon, *NetPolicy.Com,* 6–7.

57. Steven Levy, "The Internet Crash Scare: Yes, The Net is Overloaded and
    Slow, But Even a Global Gigalapse Won't Stop the Revolution," *News-
    week,* September 16, 1996, 96.

58. Anthony Flint, "Consumers Find Everything New Is Old Already," *The
    Boston Globe,* April 2, 1995, 1; Stephen Hegarty, "Technology is Great—
    For Those Who Can Afford It," *St. Petersburg Times,* December 12, 1994,
    1A; Leslie Helm, "Americans Rushing into Technology Trap; Unpre-
    pared Computer Buyers Learn Machines Can Turn into Costly Toys,"
    The Houston Chronicle, December 25, 1994, A1; Barbara Presley Noble,
    "At Work; The Office as a Work in Progress," *New York Times,* December
    18, 1994, C23; Vic Sussman, "Policing Cyberspace," *U.S. News & World
    Report,* January 23, 1995, 54; "The Next 25: What Today's Leading CEOs,
    Management Gurus, and Futurists See Coming for Your Company,
    Your Job, and Your Life," *Industry Week,* August 21, 1995, 40; Steven
    Levy, "The Encryption Wars: Is Privacy Good or Bad? Computers: The
    Government Says Encoding Your E-Mail Could Threaten National
    Security," *Newsweek,* April 24, 1995, 55.

59. Robert O'Harrow Jr., "Computing the Cost of Obsolescence," *Washington Post*, April 14, 1994, A1; Maureen M. Smith, "'Low-tech' Woes: Many Urban Students Using Outdated Computers," *Minneapolis Star Tribune*, May 30, 1994, 1B; Steve Lohr, "Recycling Answer Sought for Computer Junk," *New York Times*, April 14, 1993, A1; Peter Lewis, "Facing the Price of a Home Computer," *New York Times*, August 10, 1993, C7; Stephen Barr, "Federal Spending on Computers Hit," *Chicago Sun-Times,* October 12, 1994, 36; Kathleen Glanville, "Planned Obsolescence Prompts One Consumer to Cry 'Enough!'" *The Oregonian*, October 3, 1991, O2; Ken Siegmann, "Giving New Life to Old PCs Nonprofit Firm Repairs, Donates Them to Schools," *The San Francisco Chronicle*, May 7, 1993, D1; Barbara Kantrowitz, "The Information Gap," *Newsweek,* March 21, 1994, 78; Barbara Kantrowitz, "The Metaphor Is the Message," *Newsweek*, February 14, 1994, 49; John McCormick and Marc Levinson, "Are Cities Obsolete?" *Newsweek*, September 9, 1991, 42; Leonard Wiener, "Buying in a Buyer's Market," *U.S. News & World Report*, July 26, 1993, 50; "The College of Tomorrow," *U.S. News & World Report*, September 28, 1992, 110; Stephen Budiansky and Bruce B. Auster, "Missions Implausible," *U.S. News & World Report*, October 14, 1991, 24; Jennifer Tanaka, "What You Need," *Newsweek*, November, 1994, 20.

60. Ronald Taylor, "Explosion of Hi-Tech Products for the Home," *U.S. News & World Report,* January 3, 1983, 65.

61. John Eckhouse, "High-Tech Execs See More Rivalry from Foreigners," *The San Francisco Chronicle,* March 13, 1991, C1; Peter N. Spotts, "Better Integration of U.S. Policy, Technology Urged," *Christian Science Monitor*, February 5, 1992, 8; Thomas Omestad "Cloak and Dagger as R&D; The French Do It. The Brits Do It. But Corporate Spying May Not Be for Us," *Washington Post*, June 27, 1993, C2; Bill Gertz, "The New Spy: '90s Espionage Turns Economic," *The Washington Times*, February 9, 1992, A1; Robert Samuelson, "The New (Old) Industrial Policy," *Newsweek*, May 23, 1994, 53; Susan Dentzer, "Staying Ahead in High Tech," *U.S. News & World Report*, April 1, 1991, 53; Jim Impoco, "With Communism Dead, Now It's Capitalist vs. Capitalist," *U.S. News & World Report*, December 30, 1991, 50; Steven Butler, Robin Knight, Monika Guttman, and Marta Williams, "Sinking Deeper in the Drowning Pool," *U.S. News & World Report*, May 16, 1994, 56; Time Padgett, "The Gloom Behind the Boom," *Newsweek*, March 23, 1992, 48; Jim Impoco, "The Sultan of Silicon Valley," *U.S. News & World Report*, March 1, 1993, 56.

62. Ronald Steel, "Getting Ahead; America Remains No. 1," *New York Times*, September 29, 1996, A1.

63. Although the James Bond film series features cutting-edge technology prominently in its plots, the 1989 film *License to Kill* pictured only one computer, and it was not obviously networked.

64. *Golden Eye* grossed $26,205,007 in its opening weekend; *Tomorrow Never Dies* grossed $25,143,007 in its opening weekend.

65. Janet Maslin, "Film Review," *New York Times*, November 17, 1995, C17.

66. Kenna, "James Bond's Gender."

67. Gibson, *Neuromancer*; *Tron*. David Landis, "Exploring the Online Universe," *USA Today*, October 7, 1993, 4D; William Powers, "Wired: Plugged into the Computer World; Savvy Monthly Isn't Just for Nerds," *Washington Post*, February 1, 1994, C7; David Perlman, "A Ride on Internet Highway: It's Part of Exhibit at Exploratorium," *The San Francisco Chronicle*, February 11, 1994, C1; Peter Lewis, "Personal Computers: A Cyberspace Atlas: America Online," *New York Times*, November 15, 1994, C8; Ross Daly and Joshua Quittner, "Online to a Revolution: The Amazing—And Some Would Say Ominous—New World of TV, Telephone and Computer Is Heading Your Way," *New York Newsday*, July 18, 1993, A50; Michelle Levander, "A Cyberspace Gang Fans the Flames on the Internet," *San Jose Mercury News*, May 15, 1994 1E; Joel Achenbach, "Wire Me Up, Scotty; We have Seen the Future, but We Still Can't Tell You What It Means," *Washington Post*, May 29, 1994, W10; William Safire, "On Language; Virtual Reality," *New York Times*, September 13, 1992, F18; Charles W. Hall, "The Future Is Now; Visitors Trek Down Information Highway," *Washington Post*, April 27, 1994, D3; "Whole Earth Review Editor to Explore Virtual Reality," *The Oregonian*, November 3, 1993, C8; "Plug into the Cyber Frontier," *Computerworld*, October 30, 1994, 6.

68. "Computers of the Future," *Time*, March 28, 1988; "Computer Viruses," *Time*, September 26, 1988; "Cyberpunk: Virtual Sex, Smart Drugs, and Synthetic Rock'n'Roll! A Futuristic Subculture Erupts from the Electronic Underground," *Time*, February 8, 1993; "Coming Soon to Your TV Screen: The Info Highway: Bringing a Revolution in Entertainment, News, and Communication," *Time*, April 12, 1993; "The Strange New World of the Internet: Battles on the Frontiers of Cyberspace," *Time*, July 25, 1994; "Welcome to Cyberspace," *Time*, March 1, 1995.

69. "Computer Viruses," *Time*, September 26, 1988.

70. "Welcome to Cyberspace," *Time*, March 1, 1995.

71. The first mention of virtual reality in the *New York Times* occurred in 1989: Andrew Pollack, "For Artificial Reality, Wear A Computer," *New York Times*, April 10, 1989, A1; David Landis, "Exploring the Online

Universe," *USA Today,* October 7, 1993, 4D; Peter Lewis, "Personal
Computers: A Cyberspace Atlas: America Online," *New York Times,*
November 15, 1994, C8; Joel Achenbach, "Wire Me Up, Scotty; We have
Seen the Future, but We Still Can't Tell You What It Means," *Washington
Post,* May 29, 1994, W10; William Safire, "On Language; Virtual Reality,"
New York Times, September 13, 1992, F18; "Whole Earth Review Editor
to Explore Virtual Reality," *The Oregonian,* November 3, 1993, C8; "Plug
into the Cyber Frontier," *Computerworld,* October 30, 1994, 6; Steve
Ditlea, "Another World: Inside Artificial Reality; Computer-generated
Environments," *PC-Computing* 2 (November 1989), 90.
72. Sconce, *Haunted,* 204.
73. Gibson, *Neuromancer.*
74. De la Peña, *Body Electric,* 220.
75. Turner, *From Counterculture to Cyberculture,* 162–65.
76. Barlow, "Being in Nothingness." As Turner notes, Barlow visited Jaron
Lanier, the scientist and computer researcher, who had years earlier
named his three-dimensional imaging systems "virtual reality" after the
electronic space described by Gibson. Turner, *From Counterculture to
Cyberculture,* 163, citing Stone, *The War of Desire.*
77. *The Matrix*; Barnett, "Reviving Cyberpunk"; Adams, "Cyberspace and
Virtual Places"; Ryan, "Introduction"; Strate, "Varieties of Cyberspace."
78. *The Lawnmower Man* grossed $32,101,000 domestically.
79. Vincent Canby, "Reviews/Film; This Man Is Dangerous, and Armed
with Science," *New York Times,* March 7, 1992, A20; Jay Carr, "'Lawnmower Man': Faust Goes to the Lab," *The Boston Globe,* March 6, 1992,
30; John Marshall, "Get Virtual: We're Entering a Brave New World
of Virtual Reality," *The Seattle Post-Intelligencer,* March 14, 1992, C1;
Bradley J. Fikes, "Will Lawnmower Man Put Tiny Angel Studios on Big
Celluloid Map? Company Profile," *San Diego Business Journal,* March 9,
1992, 11; David Elliott, "'Lawnmower' a Cut Above 'Frankenstein,'" *San
Diego Union-Tribune,* March 5, 1992, 15; Steven Rea, "Review: Film—
The Otherworld of 'Lawnmower Man,'" *Philadelphia Inquirer,* March 9,
1992, E5.
80. John Marshall, "Get Virtual: We're Entering a Brave New World of Virtual Reality," *The Seattle Post-Intelligencer,* March 14, 1992, C1.
81. Castells, *The Internet Galaxy,* 16.
82. In 1994, one of the first programs designed as a commercial enterprise,
Mosaic, became Netscape Navigator, the first commercial browser
developed explicitly to make money and not simply to develop
the online world. Mosaic changed the functionality and cultural

understanding of computer network and sparked one of the first commercial technology wars (Netscape vs. Microsoft). Castells, *The Internet Galaxy*, 17.

83. Gitelman, *Always Already New*, 10.
84. Ibid., 114.
85. Heiddigger, *Being and Time*.
86. Polly, "Surfing the Internet."
87. Gitelman, *Always Already New*, 95 citing Hayles, *How We Became Posthuman*.
88. Gitelman, *Always Already New*, 96.
89. "Deterritorialized" means it rises to its own power. Goldsmith and Wu, *Who Controls the Internet?*, citing Deleuze and Guattari, *A Thousand Plateaus*, 142; Appadurai, "Disjuncture and Difference."
90. Turner, *From Counterculture to Cyberculture*, 162.
91. Ibid., 173, quoting Barlow, "Crime and Puzzlement."
92. Turner, *From Counterculture to Cyberculture*, 162.
93. Rheingold, *The Virtual Community*.
94. Philip Elmer-DeWitt, "Take a Trip into the Future on the Electronic Superhighway: A New World of Video Entertainment and Interactive Services Will Be Available Sooner than Many Think," *Time*, April 12, 1993, 42: http://www.time.com/time/magazine/article/0,9171,978216,00.html (accessed August 12, 2007).
95. Habermas, *The Structural Transformation*.
96. Norris, *Digital Divide*.
97. De la Peña, *Body Electric*, 220.
98. Bourdieu, *Outline of a Theory*.
99. Gitelman, *Always Already New*, 9.
100. Harvey, "Communication Issues."
101. Wise, "Community," 126, citing Slotkin, *Fatal Environment*.
102. High Performance Computing and Communication Act of 1991, U.S. Public Law 102-194, 102nd Cong., December 9, 1991; High Performance Computing and High Speed Networking Applications Act of 1993, H.R.1757, 103rd Cong., September 14, 1993; National Competitiveness Act of 1993, S.4.1, 103rd Cong., March 16, 1994; National Communications Competition and Information Infrastructure Act of 1994, H.R.3636. 104th Cong., June 28, 1994.
103. High Performance Computing and Communication Act of 1991, U.S. Public Law 102-194, 102nd Cong., December 9, 1991.. The term was actually coined in the 1970s in reference to cable television, and was applied to computing systems by Gore. Steven E. Miller, *Civilizing Cyberspace:*

Policy, Power, and the Information Superhighway (New York: Addison-Wesley Publishing Company, 1996), 73.

104. Standage, *Victorian Internet*, xiii.

105. Some argue superhighway mythology deliberately masked the internet's design to deliver consumers to corporations. Kroker and Weinstein, "Theory of the Virtual Class."

106. Anderson, *Imagining the Internet*, 78.

107. Philip Elmer-DeWitt, "Take a Trip on into the Future on the Electronic Superhighway: A New World of Video Entertainment and Interactive Services Will Be Available Sooner than Many Think," *Time*, April 12, 1993, 42: http://www.time.com/time/magazine/article/0,9171,978216,00.html (accessed August 12, 2007).

108. Miller, *Civilizing Cyberspace*, 129.

109. Ibid., 129.

110. Ibid., 75–76.

111. Renee Graham, "Training Wheels for the Information Superhighway; Computer Museum Eases Access," *The Boston Globe*, November 12, 1994, 61; Laurent Belsie, "Info Superhighway: Metaphor in Concrete," *Christian Science Monitor*, February 2, 1994, 1; James Lileks, "Information Superhighway Delivers Less than Promised," *The Oregonian*, February 10, 1994, E7; Mike Royko, "Taxpayers Shouldn't Foot Bill for Information Superhighway," *The Oregonian*, February 16, 1994, C9; Audrie Krause, "Hazards on the Information Highway," *San Diego Union-Tribune*, June 12, 1994, G3; "Living on the Internet—Rapidly Growing Lane in the Information Superhighway Is Full of Promise and Users," *The Seattle Times*, February 20, 1994, A1; Richard Louv, "Information Highway Could be a Toll Road," *San Diego Union-Tribune*, October 19, 1994, A2; Doug Abrahms, "Information Superhighway Provides a Vehicle for Scams," *The Washington Times*, July 2, 1994, D5; Russell Baker, "The Superhypeway," *San Jose Mercury News*, January 5, 1994, 7B; Graeme Browning, "Stuck in the Slow Lane," *The National Journal*, August 7, 1993, 32; Laura B. Randolph, "Blacks in the Fast Lane of the Information Superhighway," *Ebony*, January, 1995, 98B; Christopher Farrell and Michael J. Mandel, "What's Arriving on the Information Highway? Growth," *Business Week*, November 29, 1993, 40; Robert Samuelson, "Lost on the Information Highway," *Newsweek*, December 20, 1993, 111; "A Hitch-hiker's Guide: America's Information Highway," *The Economist*, December 25, 1993, 35; Sherry Keene-Osborn, "Full Speed Ahead—Maybe," *Newsweek*, March 7, 1994, 44; "Bill Gates and the Open Road," *The Economist*, June 3, 1995, 29.

112. Anderson, *Imagined Communities*, 80.
113. "Coming Soon to Your TV Screen: The Info Highway: Bringing a Revolution in Entertainment, News and Communication," *Time*, April 12, 1993.
114. Moschovitis, et al., *History of the Internet*, 118.
115. Ibid., 228.
116. "Internet," *Economist*, February 8, 1997, 88; Moschovitis, et al., *History of the Internet*; Murray, *The Regulation of Cyberspace*.
117. Malamud, *A World's Fair*, 9.
118. Anderson, *Imagined Communities*, 12.
119. Ibid., 35
120. Ibid., 44
121. Moschovitis, et al., *History of the Internet*.
122. Internet 1996 World Exposition archive: http://park.org/ (accessed September 3, 2007).
123. Ibid.
124. "Excerpt from Bill Clinton's Letter."
125. Malamud, *A World's Fair*, 38.
126. "Excerpt from Boris Yeltsin's Letter."
127. Malamud, *World's Fair*, 31.
128. Ibid., 4–5.
129. Ibid., 9.
130. Rodman, "The Net Effect," 16; Bagdikian, *Media Monopoly*.
131. McChesney, *Corporate Media*, 42–43.
132. Thank you to Adrian Johns for drawing this connection.
133. Thank you to Julie Elman.
134. Swisher, *Aol.com*, 55. In 2006 America Online officially changed its name to "AOL." At the time, Chairman and CEO of AOL Jon Miller said, "Our company long ago accomplished the mission implied by our old name … we literally got America online…."
135. Miller, *Civilizing Cyberspace*, 172.
136. Moschovitis, et al., *History of the Internet*, 183.
137. Vaidhyanathan, *Anarchist*, 150.
138. Wu, *Master Switch*, 262.
139. Swisher, *Aol.com*, 7; Turner, *From Counterculture to Cyberculture*, 213.
140. Moschovitis, et al., *History of the Internet*, 183.
141. Stross, *The Microsoft Way*; although Microsoft was late to enter the internet market (after the emergence of Netscape), because of the conflation of computing and networking, Gates was represented as important to both. Moschovitis, et al., *History of the Internet*.

142. He was the focus of numerous newspaper features, magazine articles and covers, and the subject of several books: Ichbiah and Knepper. *Making of Microsoft*; Wallace and Erickson, *Hard Drive*; Manes and Andrews, *Gates*; Stross, *Microsoft Way*; Wallace, *Overdrive*; for more on Gates as the richest person in the world by the early 1980s, see: Schaller, *Right Turn*, 173.

143. *ABC Nightline with Forrest Sawyer*, "The World According To Gates," November 23, 1995.

144. John Markoff, "Nothing Up Their Sleeves?: Masters of the High-Tech Demo Spin Their Magic," *New York Times,* March 11, 1996, D1.

145. "Driven:" Timothy Egan, "Microsoft's Unlikely Millionaires," *New York Times,* June 28, 1992, C1; "Visionary:" *NBC Evening News with Tom Brokaw*, "Seattle, Washington / Gates' Microsoft,"May 29, 1992; "Genius:" Ichbiah and L. Knepper, *Making of Microsoft*.

146. L.R. Shannon, "He Is an Operating System," *New York Times,* May 24, 1992, G12.

147. Zickgraf, *William Gates.*

148. Timothy Egan, "Microsoft's Unlikely Millionaires," *New York Times,* June 28, 1992, C1.

149. Stross, *Microsoft Way.*

150. *NBC Evening News with Tom Brokaw and George Lewis*, "America Close Up (Business: Microsoft)," February 4, 1993; David Einstein, "No Stopping Microsoft Nothing Seems to Faze the Software Juggernaut," *The San Francisco Chronicle*, July 19, 1994, B1; Casey Corr, "Dominant Microsoft Faces Rush of Criticism," *Oregonian*, April 14, 1991, R01; Andrew Pollack, "Microsoft's Tactics Questioned by Rivals," *New York Times*, March 15, 1991, D1; Casey Corr, "Hi-Tech—Microsoft Plays Hardball—Some Question Its Growing Industry Dominance," *The Seattle Times*, April 8, 1991, B1; Jim Erickson, "Microsoft Practices Target Federal Probe," *Seattle Post-Intelligencer*, March 13, 1991, P1; Michael Schrage, "Windows of Opportunity Open For Microsoft and Bill Gates," *Washington Post*, July 22, 1994, D3; Elizabeth Corcoran, "Microsoft Settles Case With Justice; Software Giant Accused Of Boosting Prices, Thwarting Competitors," *Washington Post*, July 17, 1994, A1; Michael Schrage, "Microsoft's Gates in the Middle of an Ethical Muddle Over Multimedia," *Washington Post*, January 8, 1993, F3.

151. "Microsoft Trial Timeline," *Washington Post*: http://www.washingtonpost.com/wp-dyn/business/specials/microsofttrial/timeline/ (accessed August 13, 2007).

152. "*U.S. vs. Microsoft* Timeline," *Wired*: http://www.wired.com/techbiz/it/news/2002/11/35212 (accessed August 13, 2007).

153. "Tycoon:" *NBC Evening News with Giselle Fernandez*, "On Line (Computers / Bill Gates)," May 26, 1995; "Bully:" James Wallace and Jim Erickson, *Hard Drive: Bill Gates and the Making of the Microsoft Empire* (New York: Wiley, 1992).
154. Wallace and Erickson, *Hard Drive*.
155. Ibid.; L.R. Shannon, "He Is an Operating System," *New York Times*, May 24, 1992, G12.
156. Wallace and Erickson, *Hard Drive*.
157. *NBC Evening News with Tom Brokaw, George Lewis and Andrea Mitchell*, "Economy: North American Free Trade Agreement / Congress / Gore Interview / Computer Industry," November 15, 1993; David Hamilton, "Gates to Clinton: Don't Manage Trade," *New York Times*, May 24, 1993, A10.

CHAPTER 4

1. *½ Miete*. The film was produced by Ute Schneider and Wim Wenders. The film won awards from the Bermuda International Film Festival, Internationale Hofer Filmtage, Brooklyn International Film Festival, and the Europäisches Filmfest.

    This chapter focuses in particular on German popular culture and news media as Germany was and is the main economic- and policy-driver in the European Union.
2. In a pay-phone call shortly after arriving in Cologne, he says, "*Ich bin nicht mehr erreichbar.*" *½ Miete*.
3. Worth noting is that characters in technology-genre films not specifically about the internet (such as *Terminator*) do decide to unplug. Internet movies: *The Lawnmower Man; Golden Eye; Tomorrow Never Dies; Johnny Mnemonic; The Net; Hackers; Lawnmower Man 2: Beyond Cyberspace; You've Got Mail; The Matrix; Minority Report; The Matrix Reloaded; The Matrix Revolutions*.
4. Burns, "Introduction," 6, citing Waldman, "Critical Theory," 56. Fear of technology is related to historical fears of Americanization in the eighteenth and nineteenth century. Wise, "Community," 126.
5. "The Strange New World of the Internet: Battles on the Frontiers of Cyberspace," *Time*, July 25, 1994; "Lernen mit Computer: schöne neue Schule" ("Learning with Computers: Beautiful New Schools"), *Der Spiegel*, September 1994.
6. The press was subject to less regulation than broadcasting media in terms of content, but was also heavily subsidized. Harcourt, *The European Union*.

7. Although "deregulation" is the popular term for this kind of pro-business regulation, the term is misleading because this type of legislation does not regulate less, but regulates in a different way. See, for example, the 1996 Information Superhighway Law in France, the 1996 Interstate Agreement on the Regulation of Broadcasting in Germany, the 1997 New Media Act in Italy, the 1998 Law on Digital Television in Spain, and the 1996 Broadcasting Act in the United Kingdom. For more on these regulations, see Harcourt, *The European Union*, 161.

8. "eEurope: An Information Society for All," *Communication on a Commission Initiative for the Special European Council of Lisbon*, March 23 and 24, 2000: http://europa.eu.int/abc/off/index_en.htm.

9. De Sola Pool notes that to argue U.S. dominance is not necessarily to argue imperialism. De Sola Pool, *Technologies Without Boundaries*, 214–15.

10. Wagnleitner, *Coca-Colonization*.

11. For documentation and analysis of the newfound interest in the digital divide in the United States, see Katz and Asbden, "Motivations for and Barriers to Internet Usage," 170, citing "Commerce Net Survey," Nielsen Media, 1996: http://www.nielsonmedia.com; "Internet Users: Who They Are: What They Want," Dataquest Report, 1995: OLST-WWW-UW-9501; "Caught in the Net;" Anderson and Bickson, *Feasibility*; and Edmondson, "The Point-and-Click Government."

12. Neuchterlein and Weiser, *Digital Crossroads*, 14.

13. Simon details these policies as follows: "Member-state regulation of commercial broadcasting focuses on ownership limits, caps on advertising and rules on media content. Laws provide percentage requirements for news and documentary programming, the promotion of European and national content and time devoted to minority audience programming or representation of identifiable societal groups." Simon, *NetPolicy.Com*, 159.

14. Blumler notes the variations among E.U. states, observing that regulations in France, Greece, Italy, Ireland, Portugal, and Spain are the most subject to fluctuating politics, while German and British regulations are more independent of shifting political contexts. Blumler, *Television*.

15. Thomas Crampton, "In France, a Toaster-Size Computer with Web Access," *New York Times*, April 2, 2007, C1. Many states—including Austria, Belgium, France, Germany, Denmark, Finland, Italy, Netherlands, Norway, Spain, and Sweden—had some kind of teletext or videotext by 1985; David Carlson, "Online Timeline," The Virtual World: http://iml.jou.ufl.edu/carlson/1980s.shtml (accessed January 3, 2008). Figures

from "The Guide of the Services Minitel," Minitel, English: http://www.minitelfr.com/Uk/divers/f_faq.html (accessed April 2, 2008).

16. Shlomo Maital, "The Global Telecommunications Picture: Is America Being Outstripped? By France?" *The Brookings Review 10,* (Summer 1992): 40–44.

17. Al Gore argued that the success of U.S. commerce depended on continued private sector leadership in development of the internet. Gore, "A Framework for Global Electronic Commerce."

18. Simon, *NetPolicy.Com,* 338.

19. Ibid. For more on this shift and the context of the French Minister's remarks, see Schlesinger, "Tension," 115.

20. Ibid.

21. For an overview of this debate, see Schlesinger, "Tension."

22. For the use of photography and postcards in pornography as early as 1880, see Sigel, "Filth." For a history of pornographic film, see Schaefer, "Gauging a Revolution." For a comprehensive history of pornography and media from the ancient Greeks to the internet, see McNair, *Mediated Sex.*

23. Miller, *Civilizing Cyberspace,* 243.

24. Shlomo Maital. "The Global Telecommunications Picture: Is America Being Outstripped? By France?" *The Brookings Review 10,* (Summer 1992): 40–44; and Cross et al., *Networks.*

25. Van Os et al., "Presentations of Europe."

26. Schlesinger, "Tension."

27. CompuServe, an internet provider that was owned by H&R Block and headquartered in Columbus, Ohio, was one of the main internet providers in the mid-1990s before it was purchased by AOL in 1998. In December 1995, when Germany acted against CompuServe, the corporation provided internet and email access to over four million subscribers in 140 countries. John Markoff, "On-Line Service Blocks Access to Topics Called Pornographic," *New York Times,* December 29, 1995, A1.

28. For a summary of this case, see Goldsmith and Wu, *Who Controls the Internet,* 73–74. Also see newspaper coverage from the period: Karen Kaplan, "Germany Forces Online Services to Censor Internet," *Los Angeles Times,* December 29, 1995, A1; "Why Free-Wheeling Internet Puts Teutonic Wall over Porn," *Christian Science Monitor,* January 4, 1996, 1; Kara Swisher, "Cyberporn Debate Goes International; Germany Pulls the Shade on CompuServe, Internet," *Washington Post,* January 1, 1996, F13; Jon Auerbach, "Fences in Cyberspace: Governments Move to Limit Free Flow of the Internet," *Boston Globe,* February 1, 1996, 1.

29. Goldsmith and Wu, *Who Controls the Internet*, 73–74.
30. Paul Taylor, "Internet Groups Suspended Over Pornography Fears," *Financial Times* (London), December 29, 1995, 1.
31. Ibid.
32. "Justiz verzweifelt am anarchischen Internet: Staatsanwalt beklagt fehlende Regelungen" ("Law Despairs at the Anarchist Internet: Public Prosecutor Deplores Lack of Regulation"), *Süddeutsche Zeitung*, December 6, 1995, 12.
33. Reidenberg, "Governing Networks," 97.
34. Johnson and Post, "Rise of Law," 7–8. For a more extensive list of banned sites and more information on the homosexuality portions, see John Markoff, "On-Line Service Blocks Access to Topics Called Pornographic," *New York Times*, December 29, 1995, A1.
35. Markoff, "On-Line Service Blocks Access," A1.
36. Michael Meyer and Jennifer Tanaka, "A Bad Dream Comes True in Cyberspace," *Newsweek*, January 8, 1996, 65.
37. For more on the hearings, see Markoff, "On-Line Service Blocks Access," A1.
38. For more on European approaches to policymaking, see Murray, *The Regulation of Cyberspace*; Baldwin, et al., *A Reader on Regulation*; Maastricht Treaty on European Union, done at Maastricht, February 7, 1992, Eur. O.J. C 224/1 (August 31, 1992). See Bermann et al., *Cases and Materials*.
39. Common Position (EC) No/95 With a View to Adopting Directive 94/EC of the European Parliament and of the Council on the Protection of Individuals with Regard to the Processing of Personal Data and on the Free Movement of Such Data, 1994, O.J. (C 93, April 13, 1995), reprinted in Appendix, *Iowa Law Review* (1995): 697. This initiative allowed "transborder data flows only if the recipient country offered 'an adequate level of data protection." Schwartz, "European Data Protection Law," 471.
40. Reidenberg, "Governing Networks," 97.
41. For examples of *extension*-focused news reports, see "Gnädige Frau, darf ich Ihnen meinen Cyber zeigen?" ("Madam, May I Show You My Cyber?"), *Frankfurter Allgemeine Zeitung*, March 10, 1997, 36; Michael Mertes, "Das Internet revolutioniert die Politic: Das Netz als globales Dorf oder Metropolis" ("The Internet Revolutionizes Politics: The Net as Global Village or Metropolis"), *Welt am Sonntag*, April 19, 1998, 34; "Publizieren im Cyberspace" ("Publishing in Cyberspace"), *Frankfurter Allgemeine Zeitung*, July 22, 1994, N1; "Bibliotheken im Cyberspace:

Grenzen der Digitalisierung" ("Libraries in Cyberspace: Limits of Digitalization"), *Frankfurter Allgemeine Zeitung*, September 25, 1996, N6; "Unterwegs nach Suburbia" ("On the Road to Suburbia"), *Frankfurter Allgemeine Zeitung*, January 22, 1996, 11; "Kaufhaus von morgen plus Computer E-Commerce; globale Shopping-Center sind nur einen Mausklick vom Kunden entfernt. Firmen erhoffen sich vom Handel über Datennetze fette Gewinne" ("Department Store of the Future plus Computer E-Commerce; Global Shopping Centers Are only a Mouse Click Away from the Customer. Companies Hope to Win Fat Profits from Data Networks"), *Stern*, March 19, 1998, 137; Nick Clayton, "Solicitors Set up Shop in Cyberspace," *The Scotsman*, February 18, 1998, 3; Andrew Bibby, "A Phoenix Rises and Heads for Cyberspace," *The Independent* (London), February 13, 1995, 21; Helen Jones, "Now You Can Surf the Net for a Job; Cyberspace now Offers Thousands of Opportunities," *The Independent* (London), April 18, 1996, 22; Gary Buchanan, "Simple, Low-cost Ways to Make the Right Connections," *The Herald* (Glasgow), January 26, 1998, 16; Andreas Heimann and Jay Dougherty, "Cemeteries in Cyberspace: Visiting Eternity on the Web," *Deutsche Presse-Agentur*, October 5, 1997; Bob Swain, "The Holy and the Interface: Sitting Miles Apart, People Can Take a Tour of a French Abbey, or Help Run a Cable TV Show in New York: It's Called Televirtuality," *The Guardian* (London), April 15, 1993, 17; Jay Dougherty, "Playboy Steams Up Cyberspace," *Deutsche Presse-Agentur*, January 12, 1995; Roger Trapp, "Virtual and Vinyl-like, It's the Cyber CD Shop; From Obscure Indie to Early Elvis Costello, You Can Buy It on the Net," *The Independent* (London), October 7, 1996, 11; Kirsten Foster, "Surf's Up: Queer and Loathing in Cyberspace: Just in Case You Hadn't Noticed, the Net is Turning Pink. Forget Dodgy Pick-Up Bars and Go Cruising By Computer," *The Independent* (London), August 20, 1995, 11; Joan Grady, "Launched into Cyberspace," *The Herald* (Glasgow), October 31, 1995, 14.

For examples of *amputation*-focused news reports, see "Cyberspace und der amerikanische Traum" ("Cyberspace and the American Dream"), *Frankfurter Allgemeine Zeitung*, August 26, 1995, 30; "Der Kopf schrumpft" ("The Head Shrinks"), *Frankfurter Allgemeine Zeitung*, September 9, 1995, 29; "Die verflüchtigte Materie" ("The Vaporized Matter"), *Frankfurter Allgemeine Zeitung*, October 4, 1995, N5; "Datenautobahn als Eckpfeiler der amerikanischen Technikpolitik" ("Information Superhighway as Cornerstone of American Technology Policy"), *Frankfurter Allgemeine Zeitung*, January 25, 1994, 14; "Mit zehn Gigabyte"

("With 10 Gigabytes"), *Frankfurter Allgemeine Zeitung*, January 9, 1995, 1; "Schnäppchen aus dem Internet" ("Bargains on the Internet"), *Focus Magazin* 31, July 29, 1996, 132–36; "Klassenkampf im Cybersp@ce" ("Class Struggle in Cybersp@ce"), *Focus Magazin* 41, October 7, 1996, 286–87; "Tödlicher Mausklick" ("Fatal Mouse Click"), *Focus Magazin* 39, September 25, 1995, 192–94; "Per Fahrrad auf die Datenautobahn" ("Bicycling on the Information Superhighway"), *Focus Magazin* 50, December 11, 1995, 142; Walter Dreher, "Gesellschaft: Ein Volk auf dem Ego-Trip" ("Society: A People on an Ego Trip"), *Focus Magazin* 27, July 31, 1995, 52–60; Marion Meiners, "Datennetze: Anarchie in Digitalien" ("Data Networks: Anarchy in Digitalia"), *Focus Magazin* 27, July 1, 1996, 134–35.

42. "Internet—das Netz der Netze? Chaotische Strukturen und zunehmende kommerzielle Angebote. Immer schneller webt die Spinne ihr Netz um die Welt. Noch lassen sich auf der Datenautobahn nur begrenzt Geschäfte machen / Probleme mit Datensicherheit und Tempo" ("Internet—the Net of the Nets? Chaotic Structures and Increasing Commercial Offers. Faster and faster the Spider Weaves Its Net around the World. At this point, there are still only limited business opportunities on the Information Superhighway / Problems with Data Security and Speed"), *Süddeutsche Zeitung*, July 18, 1995, 28.

43. Jeanne Rubner, "Das Web ist das Ziel: Internet, Internat: Müssen wirklich alle ans Netz?" ("The Web Is the Goal: Internet, Boarding School [play on words]: Must We All Really Live Online?"), *Süddeutsche Zeitung*, December 17, 1997, 17.

44. *½ Miete.*

45. Translated from "Wegen Typen wie uns wird alles irgendwann zur Gründe gehen."

46. Deborah Young, "1/2 The Rent," *Variety*, April 14, 2003.

47. Matthias Heine, "Wer wohnt hier? *Halbe Miete* von Marc Ottiker" ("Who Lives Here? *Halbe Miete* by Marc Ottiker,") *Die Welt*, December, 31, 2003, 28: http://www.welt.de/print-welt/article283043/Wer-wohnt-hier-Halbe-Miete-von-Marc-Ottiker.html (accessed July 29, 2012).

48. For more on American technological determinism, see Segal, *Technological Utopianism*; Williams, *Television*; and Volti, *Society and Technological Change*.

49. Murray, *The Regulation of Cyberspace*, 35.

50. "Digitale Stad" from November 1996, accessed through waybackmachine.com: http://web.archive.org/web/19970618155059/www.dds.nl/dds/info/english/dds-engl.html (accessed March 5, 2008).

51. Ibid.
52. Malamud, *A World's Fair*, 37–38. Founders hoped to quickly transition to "end its dependence on receiving ad hoc subsidies within two years." "Digitale Stad" from November 1996.
53. De Waag was built in 1488 to house and weigh goods, but soon became a labor guild headquarters, then a make-shift medical school in the 1500s, and eventually a theater in the 1600s. Malamud, *A World's Fair*, 37–38.
54. 1996 is the earliest archived version available through Archive.org.
55. "Digitale Stad" from November 1996.
56. "The Digital City Foundation" page of "Digitale Stad."
57. "Digitale Stad."
58. Tan, "An Interview."
59. Ibid.
60. Founder Marleen Stikker wanted to connect women, senior citizens, and minority groups. "Digitale Stad."
61. Jenkins, *Convergence Culture*; Shirky, *Cognitive Surplus*.
62. Globalization and "automation" threatened "employment, and thereby the social cohesion of a society, under pressure." "Digitale Stad."
63. Frankfurt was the first digital city in Germany, at http://www.frankfurt. de: "Frankfurt erhaelt eine Adresse im Computer: Stadt will Sich über Internet Vermarkten" ("Frankfurt Gets a Computer Address: The City Wants to Market Itself Online"), *Frankfurter Allgemeine*, April 30, 1995, 9.
64. "Digitale Stad."
65. This representation was also present in German newspapers. See for example, "Postkarten per Internet. Im Kaffeehaus des 21. Jahrhunderts" ("Postcards from the Internet: In the Coffeehouse of the 21st Century"), *Süddeutsche Zeitung*, July 19, 1995, 13.
66. Malamud, *A World's Fair*, 37–38.
67. For more on the specific differences between member-states, see the thorough work done by Eli Noam in Part II of his *Telecommunications in Europe*.
68. For more on American technological determinism, see Segal, *Technological Utopianism*; Wise, "Community, Affect, and the Virtual: The Politics of Cyberspace," in *Virtual Publics*; Williams, *Television;* Volti, *Society and Technological Change*; and Adas, *Machines*.
69. Harvey, "Privacy," 243.
70. For more on the history of the European Union, see Rogowski and Turner, *Shape of the New Europe*; Menon and Schain, *Comparative*

Federalism; Egan, *Constructing a European Market;* Richardson, *European Union.*

71. First: West Germany, France, Italy, Belgium, Netherlands, and Luxembourg; Second: Ireland, the United Kingdom, Denmark, Greece, Portugal, Spain, Austria, Finland, and Sweden. For more on the history of the European Union, see Rogowski and Turner, *The Shape of the New Europe;* Menon and Schain, *Comparative Federalism;* Egan, *Constructing a European Market;* Richardson, *European Union.*

72. This similarity was demonstrated even in the Union's name when the Maastricht Treaty of 1993 changed the official name from the "European Community" to "European Union," signifying a more "united states" model. The name shift became official with the Lisbon Treaty in 2009. Maastricht Treaty on European Union, done at Maastricht, February 7, 1992, Eur. O.J. C 224/1 (August 31, 1992). See Bermann et al., *Cases and Materials.*73.

73. Harcourt writes that "E.U. regulation is often seen as a response to national initiatives." Harcourt, *The European Union,* 3. Also see Levy, *Europe's Digital Revolution.*

74. The "Liberalization Directive," which was created under Article 90 of the Treaty of Rome, "requires Member-states to remove measures which are contrary to the rules of the Treaty, and specifically the competition rules, with regard to public undertakings and those with special and exclusive rights which includes former telecommunications monopolists." Watson and Wheatdon, *Telecommunications,* xiii.

75. Schlesinger, "Tension," 95.

76. For more on how national identity is formed in opposition to other national identities, see Anderson, *Imagined Communities.*

77. Although the United States is by no means linguistically homogenous, cultural inclusion does presume English-language ability. For more on languages and the European Union, see Rogowski and Turner, *The Shape of the New Europe;* Egan, *Constructing a European Market;* Richardson, *European Union.*

78. Schlesinger, "Tension," 103–104.

79. E.U. Public Law, Council Directive 89/552/EEC. European Commission, October 3, 1989. *Television Without Frontiers Directive.* "Summaries of Legislation," European Union: http://europa.eu/scadplus/leg/en/lvb/l24101.htm (accessed April 18, 2008).

80. Patterson, "Introduction."

81. Note, for example, the 1996 Information Superhighway Law in France, the 1996 Interstate Agreement on the Regulation of Broadcasting in

Germany, the 1997 New Media Act in Italy, the 1998 Law on Digital Television in Spain, and the 1996 Broadcasting Act in the United Kingdom; For more, see Harcourt, *The European Union*, 161.

82. In the early 1970s, interaction between American and British academics and strong British governmental support for the establishment of a British network meant that the United States and the United Kingdom were continuously interconnected via satellite computer links. These connections allowed the two nations to avoid much "of the political in-fighting which had dogged the French and German scenes at the time." Peter T. Kirstein, "Early Experiences with the ARPANET and INTERNET in the U.K.:" http://www.cs.ucl.ac.uk/staff/jon/arpa/internet-history.html (accessed January 3, 2008).

83. Ibid.

84. Market liberalization began as early as 1983. Giovannetti, "IT Revolution," 126.

85. Kirstein, "Early Experiences." Eventually, the Deutsche Bundespost, the postal service of West Germany, contracted with British Telecom to begin Germany's version of France's Minitel, called Bildschirmtext (or "screen text"), which became functional in the early 1980s, and had 28,000 subscribers and 3,700 sites by 1985. Giovannetti, "IT Revolution," 126.

86. "Deutsche Bundesregierung:" http://www.bundesregierung.de.

87. The website featured a box where users could search press releases. The title of the page was "Search White House Press Releases, Radio Addresses, Photos and Web Pages." "White House" main website: http://www.whitehouse.gov/ accessed through Archive.org's WayBackMachine: http://www.archive.org/ (accessed April 23, 2008).

88. "eEurope: An Information Society for All," *Communication on a Commission Initiative for the Special European Council of Lisbon*, March 23 and 24, 2000: http://europa.eu.int/abc/off/index_en.htm. In the same year, the European Union launched a seven-year program designed to promote European collective culture. Although a specifically European internet site dated back to 1971—when the Commission of the European Community passed a resolution to create a network to be called "Euronet"—a major part of the 2000 E.U. initiatives was the creation of a new European internet site. For more on the history of Euronet, see Roberts, "The Evolution of Packet Switching."

89. "eEurope: An Information Society for All," *Communication on a Commission Initiative for the Special European Council of Lisbon*, March 23 and 24, 2000: http://europa.eu.int/abc/off/index_en.htm

90. Ibid., 4.
91. In 1999, the United States had 25 internet hosts per 1,000 inhabitants, compared to 5 in the United Kingdom, 4 in Japan, 3 in Germany, and 3 in France. Giovannetti, "IT Revolution," 126-27.
92. Ibid., 136.
93. The publication of the "White Papers" in the 1990s marked the European Community's focus on new technology. These papers argued for market liberalization, placing technological convergence centrally in those arguments. In particular, the so-called 1994 Bangemann White Paper on "Europe and the Global Information Society" was considered especially formative in the drafting of the eEurope project. Bangemann's paper focuses on the importance of media policy integration "for both job growth and international trade." Commission of the European Communities, "Europe and the Global Information Society." For more on the "Harmonization Directives," see Harcourt, *The European Union*; and Watson and Wheatdon, *Telecommunications*.
94. "eEurope 2005 Resolution," 4.
95. E.U. household internet penetration increased from 18% in March 2000 to 28% in October to 36% in June 2001 and to 38% in December 2001. Average costs decreased "continuously and substantially" between 1999 and 2001. In May of 2001, 80% of E.U. schools were online. "eEurope: Benchmarking Report."
96. "1) Bringing every citizen, home and school, every business and administration, into the digital age and online. 2) Creating a digitally literate Europe, supported by an entrepreneurial culture ready to finance and develop new ideas. 3) Ensuring the whole process is socially inclusive, builds consumer trust and strengthens social cohesion." "eEurope: An Information Society for All," *Communication on a Commission Initiative for the Special European Council of Lisbon*, March 23 and 24, 2000: http://europa.eu.int/abc/off/index_en.htm; also cited in Giovannetti, "IT Revolution," 124–42.
97. This Bangemann Report was the origin of the term. Commission of the European Communities, "Europe and the Global Information Society."
98. "eEurope: An Information Society for All," *Communication on a Commission Initiative for the Special European Council of Lisbon*, March 23 and 24, 2000: http://europa.eu.int/abc/off/index_en.htm, 4.
99. Hardt and Negri, *Multitude*, 280.
100. Although I agree with Hardt and Negri that free–market capitalism is paradoxically impossible without regulation from the state and wish to acknowledge the influence of political and industry leaders enacted

through international meetings such those in Davos, I do not intend to reinforce the conspiratorial tone they express. Hardt and Negri, *Multitude*, 167.

101. Hardt and Negri argue that "imperial" power involves networked power that works through supranational organizations and other powers, while "imperialist" is an extension of state sovereignty over new territories. Hardt and Negri, *Empire*.
    For more on the debates about what "Americanization" is, how it works, and why it is or is not important, see Wagnleitner, *Coca-Colonization;* Poiger, *Jazz, Rock and Rebels;* Krige, *American Hegemony*.

102. Harcourt, *The European Union*, 9.

103. Ibid., 3.

104. Vaidhyanathan has written about the assumption that the nation was dead: "Just yesterday, it seems, influential thinkers were imagining a world in which the nation-state would wither, and many decisions that affect everyday life would be shifted up to multilateral institutions or down to individual market actors. Technologies were to play a leading part in that change, linking cosmopolitan citizens and transnational markets in a way that would enable crude governance, cultural creolization, and efficient commercial transactions. Human beings were on the verge of finding new and exciting ways of relating to one another. Arbitrary barriers of ethnicity and geography would wither. Through technology, we would master the dynamics of, and therefore control, our 'cultural evolution.'" Vaidhyanathan, *Anarchist*, 151. Vaidyanathan cites Wright, *Nonzero;* Friedman, *Lexus;* Micklethwait and Wooldridge, *A Future Perfect*.

105. Josef Joffe, "One Dollar, One Vote," *New York Times*, April 25, 1999, G14. (Josef Joffe is an editorial page editor and columnist for the *Süddeutsche Zeitung*.)

106. "Organisation and Management of the Internet," *International and European Policy Issues 1998–2000,* April 11, 2000: http://europa.eu/scadplus/leg/en/lvb/l24232.htm.

107. David J. Lynch, "Europeans Issue Wake-up Call to U.S. Dominance of Internet," *USA Today*, January 12, 2000, B3.

108. The information superhighway metaphor is also used in Europe—for example the internet is called the "Datenautobahn" (or the "data-highway") in Germany; however, German and British papers began using the term in reports about the U.S. policies in the 1990s. For example, see "Datenautobahn als Eckpfeiler der amerikanischen Technikpolitik" ("Information Superhighway as Cornerstone of American Technology

Policy"), *Frankfurter Allgemeine Zeitung*, January 25, 1994, 14; "Ein Hochgeschwindigkeitsnetz für Daten als Milliardengeschäft" ("A High Speed Data Network as a Multi-Billion-Dollar Business"), *Frankfurter Allgemeine Zeitung*, September 17, 1993, 16; "Time to Join the Super-highway," *Sunday Times*, October 17, 1993; Susana Antunes, "U.S. Phone Giants Line Up for Global 'Superhighway" Race: The Telecommunications Industry Is Going Through Major Changes," *Evening Standard*, October 15, 1993, 36; Bailey Morris, "In Washington: Crossed Wires on Telecoms," *The Independent*, August 15, 1993, 6; Lauren Chambliss, "Superhighway to a Revolution: American View," *Evening Standard*, April 22, 1993, 38; Mark Tran, "American Notebook: Clinton Aims to Act as Catalyst for Information Superhighway," *The Guardian*, April 13, 1993, 9.

109. Harcourt, *The European Union*, 19.

110. This massive internet-expansion proposal aimed to "stimulate the development of services, applications and contents" while "providing access for everyone in order to combat social exclusion, whether it is due to particular needs, a disability, age or illness." "Communication from the Commission of 11 April 2000."

111. "Der Goldrausch im Cyberspace," *Süddeutsche Zeitung*, November 11, 1995, 33. Another article noted "The gold-digger mentality on the internet could flare up anytime." "Internet—das Netz der Netze? Chaotische Strukturen und zunehmende kommerzielle Angebote. Immer schneller webt die Spinne ihr Netz um die Welt. Noch lassen sich auf der Daten-autobahn nur begrenzt Geschäfte machen / Probleme mit Datensicher-heit und Tempo" ("Internet—the Net of the Nets? Chaotic Structures and Increasing Commercial Offers. Faster and faster the Spider Weaves Its Net around the World. At this point, there are still only limited business opportunities on the Information Superhighway / Problems with Data Security and Speed"), *Süddeutsche Zeitung*, July 18, 1995, 28.

112. Lessig, *Code*; Grossman, *From Anarchy to Power*.

113. President Bill Clinton and Vice President Al Gore began speaking about the "digital divide" in a 1996 speech in Knoxville, Tennessee, in regard to computer abilities and ownership. The term quickly expanded to encompass internet and eventually broadband network access. Clinton, "Remarks by the President."

114. The National Telecommunications Infrastructure Administration (NTIA) at the Department of Commerce under the Clinton administration, conducted a series of surveys (1995), (1998), (1999), and (2000). "Falling through the Net."

115. A July 1999 report from the Department of Commerce, based on December 1998 Census Department data, revealed that "1) Better-educated Americans are more likely to be connected. In 1998, those with a college degree are more than eight times as likely to have a computer at home and nearly sixteen times as likely to have home Internet access as those with an elementary school education. 2) The gap between high- and low-income and urban and rural Americans is increasing. Urban households with incomes of $75,000 or higher are more than twenty times more likely to have access to the Internet than rural households at the lowest income levels, and more than nine times as likely to have a computer at home. 3) Whites are more likely to be connected than African-Americans or Hispanics." "Clinton-Gore Administration: A National Call to Action to Close the Digital Divide," *White House Press Release*, April 4, 2000: http://clinton4.nara.gov/WH/New/html/20000404.html

116. "Falling Through the Net: Defining the Digital Divide," National Telecommunications and Information Administration of the U.S. Commerce Department. July 8, 1999.

117. "Clinton-Gore Administration: A National Call to Action to Close the Digital Divide," *White House Press Release*, April 4, 2000: http://clinton4.nara.gov/WH/New/html/20000404.html.

118. By "Y2K," I mean the anticipated computer meltdowns as 1999 turned to 2000 because many computer programs were written using two-digit year codes (99 for 1999). For more on how the government imagined this scenario playing out, see Powell et al., *Communications Y2K*.

119. John Schwartz, "U.S. Cites Race Gap in Use of Internet; Clinton Bemoans 'Digital Divide,'" *Washington Post*, July 9, 1999, A1; Ariana Eunjung Cha, "Initiatives Outlined for 'Digital Divide,'" *Washington Post*, December 10, 1999, E3; Marc Lacey, "Clinton Enlists Top-Grade Help for Plan to Increase Computer Use," *New York Times*, February 3, 2000, A25; Martha Woodall, "Technology's Have-nots, From 2 Views: President Clinton Called for More Internet Access, While at Penn Came Talk of Places Where Phones are Foreign," *The Philadelphia Inquirer*, December 10, 1999, C1; Marc Lacey, "Clinton to Seek U.S. Subsidies to Help the Poor Get Online," *New York Times*, January 22, 2000, A9; Steve Lohr, "A Nation Ponders Its Growing Digital Divide," *New York Times*, October 21, 1996, D5; Tamara Henry, "Schools, Libraries in Line to Be in Line With Help of $2 Billion, All in USA Expected to be Linked to Net by 2000," *USA Today*, March 1, 1999, D1; Sylvia Moreno, "President Aims to Leap the 'Digital Divide'; In Visit to SE School, Clinton Vows to

Close the Gap Between the High-Tech Haves and Have-Nots," *Washington Post*, February 3, 2000, B4; Jeff Biggers, "Computers for All? Many Can't Use Them," *USA Today*, January 27, 2000, A15; Gary Andrew Poole, "A New Gulf in American Education, the Digital Divide," *New York Times*, January 29, 1996, D3.

120. "Clinton-Gore Administration: A National Call to Action to Close the Digital Divide," *White House Press Release*, April 4, 2000: http://clinton4.nara.gov/WH/New/html/20000404.html.

121. Gary Andrew Poole, "A New Gulf in American Education, the Digital Divide," *New York Times*, January 29, 1996, D3.

122. John Schwartz, "U.S. Cites Race Gap in Use of Internet; Clinton Bemoans 'Digital Divide,'" *Washington Post*, July 9, 1999, A1; Ariana Eunjung Cha, "Initiatives Outlined For 'Digital Divide,'" *Washington Post*, December 10, 1999, E3; Marc Lacey, "Clinton Enlists Top-Grade Help for Plan to Increase Computer Use," *New York Times*, February 3, 2000, A25; Tamara Henry, "Schools, Libraries In Line to Be In Line With Help of $2 Billion, All in USA Expected to be Linked to Net by 2000," *USA Today*, March 1, 1999, D1; Sylvia Moreno, "President Aims to Leap the 'Digital Divide;' In Visit to SE School, Clinton Vows to Close the Gap Between the High-Tech Haves and Have-Nots," *Washington Post*, February 3, 2000, B4; Gary Andrew Poole, "A New Gulf in American Education, the Digital Divide," *New York Times*, January 29, 1996, D3.

123. President Clinton traveled to East Palo Alto, California, the Navajo Nation in Shiprock, New Mexico, and Chicago, Illinois, to highlight private- and public-sector initiatives to help bring digital opportunity to all Americans. Later, he traveled to rural North Carolina to stress the importance of expanding rural broadband internet access. "Clinton-Gore Administration: A National Call to Action to Close the Digital Divide," *White House Press Release*, April 4, 2000: http://clinton4.nara.gov/WH/New/html/20000404.html.

124. Yahoo! dedicated $1 million to advertising this AmeriCorps program. "Clinton-Gore Administration: A National Call to Action to Close the Digital Divide," *White House Press Release*, April 4, 2000: http://clinton4.nara.gov/WH/New/html/20000404.html.

CHAPTER 5

1. The Morning Mix, "Revolution, Social Networks, and Charlie Sheen," *ABC News Transcript*, February 15, 2011; Gloria Borger, Candy Crowley, Fareed Zakaria, and Howard Kurtz. "The New World Order; What's Next for the Middle East?" *CNN*, March 27, 2011; Anderson Cooper, Jill

Dougherty, Fareed Zakaria, David Gergen, Isha Sesay, Nic Robertson, Sanjay Gupta, and Gary Tuchman, "Crackdown in Iran; Egypt's Uncertain Future," *CNN*, February 14, 2011; Piers Morgan, Nic Robertson, Arwa Damon, Ben Wedeman, and John King, "Mubarak Steps Down," *CNN*, February 11, 2011; Charles Osgood, Mo Rocca, and Steve Hartman, "For January 30, 2011," *CBS News Transcripts*, January 30, 2011; Jon Scott, Jim Pinkerton, Cal Thomas, and Judy Miller Kirsten Powers, "Fox News Watch for February 19, 2011," *Fox News Network*, February 19, 2011; Simon Mann, "Obama Pledges Support after Facebook Revolution," *Sunday Age*, February 13, 2011, 15; Jeffrey Ghannam, "Freedom, Beyond 140 Characters," *Washington Post*, February 20, 2011, B03; Ehab Lotayef, "McGill Grad Laid Groundwork for 'Facebook Revolution,'" *The Gazette*, February 23, 2011, A23, B14; Phila Siu, "Tweeting to Topple Regimes; Facebook and Twitter Proved Crucial in the Revolutions that Swept through Egypt and Tunisia," *South China Morning Post*, April 19, 2011, 6; Mohammed El-Naway, "Spread of Facebook Revolution," *Sunday Mirror*, February 20, 2011, 8; James Hider and Laura Pitel, "Google Boss Was Behind Facebook Revolution," *The Times*, February 8, 2011, 13; Sonia Verma, "How Egypt Got Here: A Brutal Beating and a Penchant for Facebook Has Protesters Eager to Brave the Streets," *The Globe and Mail*, January 27, 2011, A10; Jennifer Preston, "Movement Began with Outrage and a Facebook Page that Gave It an Outlet," *New York Times*, February 6, 2011, A10; Martin Fletcher, "Crowds Salute the Facebook Dreamer Who Led His Nation," *The Times of London*, February 9, 2011, 6.

2. Sandro Contenta, "Behind the Barricades: How Egypt Was Won," *The Toronto Star*, February 21, 2011, A6; Sonia Verma, "How Egypt Got Here: A Brutal Beating and a Penchant for Facebook Has Protesters Eager to Brave the Streets," *The Globe and Mail*, January 27, 2011, A10; Jennifer Preston, "Movement Began with Outrage and a Facebook Page that Gave It an Outlet," *New York Times*, February 6, 2011, A10; Martin Fletcher, "Crowds Salute the Facebook Dreamer Who Led His Nation," *The Times of London*, February 9, 2011, 6.

3. Sandro Contenta, "Behind the Barricades: How Egypt Was Won," *The Toronto Star*, February 21, 2011, A6.

4. Linda Herrera, "Egypt's Revolution 2.0: The Facebook Factor," *Jadaliyya*, February 12, 2011: http://www.jadaliyya.com/pages/index/612/egypts-revolution-2.0_the-facebook-factor (accessed July 29, 2012).

5. Mark Pfeifle, "A Nobel Peace Prize for Twitter?" *Christian Science Monitor*, July 6, 2009: http://www.csmonitor.com/Commentary/Opinion/2009/0706/p09s02-coop.html (accessed July 29, 2012).

6. E. Morozov, "Iran Elections: A Twitter Revolution?" *Washington Post*: http://www.washingtonpost.com/wp-dyn/content/discussion/2009/06/17/DI2009061702232.html.

7. Work on cybersecurity and cyberwar makes this point in especially clear (and frightening) terms. Clarke, *Cyberwar*.

8. Malcolm Gladwell, "Small Change: Why the Revolution Will Not Be Tweeted," *The New Yorker*, October 4, 2010: http://www.newyorker.com/reporting/2010/10/04/101004fa_fact_gladwell (accessed July 29, 2012).

9. Malcolm Gladwell, "Does Egypt Need Twitter?" *The New Yorker*, February 2, 2011: http://www.newyorker.com/online/blogs/newsdesk/2011/02/does-egypt-need-twitter.html (accessed July 29, 2012)

10. Kraidy and Mourad, "Hypermedia Space."

11. Drezner and Farrell, "Introduction"; Julia Keller, "She Has Seen the Future and It Is—Weblogs," *Chicago Tribune*, September 7, 1999, 1.

12. Andrew Brown, "It's a Blog's Life; Internet—Andrew Brown Succumbs to the Anarchic Appeal of the Web Log," *New Statesman*, October 11, 1999: http://www.newstatesman.com/node/135854 (accessed July 29, 2012).

13. John Leo, "Flogged by Bloggers," *U.S. News & World Report*, August 5, 2002, 41; Doug Bedell, "Weblogs Are Alternative Voices, Offering Entry into Online World," *San Diego Union-Tribune*, May 16, 2000, 8; "A Blog about Writing about Blogs," *Newsweek,* August 26, 2002, 44; Craig Colgan, "Creatures from the Web Lagoon: The Blogs," *The National Journal*, August 3, 2002, 2323; John Leo "A Blog's Bark Has Bite," *U.S. News & World Report*, May 13, 2002, 48; David Gallagher, "Invasion of the 'Blog': A Parallel Web of Personal Journals," *New York Times*, December 28, 2000, G11; Michael Saunders and Jim Sullivan, "Fame Sometimes Blogs Her Down," *The Boston Globe,* November 11, 2000.

14. Thank you to Laura Kenna. Sconce writes about electronic media as being imagined as unmediated. Sconce, *Haunted Media*, 4–5.

15. Ibid., 8.

16. Frances Katz, "NetWatcher: Pithy Commentary Found in Web Logs," *The Atlanta Journal and Constitution*, October 3, 1999, P2.

17. Paul Boutin, "Robot Wisdom on the Street," *Wired,* July 13, 2005.

18. Jorn Barger, "Top 10 Tips for New Bloggers From Original Blogger," *Wired,* December 15, 2007.

19. Levy, *Hackers*; Manes and Andrews, *Gates*.

20. Drezner and Farrell, "Introduction."

21. Burstein, "Cave Painting," xvi.

22. Holly J. Morris, "Blogging Burgeons as a Form of Web Expression," *U.S. News & World Report*, January 15, 2001, 52; Drezner and Farrell, "Introduction."
23. Total identified blogs came to 161,691,735. Blogpulse Statistics, May 12, 2011: http://www.blogpulse.com/.
24. "Weblogs, Weblogs Everywhere; We Tell You Where to Find Them," *Milwaukee Journal Sentinel*, July 16, 2000, 5E.
25. "'Blog' Tops U.S. Dictionary's Words of the Year," *Reuters*, November 30, 2004, cited in Burstein, "Cave Painting," xvi.
26. Morris, "Blogging Burgeons as a Form of Web Expression," *U.S. News & World Report*, January 15, 2001, 52.
27. Julia Keller, "She Has Seen the Future and It Is—Weblogs," *Chicago Tribune*, September 7, 1999, 1.
28. Doug Bedell, "Weblogs are Alternative Voices, Offering Entry into Online World," *San Diego Union-Tribune*, May 16, 2000, 8.
29. Ibid.
30. Julia Keller, "She Has Seen the Future and It Is—Weblogs," *Chicago Tribune*, September 7, 1999, 1..
31. Ibid.
32. Grossberg et al., *MediaMaking*, 389–90.
33. Lovink, *Zero Comments*.
34. Burstein, "Cave Painting," xv.
35. Ibid..
36. Ibid., xiv.
37. Steven Levy, "Will the Blogs Kill Old Media?" *Newsweek*, May 20, 2002, 52; Marvin, *Old Technologies*.
38. Steven Levy, "Will the Blogs Kill Old Media?" *Newsweek*, May 20, 2002, 52.
39. Ibid.
40. John Leo, "Flogged by Bloggers," *U.S. News & World Report*, August 5, 2002, 41.
41. Ibid.
42. Ibid.
43. "Full Disclosure," transcript, *The NewsHour with Jim Lehrer*, September 14, 1998: http://www.pbs.org/newshour/bb/media/july-dec98/media_9-14a.html (accessed April 30, 2009).
44. Thomas B. Edsall, "Lott Decried for Part of Salute to Thurmond: GOP Senate Leader Hails Colleague's Run as Segregationist," *Washington Post*, December 7, 2002, A6.

45. John King, Mark Preston, Dana Bash, and Jessica Yellin, "Senate's No. 2 Republican to Resign by End of Year," *CNN.com*, November 26, 2007: http://www.cnn.com/2007/POLITICS/11/26/lott.resign/ (accessed April 20, 2009).

46. Michael Barone, "Showing Where They Stand," *U.S. News & World Report*, December 30, 2002, 25.

47. Ibid.

48. John Podhoretz, "The Internet's First Scalp," *New York Post*, December 13, 2002: http://www.nypost.com/p/news/opinion/opedcolumnists/item_UUez8Uof36H9jyY3xTfRLO (accessed July 29, 2012).

49. Julia Keller, "She has Seen the Future and It Is—Weblogs," *Chicago Tribune*, September 7, 1999, 1.

50. Steven Levy, Ana Figueroa, Arian Campo-Flores, Jennifer Lin, and Marcia Hill Gossard, "Living in the Blog-o-sphere," *Newsweek*, August 26, 2002, 42.

51. Ibid.

52. Paul Boutin, "Kill Your Blog: Still Posting Like It's 2004? Well, Knock It Off. There are Chirpier Ways to Get Your Word Out." *Wired*, November 1, 2008, 27.

53. Kathleen Hall Jamieson and Joseph N. Cappella, *Echo Chamber: Rush Limbaugh and the Conservative Media Establishment* (New York: Oxford University Press, 2009), 4.

54. Drezner and Farrell, "Introduction"; Sunstein, *Republic.com*; Putnam, *Bowling Alone*. Also see Jamieson and Cappella, *Echo Chamber*.

55. Jose Antonia Vargas, "Obama's Wide Web: From Youtube to Text Messaging, Candidate's Team Connects to Voters." *Washington Post*, August 20, 2008, C1.

56. Jamieson and Cappella, *Echo Chamber*.

57. Sifry, *WikiLeaks*, 62.

58. Pew, *Portrait of Generation Next*.

59. "Flickering Here, Twittering There: Technology and the Campaigns." *The Economist*, August 16, 2009; Jose Antonia Vargas, "Obama's Wide Web: From Youtube to Text Messaging, Candidate's Team Connects to Voters." *Washington Post*, August 20, 2008, C1.

60. Cecilia Kang, "Twitter CEO Named to Presidential Advisory Panel," *PostTech Washington Post*, May 26, 2011: http://www.washingtonpost.com/blogs/post-tech/post/twitter-ceo-named-to-presidential-advisory-panel/2011/05/26/AGhB5OCH_blog.html#pagebreak (accessed May 25, 2011).

61. Andy Borowitz, "How Technology Played a Role in the Presidential Campaigns," transcript, *NBC News*, November 5, 2008; Andy Borowitz, "McCain Makes Historic First Visit to Web," *St. PetersburgTimes*, July 27, 2008, 5P; Mark Leibovich, "Hail to the Twitterer," *New York Times*, August 3, 2008, A1; "How the Obama Campaign has Harnessed the Power of the Internet," transcript, *NBC News with Luke Russert*, August 27, 2008; "The Kids Are Alright; The Net Generation," *The Economist*, November 15, 2008.

62. Andy Borowitz, "McCain Makes Historic First Visit to Web," *St. PetersburgTimes*, July 27, 2008, 5P.

63. Sifry, *WikiLeaks*, 44, 46.

64. Bruns, *Blogs*; Jenkins, *Convergence Culture*; and Shirky, *Cognitive Surplus*.

65. Sifry, *WikiLeaks*, 56.

66. Ibid. 50.

67. Jay Rosen, "The People Formerly Known as the Audience," *PressThink*, June 27, 2006: http://archive.pressthink.org/2006/06/27/ppl_frmr.html.

68. Smith, "Government Online."

69. E-Government Act, U.S. Public Law 107-347, 107th Cong., December 17, 2002; Dot Kids Implementation and Efficiency Act, U.S. Public Law 107-317, 107th Cong., December 4, 2002; Internet False Identification Prevention Act, U.S. Public Law 106-578, 106th Cong., December 28, 2000. U.S. Congress, House, Committee on Government Reform, *Turning the Tortoise into the Hare: How the Federal Government Can Transition from Old Economy Speed to Become a Model for Electronic Government*, May 2003, H. 401; U.S. Congress, House, Committee on Energy and Commerce, *Establishing Kid-friendly Top-level Domain: Dot Kids Name Act of 2001*, February 2002, H. 361; U.S. Congress, Senate, Committee on Commerce, Science, and Transportation, *Holes in the Net: Security Risks and the E-Consumer*, July 2004, S. 107-674; U.S. Congress, House, Committee on the Judiciary, *WHOIS Database: Privacy and Intellectual Property Issues*, September 2001, H. 521.

70. For documentation and analysis of interest in the digital divide in the United States, see Katz and Asbden, "Motivations for and Barriers," 170; "Caught in the Net: What to Make of User Estimates." *Public Perspective* 6 (July 1996): 37–40; Anderson and Bickson, *Feasibility and Societal Implications*; and Edmondson, "The Point-and-Click Government."

71. U.S. Congress, House, Congressional-Executive Commission on China, *China's Cyber-Wall: Can Technology Break Through?* February 2003, H. 891; U.S. Congress, House, Congressional-Executive Commission on China, *Wired China: Who's Hand Is on the Switch?* August 2002, H.

891; U.S. Congress, Senate, Committee on Foreign Relations, *America's Global Dialog: Sharing American Values and the Way Ahead for Public Diplomacy,* January 2003, S. 381.

72. U.S. Congress, House, Committee on Energy and Commerce, *Cyber Security: Private-Sector Efforts Addressing Cyber Threats,* February 2002, H. 361; U.S. Congress, House, Committee on the Judiciary, *Immigration and Naturalization Service's (INS's) Implementation of the Foreign Student Tracking Program,* January 2003, H. 521.

73. Federal Funding Accountability and Transparency Act, U.S. Public Law 109-282, 109th Cong., September 26, 2006.

74. Sifry, *WikiLeaks,* 74, 78.

75. Weinberger, "Transparency."

76. Thanks to Julie Elman. Berlant, *Female Complaint,* x.

77. Ibid., vii.

78. Ibid., x–xi.

79. Ibid.

80. Carr, *Shallows*; Lanier, *You Are Not a Gadget*; Johnson, *Everything.*

81. Calum MacLeod, "China Vaults Past USA in Number of Internet Users." *USA Today,* April 21, 2008, A1.

82. Ibid.

83. "U.S. Web Giants Cower at Great Firewall of China." *USA Today,* March 8, 2006, A10.

84. Goldsmith and Wu, *Who Controls the Internet?* 93.

85. Wu, *Master Switch,* 279.

86. Vaidhyanathan, *Googlization of Everything,* xi.

87. Brian Whitaker, "Computing and the Net: Stake Me to Your Breeder; Brian Whitaker Tests the Toils of Surfing in Arabic," *The Guardian,* April 23, 1998, 6.

88. Even though the internet could "produce documents in Hindi or Japanese, computers and networks themselves speak and operate in only a fragmentary, math- and logic-oriented chink of English." Golumbia, *Cultural Logic,* 120.

89. Ibid., 123.

90. Matt Warman, "Internet Finally Changes the Script," *The Daily Telegraph,* May 7, 2010, 11.

91. Ian Black and Jemima Kiss, "Worldwide Web Goes Truly Global with Arabic URLs," *The Guardian,* May 7, 2010, 28.

92. Rashid Khalidi, "The Arab Spring," *The Nation,* March 3, 2011: http://www.thenation.com/print/article/158991/arab-spring (accessed May 28, 2011).

93. McAlister, *Epic Encounters*. In particular, in the moment before military leadership stepped in, news reports tapped a "Clash of the Civilizations" anxiety, which suggested that a people with differing values, religions, cultures were gaining power. Huntington, "The Clash of Civilizations?"

94. Thanks to Julie Elman.

95. Ryan Lizza, "The Consequentialist: How the Arab Spring Remade Obama's Foreign Policy," *The New Yorker*, May 2, 2011: http://www.newyorker.com/reporting/2011/05/02/110502fa_fact_lizza#ixzz1O506P98L (accessed May 31, 2011).

96. Ken Dilanian and W. J. Hennigan, "Plan to Thwart Cyber Attack Urged," *Los Angeles Times*, May 13, 2011, B1; Dave Boyer, "Obama Unveils Cyber Security Plan," *Washington Times*, May 13, 2011, A4; Jon Swartz, "Should the Internet have an 'Off' Switch? Bill Gives President Power to Shut It Down during Cyber Attack," *USA Today*, February 16, 2011, 1B.

97. Shirky, *Cognitive Surplus*.

98. Douglas, "The Turn Within," 625–26.

99. McAlister, "Facebook Revolution?"

100. Morozov, "Freedom.gov." Also see Morozov, *The Net Delusion*.

101. James Hider and Laura Pitel, "Google Boss Was Behind Facebook Revolution," *The Times*, February 8, 2011, 13.

102. Wu, *Master Switch*, 273.

103. Kraidy and Mourad, "Hypermedia."

104. Khanfar, "A Historic Moment."

105. Sifry, *WikiLeaks*, 63.

106. Fresh Air, "A Look At The Youth Of Egypt's Muslim Brotherhood," *National Public Radio*, February 17, 2011; Don Imus, Connell McShane, Charles McCord, Dagen McDowell, Ashley Webster, Rob Bartlett, Tony Powell, Maria Molina, Bernard McGuirk, Lou Rufino, Warner Wolf, "Update on Egypt," *Imus Simulcast*, February 7, 2011; Greta Van Susteren, John Bolton, Rick Santorum, "Situations Remain Uncertain," *Fox News Network*, March 30, 2011.

107. Jeffrey Fleishman, "Islamists' Message on Hold: The Muslim Brotherhood Joins the Revolt but Keeps Its Agenda Out—For Now," *Los Angeles Times*, January 31, 2011, A1.

108. Samantha Shapiro, "Revolution, Facebook Style," *New York Times*, January 25, 2009, MM34.

109. McAlister, *Epic Encounters*, 47.

110. Jon Stewart, "Gigi Ibrahim," *Daily Show*, April 25, 2011: http://www.thedailyshow.com/watch/mon-april-25-2011/gigi-ibrahim (accessed May 2, 2011).

CONCLUSION

1. Sconce, *Haunted Media*, 200.

2. WikiLeaks: http://www.WikiLeaks.ch/.

3. "Afghanistan War Logs: The Unvarnished Picture," *Guardian*, July 25, 2010: http://www.guardian.co.uk/commentisfree/2010/jul/25/afghani-stan-war-logs-guardian-editorial?intcmp=239 (accessed May 25, 2011); "U.S. Embassy Cables," *Guardian*: http://www.guardian.co.uk/world/the-us-embassy-cables?INTCMP=SRCH (accessed May 25, 2011).

4. Vice President Joe Biden called Julian Assange closer to a "hi-tech terrorist" than a "whistleblower," and Secretary of State Hillary Clinton said WikiLeaks' releases were an "an attack" on the world. Ewen MacAskill, "Julian Assange Like a Hi-Tech Terrorist, Says Joe Biden." *Guardian*, December 19, 2010: http://www.guardian.co.uk/media/2010/dec/19/assange-high-tech-terrorist-biden (accessed May 9, 2011).

5. Sifry, *WikiLeaks*; Brad Knickerbocker, "WikiLeaks and Julian Assange: Stateless, Penniless Pariahs?" *The Christian Science Monitor*, December 4, 2010: http://www.csmonitor.com/USA/2010/1204/WikiLeaks-and-Julian-Assange-Stateless-penniless-pariahs (accessed July 29, 2012); James Silver and Alexi Mostrous, "Stop Dragging WikiLeaks Down and Hand Yourself In, Assange Is Told by One of His Main Allies," *The Times*, December 23, 2010, 17; Patrick Lannin, "WikiLeaks Boss Fights Warrant; Denies Swedish Rape Allegations," *The Toronto Sun*, December 2, 2010, 34; Martin Beckford, "Hunt Down the WikiLeaks Chief Like Al-Qaeda, Demands Palin," *The Daily Telegraph*, December 1, 2010, 2; Robert Booth, "The US Embassy Cables Assange and WikiLeaks: Future of WikiLeaks," *The Guardian*, December 8, 2010, 4.

6. Sifry, *WikiLeaks*, 187; Domscheit-Berg, *Inside WikiLeaks*, 211; Brad Knickerbocker, "WikiLeaks and Julian Assange: Stateless, Penniless Pariahs?" *The Christian Science Monitor*, December 4, 2010: http://www.csmonitor.com/USA/2010/1204/WikiLeaks-and-Julian-Assange-State-less-penniless-pariahs (accessed July 29, 2012).

7. Goldsmith and Wu, *Who Controls the Internet?*; Jayson Harsin, "WikiLeaks' Lessons for Media Theory and Politics," *Flow* 13, January 15, 2011: http://flowtv.org/2011/01/WikiLeaks-lessons-for-media-theory/ (accessed May 28, 2011).

8. Sifry, *WikiLeaks*, 39: citing http://WikiLeaks.ch/cable/2008/06/08TUNIS679.html.

9. Katla McGlynn "'SNL': Julian Assange Responds to Mark Zuckerberg Being Named 'Person of the Year,'" *Huffington Post*, December 19,

2010: http://www.huffingtonpost.com/2010/12/19/snl-julian-assange-zuckerberg_n_798836.html (accessed May 28, 2011).

10. Several books were published as I finished my manuscript: Streeter, *The Net Effect*; Wu, *Master Switch*; Gitelman, *Always Already New*; Goldsmith and Wu, *Who Controls the Internet?*; Poster, *Information Please*; and Friedman, *Electric Dreams*.

½ *Miete*. Dir. Marc Ottiker. 2002, Filmstiftung Nordrhein-Westfalen.

1996 Internet World's Fair. http://park.org.

2001: A Space Odyssey. Dir. Stanley Kubrick. 1969; Los Angeles: Metro-Goldwyn-Mayer.

Adams, Paul. "Cyberspace and Virtual Places." *Geographical Review* 87 (April 1997): 155–171.

Adas, Michael. *Machines as the Measure of Men: Science, Technology, and Ideologies of Western Dominance*. Ithaca: Cornell University Press, 1989.

Anderson, Benedict. *Imagined Communities: Reflections on the Origin and Spread of Nationalism*. New York: Verso, 1983.

Anderson, Janna. *Imagining the Internet: Personalities, Predictions, Perspectives*. New York: Rowman & Littlefield, 2005.

Anderson, R., and T. Bickson. *Feasibility and Societal Implications*. Santa Monica, CA: Rand Corporation, 1995.

Appadurai, Arjun. "Disjuncture and Difference in the Global Cultural Economy." In *Modernity at Large*. Minneapolis: University of Minnesota Press, 1996.

Armour, Polly. "Surfing the Internet," Wilson Library Bulletin 66 (June 1992): 38-42.

Bagdikian, Benjamin. *The Media Monopoly*. Boston, Beacon, 2000.

Baldwin, R., C. Scott, and C. Hood. *A Reader on Regulation*. Oxford: Oxford University Press, 1998.

Barlow, John Perry. "Being in Nothingness: Virtual Reality and the Pioneers of Cyberspace." Originally posted 1990, *Electronic Frontier Foundation Archives*. http://w2.eff.org/Misc/Publications/John_Perry_Barlow/HTML/being_in_nothingness.html

———. "Crime and Puzzlement." *WELL*, June 8, 1990. Reprinted in *Whole Earth Review* 68 (Fall 1990): 44–57.

Barnett, Chad. "Reviving Cyberpunk: (Re)constructing the Subject and Mapping Cyberspace in the Wachowski Brother's Film *The Matrix*." *Extrapolation* 41 (Winter 2000): 359–375.

Barry, Dave. *Dave Barry in Cyberspace*. New York: Ballantine Books, 1997.

Barthes, Roland. *Mythologies*. Trans. Annette Lavers. New York: Noonday Press, 1972.

Battlestar Galactica. Dir. Glen Larson. 1978; Los Angeles: Glen A. Larson Productions.

Baumgartner, Frank, and Brian Jones. *Agendas and Instability in American Politics*. Chicago: University of Chicago Press, 1993.

Berlant, Lauren. *The Female Complaint: The Unfinished Business of Sentimentality in American Culture*. Durham: Duke University Press, 2008.

———. *The Queen of America Goes to Washington City: Essays on Sex and Citizenship*. Durham: Duke University Press, 1997.

Bermann, George, Roger Goebel, William Davey, and Eleanor Fox. *Cases and Materials on European Community Law*. St. Paul, MN: West, 1995.

Bhabha, Homi. *Nation and Narration*. London: Routledge, 1990.

Blade Runner. Dir. Ridley Scott. 1982; Los Angeles: Blade Runner Partnership.

Blumler, J. *Television and the Public Interest: Vulnerable Values in European Broadcasting*. London: Sage, 1992.

Bourdieu, Pierre. *Field of Cultural Production: Essays on Art and Literature*. Randal Johnson, ed. New York: Columbia University Press, 1993.

———. *Outline of a Theory of Practice*. Richard Nice, trans. Cambridge: Cambridge University Press, 1977.

Broderick, Damien. *Reading by Starlight: Postmodern Science Fiction*. London: Routledge, 1995.

Bruns, Axel. *Blogs, Wikipedia, Second Life, and Beyond: From Production to Produsage*. New York: Peter Lang, 2008.

Buck Rogers in the 25th Century. Dirs. Bob Bender and Harvey Laidman. 1979; Los Angeles: John Mantley Productions.

Burns, Rob. "Introduction." In *German Cultural Studies: An Introduction*. Rob Burns, ed. Oxford: Oxford University Press, 1995, 1–8.

Burstein, Dan. *In blog! How the Newest Media Revolution Is Changing Politics, Business, and Culture*. New York: CDS Books, 2005.

Bush, George H. W. "Address to the Nation on the Invasion of Iraq," January 16, 1991. http://www.millercenter.virginia.edu/scripps/digitalarchive/speeches/spe_1991_0116_bush.

Campbell, John, and Matt Carlson. "Panopticon.com: Online Surveillance and the Commodification of Privacy." *Journal of Broadcasting and Electronic Media* 46 (Winter 2002): 586–606.

Cappella, Joseph N. and Kathleen Hall Jamieson. *Spiral of Cynicism: The Press and the Public Good*. Oxford: Oxford University Press, 1997.

Carr, Nicholas. *The Shallows: What the Internet Is Doing to Our Brains.* New York: W. W. Norton, 2010.

Cassidy, John. *Dot.con: The Greatest Story Ever Sold.* New York: HarperCollins, 2002.

Castells, Manuel. "Communication, Power and Counterpower in the Network Society." *International Journal of Communication* 1 (2007): 238–266.

———. *The Internet Galaxy: Reflections on the Internet, Business, and Society.* New York: Oxford University Press, 2001.

———. *The Rise of the Network Society.* New York: Blackwell, 2000.

"Caught in the Net: What to Make of User Estimates." *Public Perspective* 6 (July 1996): 37–40.

Chauncey, George. "The Post-War Sex Crime Panic." In *True Stories from the American Past.* William Graebner, ed. New York: McGraw-Hill, 1993.

Chevan, Albert, and Randall Stokes. "Growth in Family Income Inequality, 1970–1990: Industrial Restructuring and Demographic Change." *Demography* 37 (August 2000): 365–380.

Clarke, Richard. *Cyberwar: The Next Threat to National Security and What to Do about It.* New York: HarperCollins, 2010.

"Clinton-Gore Administration: A National Call to Action to Close the Digital Divide." *White House Press Release,* April 4, 2000. http://clinton4.nara.gov/WH/New/html/20000404.html.

Clinton, William. "Remarks by the President and the Vice President to the People of Knoxville." Speech, Knoxville Auditorium Coliseum, Knoxville, TN, October 10, 1996.

Cohen, Jeffrey Jerome. "Masoch / Lancelotism." *New Literary History* 28 (1997): 231–260.

Cohen, Stanley. *Folk Devils and Moral Panics: The Creation of Mods and Rockers.* New York: Routledge, 2002.

Commission of the European Communities. "Europe and the Global Information Society: Recommendations to the European Council." *Report by the High Level Group on the Information Society.* Brussels, May 1994.

"Communication from the Commission of 11 April 2000 to the Council and the European Parliament." In *The Organisation and Management of the Internet: International and European Policy Issues 1998–2000,* April 11, 2000. http://europa.eu/scadplus/leg/en/lvb/l24232.htm.

Computer Crime Prevention Act of 1984, S. 2270.

Computer Fraud and Abuse Act of 1984, S. 2864.

Counterfeit Access Device and Computer Fraud and Abuse Act of 1984. H.R. 5112.

Crichton, Michael. *Rising Sun.* New York: Ballantine Books, 1995.

Critcher, Chas. *Critical Readings: Moral Panics and the Media*. New York: Open University Press, 2006.

Cross, Robert L., Andrew Parker, and Lisa Sasson. *Networks in the Knowledge Economy*. Oxford : Oxford University Press, 2003.

Davis, Erik. *Techgnosis: Myth, Magic plus Mysticism in the Age of Information*. New York: Three Rivers Press, 1998.

"De Digitale Stad." http://www.dds.nl/.

De la Peña, Carolyn. *Body Electric: How Strange Machines Built the Modern America*. New York: New York University Press, 2003.

De Sola Pool, Ithiel. *Technologies without Boundaries: On Telecommunications in a Global Age*. Cambridge: Harvard University Press, 1990.

Deleuze, Gilles, and Félix Guattari. *A Thousand Plateaus: Capitalism and Schizophrenia*. Minneapolis: University of Minnesota Press, 1987.

"Deutsche Bundesregierung." http://www.bundesregierung.de.

Domscheit-Berg, Daniel. *Inside WikiLeaks: My Time with Julian Assange at the World's Most Dangerous Website*. New York: Crown, 2011.

Douglas, Susan. "The Turn Within: The Irony of Technology in a Globalized World." *American Quarterly* 58 (2006): 619–640.

Downs, Anthony. *Political Theory and Public Choice*. Northhampton, MA: Elgar, 1998.

Drezner, Daniel W. and Henry Farrell. "Introduction: Blogs, Politics and Power." *Public Choice* 134 (2008): 1–13.

Ebo, Bosah, ed. *Cyberimperialism? Global Relations in the New Electronic Frontier*. Westport, CT: Praeger, 2000.

Edelman, Murry. *Constructing the Political Spectacle*. Chicago: University of Chicago Press, 1988.

Edmondson, B. "The Point-and-Click Government." *Marketing Tools* (July/August 1996).

Edwards, Paul. *The Closed World: Computers and the Politics of Discourse in Cold War America*. Cambridge: MIT Press, 1996.

Egan, Michelle. *Constructing a European Market: Standards, Regulation, and Governance*. Oxford: Oxford University Press, 2001.

Entman, Robert. "Framing: Toward Clarification of a Fractured Paradigm." *Journal of Communication* 43 (1993): 51–59.

"eEurope: An Information Society for All." *Communication on a Commission Initiative for the Special European Council of Lisbon*, March 23 and 24, 2000, http://europa.eu.int/abc/off/index_en.htm.

"eEurope: Benchmarking Report." *Communication from the Commission to the Council, the European Parliament, the Economic and Social Committee, and the Committee of the Regions*, Brussels, May 2, 2002.

"eEurope 2005 Resolution." Council of the European Union, 5197/03, January 28, 2003.

E.U. Public Law, Council Directive 89/552/EEC. European Commission, October 3, 1989. *Television without Frontiers Directive.* "Summaries of Legislation." http://europa.eu/scadplus/leg/en/lvb/l24101.htm.

"Excerpt from Bill Clinton's Letter of Support." 1996 Internet World Exposition, March 28, 1995. http://parallel.park.org/Guests/WWWvoice/.

"Excerpt from Boris Yeltsin's Letter of Support." 1996 Internet World Exposition, November 1, 1995. http://parallel.park.org/Guests/WWWvoice/.

"Falling Through the Net: Defining the Digital Divide." National Telecommunications and Information Administration of the U.S. Commerce Department. July 8, 1999.

Federal Computer Systems Protection Act of 1983, S. 1733.

Federal Criminal Code Amendment, H.R. 4301.

Fishman, Robert. *Bourgeois Utopias: The Rise and Fall of Suburbia.* New York: Basic Books, 1987.

Friedman, Ted. *Electric Dream: Computers in American Culture.* New York: New York University Press, 2005.

Friedman, Thomas. *The Lexus and the Olive Tree.* New York: Anchor, 2000.

Gaddis, John. *Surprise, Security, and the American Experience.* Cambridge: Harvard University Press, 2004.

Gauntlett, David. "Introduction to the New Edition." In *Web.Studies: Rewiring Media Studies for the Digital Age.* David Gauntlett and Ross Horsley, eds. Oxford: Oxford University Press, 2004.

Gibson, William. *Neuromancer.* New York: Ace Books, 1984.

Giovannetti, Emanuele. "The IT Revolution, the Internet, and Telecommunications: The Transition Towards a Competitive Industry in the European Union." In *Internet Revolution: A Global Perspective.* Mitsuhior Kagami and Masatsugu Tsuji, eds. Cambridge: Cambridge University Press, 2003.

Gitelman, Lisa. *Always Already New: Media, History, and the Data of Culture.* Cambridge: MIT Press, 2006.

Gitlin, Todd. *The Whole World Is Watching: Mass Media in the Making and Unmaking of the New Left.* Berkeley: University of California Press, 1980.

Gladwell, Malcolm. "Does Egypt Need Twitter?" *The New Yorker,* February 2, 2011.

———. "Small Change: Why the Revolution Will Not Be Tweeted." *The New Yorker,* October 4, 2010.

Golden Eye. Dir. Martin Campbell.1995; Los Angeles: Danjag.

Golding, P., and P. Harris. *Beyond Cultural Imperialism: Globalization, Communication and the New International Order.* London: Sage, 1977.

Golding, Peter. "Worldwide Wedge: Division and Contradiction in the Global Information Infrastructure." In *Media Studies: A Reader*. Paul Marris and Sue Thornham, eds. New York: New York University Press, 1999.

Goldsmith, Jack, and Tim Wu. *Who Controls the Internet? Illusions of a Borderless World*. New York: Oxford University Press, 2006.

Golumbia, David. *The Cultural Logic of Computation*. Cambridge: Harvard University Press, 2009.

Gore, Al. "A Framework for Global Electronic Commerce." White House, July 1, 1997. http://www.technology.gov/digeconomy/framewrk.htm.

Graber, Doris. *Mass Media and American Politics*. Washington, DC: Congressional Quarterly, 1989.

Grossberg, Lawrence, Ellen Wartella, Charles Whitney, and MacGregor Wise. *MediaMaking: Mass Media in a Popular Culture*. London: Sage Publications, 2006.

Grossman, Wendy. *From Anarchy to Power: The Net Comes of Age*. New York: New York University Press, 2001.

H.R.1757. 103rd Cong. September 14, 1993. *High Performance Computing and High Speed Networking Applications Act of 1993*.

Habermas, Jürgen. *The Structural Transformation of the Public Sphere: An Inquiry into a Category of Bourgeois Society*. Cambridge: MIT Press, 1991.

Hackers. Dir. Iain Softley.1995, United Artists.

Hall, Stuart, Chas Critcher, Tony Jefferson, John Clarke, and Bryan Roberts. "The Changing Shape of 'Panics.'" In *Critical Readings: Moral Panics and the Media*. Chas Critcher, ed. Maidenhead: Open University Press, 2006.

Haraway, Donna. "A Cyborg Manifesto: Science, Technology, and Socialist-Feminism in the Late Twentieth Century." In *Simians, Cyborgs and Women: The Reinvention of Nature*. New York; Routledge, 1991.

Harcourt, Alison. *The European Union and the Regulation of Media Markets*. Manchester: Manchester University Press, 2005.

Hardt, Michael, and Antonio Negri. *Empire*. Cambridge: Harvard University Press, 2000.

———. *Multitude: War and Democracy in the Age of Empire*. New York: Penguin, 2004.

Harsin, Jayson. "WikiLeaks' Lessons for Media Theory and Politics." *Flow* 13, January 15, 2011. http://flowtv.org/2011/01/wikileaks-lessons-for-media-theory.

Harvey, David. *The Condition of Postmodernity: An Inquiry in the Origins of Cultural Change*. Cambridge, MA: Blackwell, 1990.

Harvey, Kerric. "Privacy and Cultural Geography in the Emerging Online World." *Telecommunications and Space Journal* 6 (1999): 233–251.

Harvey, Lisa St. Clair. "Communication Issues and Policy Implications." In *Communication in the Age of Virtual Reality*. Frank Biocca and Mark R. Levy, eds. Hillsdale, NJ: Lawrence Erlbaum Associates, 1995.

Hayles, Katherine. *How We Became Posthuman: Virtual Bodies in Cybernetics, Literature, and Informatics*. Chicago: University of Chicago Press, 1999.

Hebdidge, Dick. *Subculture: The Meaning of Style*. London: Methuen, 1979.

Heiddigger, Martin. *Being and Time*. New York: Harper & Row, 1962.

Herman, E. S., and R. W. McChesney. *The Global Media: The New Missionaries of Corporate Capitalism*. London: Cassel, 1997.

Hetata, S. "Dollarization, Fragmentation, and God." In *The Cultures of Globalization*. Frederic Jameson and Masao Miyoshi, eds. Durham: Duke University Press, 1998.

Hofstadter, Douglas R., and Daniel C, Dennett, eds., *The Mind's I: Fantasies and Reflections on the Self and Soul*. New York: Basic Books, 1981.

House Subcommittee on International Finance, Trade, and Monetary Policy, Committee on Banking, Finance, and Urban Affairs, *Hearings on H. 241, U.S.-Japan Economic Relations*, June 9, 1987.

House Subcommittee on Transportation, Aviation, and Materials, Committee on Science and Technology, *Hearing on H. 701, Computer and Communications Security and Privacy* 98th Cong., September 26, October 17, 24, 1983.

H.R.3636. 104th Cong. June 28, 1994. *National Communications Competition and Information Infrastructure Act of 1994*.

Huntington, Samuel. "The Clash of Civilizations?" *Foreign Affairs* 72, no. 3 (1993): 22.

Ichbiah, Daniel, and Susan L. Knepper. *The Making of Microsoft: How Bill Gates and His Team Created the World's Most Successful Software Company*. Rocklin, CA: Prima, 1991.

Iyengar, Shanto. *Is Anyone Responsible? How Television Frames Political Issues*. Chicago: University of Chicago Press, 1991.

Jameson, Frederic. *Postmodernism, or, The Cultural Logic of Late Capitalism*. New York: Verso, 1991.

———. and Masao Miyoshi. *The Cultures of Globalization*. Durham: Duke University Press, 1998.

Jamieson, Kathleen Hall, and Joseph N. Cappella. *Echo Chamber: Rush Limbaugh and the Conservative Media*. New York: Oxford University Press, 2009.

Jenkins, Henry. *Convergence Culture: Where Old and New Media Collide*. New York: New York University Press, 2006.

Johnny Mnemonic. Dir. Robert Longo. 1995, Alliance Communications Corporation.

Johnson, David, and David Post. "The Rise of Law on the Global Network." In *Borders in Cyberspace: Information Policy and Global Information Infrastructure.* Brian Kahin and Charles Nesson, eds. Cambridge: MIT Press, 1997.

Johnson, Stephen. *Everything Bad Is Good for You: How Today's Popular Culture Is Actually Making Us Smarter.* New York: Riverhead Hardcover, 2005.

Jones, Steve. "internet@academia.com: Internet Studies and Academic Work." *Popular Communication* 1, no. 1 (2003): 33–40.

Kaplan, Amy, and Donald Pease. *Cultures of United States Imperialism.* Durham: Duke University Press, 1993.

Katz, James, and Philip Asbden. "Motivations for and Barriers to Internet Usage: Results of a National Public Opinion Survey." *Internet Research* 7 (Fall 1997): 170–188.

Kavoori, A. "Discursive Texts, Reflexive Audiences: Global Trends in Television News Texts and Audience Reception." *Journal of Broadcasting & Electronic Media* 43 (1999): 386–398.

Kenna, Laura Cook. "James Bond's Gender: Masculine Identity, Feminine Technology." *Mid-Atlantic American Popular Culture Association Conference Film Studies Panel.* Pittsburg, PA, November 2002.

Khanfar, Wadah. "A Historic Moment in the Arab World." *TED Talk.* http://www.ted.com/talks/wadah_khanfar_a_historic_moment_in_the_arab_world.html.

Kingdon, John W. *Agendas, Alternatives, and Public Policies.* New York: HarperCollins, 1995.

Kraidy, Marwan M., and Sara Mourad. "Hypermedia Space and Global Communication Studies Lessons from the Middle East." *Global Media Journal* 9, no. 16 (2010):1–19.

Krige, John. *American Hegemony and the Postwar Reconstruction of Science in Europe.* Cambridge: MIT Press, 2006.

Kroker, Andrew, and Michael Weinstein. "The Theory of the Virtual Class." In *Electronic Media and Technoculture.* John Thorton, ed. New Brunswick: Rutgers University Press, 2000.

Kurzweil, Ray. *The Singularity Is Near: When Humans Transcend Biology.* New York: Viking, 2005.

Lanier, Jaron. *You Are Not a Gadget.* New York: Alfred Knopf, 2010.

Latour, Bruno. *We Have Never Been Modern.* Catherine Porter, trans. Cambridge: Harvard University Press, 1993.

The Lawnmower Man. Dir. Brett Leonard. 1992, Allied Vision.

Lessig, Lawrence. *Code and Other Laws of Cyberspace.* New York: Basic Books, 1999.

Levy, David. *Europe's Digital Revolution: Broadcasting Regulation, the E.U., and the Nation-states.* New York: Routledge, 1999.

Levy, Steven. *Hackers: Heroes of the Computer Revolution.* New York: Penguin, 2001.

License to Kill. Dir. John Glen. 1995; Los Angeles: Danjaq.

Light, Jennifer S. "When Computers Were Women." *Technology and Culture* 40 (1999): 455–483.

Lilley, Sasha. "On Neoliberalism: An Interview with David Harvey." *Monthly Review,* June 6, 2006. http://mrzine.monthlyreview.org/2006/lilley190606.html.

Lovink, Geert. *Zero Comments: Blogging and Critical Internet Culture.* New York: Routledge, 2009.

Lowe, Lisa, and D. Lloyd. *The Politics of Culture in the Shadow of Capital.* Durham: Duke University Press, 1997.

Luckhurst, Roger. *Science Fiction.* Cambridge: Polity, 2005.

Maier, Charles. "The Politics of Productivity: Foundations of American International Economic Policy after World War II." In *In Search of Stability Explorations in Historical Political Economy.* Charles Maier, ed. Cambridge: Cambridge University Press, 1987.

Maital, Shlomo. "The Global Telecommunications Picture: Is America Being Outstripped? By France?" *The Brookings Review* 10 (Summer 1992): 40–44.

Malamud, Carl. *A World's Fair for the Global Village.* Cambridge: MIT Press, 1997.

Manes, Stephen, and Paul Andrews. *Gates: How Microsoft's Mogul Reinvented the Industry—and Made Himself the Richest Man in America.* New York: Doubleday, 1993.

Manisha, Desai. *Gender and the Politics of Possibilities: Rethinking Globalization.* New York: Rowman & Littlefield, 2009.

Marvin, Carolyn. *Old Technologies: Thinking About Electronic Communication in the Late Nineteenth Century.* New York: Oxford University Press, 1988.

Marx, Leo. *Machine in the Garden: Technology and the Pastoral Ideal.* New York: Oxford University Press, 1999.

The Matrix. Dirs. Andy Wachowski and Larry Wachowski. 1999, Groucho II Film Partnership.

The Matrix Reloaded. Dirs. Andy Wachowski and Larry Wachowski. 2003, Warner Brothers.

The Matrix Revolutions. Dirs. Andy Wachowski and Larry Wachowski. 2003, Warner Brothers.

McAlister, Melani. *Epic Encounters: Culture, Media, and U.S. Interests in the Middle East since 1945.* Berkeley: University of California Press, 2001.

———. "Facebook Revolution?" Talk at University of Pennsylvania, February 28, 2011.

McCarthy, Anna. *Ambient Television: Visual Culture and Public Space.* Durham: Duke University Press, 2001.

McChesney, Robert. *Corporate Media and the Threat to Democracy.* New York: Seven Stories Press, 1997.

McLuhan, Marshall. *Understanding Media: The Extensions of Man.* New York: McGraw-Hill, 1964.

———. and Bruce Powers. *The Global Village: Transformations in World Life and Media in the 21st Century.* New York: Oxford University Press, 1989.

McNair, Brian. *Mediated Sex: Pornography and Postmodern Culture.* New York: Arnold, 1996.

Medovoi, Leerom. *Rebels: Youth and the Cold War Origins of Identity.* Durham: Duke University Press, 2005.

Menon, Anand, and Martin Schain. *Comparative Federalism: The European Union and the United States in Comparative Perspective.* Oxford: Oxford University Press, 2006.

Metropolis. Dir. Fritz Lang. 1927; Germany: Universum Film.

Micklethwait, John, and Adrian Wooldridge. *A Future Perfect: The Challenge and Hidden Promise of Globalization.* New York: Times Books, 2000.

Miller, Daniel, and Don Slater. *The Internet: An Ethnographic Approach.* Oxford, UK: Berg, 2001.

Miller, Steven E. *Civilizing Cyberspace: Policy, Power, and the Information Superhighway.* New York: Addison-Wesley, 1996.

Minority Report. Dir. Steven Spiegberg. 2002, Cruise/Wagner Productions.

Miyoshi, Masao. "A Borderless World? From Colonialism to Trans-Nationalism and the Decline of the Nation-State." In *Global/Local: Cultural Production and the Transnational Imaginary.* Rob Wilson and Wimal Dissanayake, eds. Durham: Duke University Press, 1996.

Modern Times. Dir. Charlie Chaplin. 1936; Los Angeles: Charles Chaplin Productions.

Morozov, Evgeny. "Freedom.gov: Why Washington's Support for Online Democracy Is the Worst Thing Ever to Happen to the Internet." *Foreign*

Policy, January 2011. http://www.foreignpolicy.com/articles/2011/01/02/
freedomgov.

———. *The Net Delusion: The Dark Side of Internet Freedom*. New York:
Public Affairs, 2011.

Moschovitis, Christos, J. P. Hilary Poole, Tami Schuyler, and Theresa M.
Senft. *History of the Internet: A Chronology, 1843 to the Present*. Oxford:
ABC-CLIO, 1999.

Mumford, Lewis. *The Pentagon of Power: The Myth of the Machine*. New
York: Harcourt Brace Jovanovich, 1970.

Murray, Andrew. *The Regulation of Cyberspace: Control in the Online Environment*. New York: Routledge, 2007.

Negroponte, Nicholas. *Being Digital*. New York: Knopf, 1995.

The Net. Dir. Irwin Winkler. 1995, Columbia Pictures Corporation.

Neuchterlein, Jonathan E., and Philip J. Weiser. *Digital Crossroads: American
Telecommunications Policy in the Internet Age*. Cambridge: MIT Press, 2005.

Noam, Eli. *Telecommunications in Europe*. New York: Oxford University
Press, 1992.

Norris, Pippa. *Digital Divide: Civic Engagement, Information Poverty, and
the Internet Worldwide*. Cambridge: Cambridge University Press, 2001.

"Organisation and Management of the Internet." *Activities of the European
Union: Summaries of Legislation*. http://europa.eu.int/scadplus/leg/en/
lvb/l24232.htm.

Page, Benjamin, and Robert Shapiro. *The Rational Public: Fifty Years of
Trends in Americans' Policy Preferences*. Chicago: University of Chicago
Press, 1992.

Pan, Zhongdang, and Gerald Kosicki. "Framing Analysis: An Approach to
News Discourse." *Political Communication* 10, no. 1 (1993): 59–79.

Papson, Stephen. "The IBM Tramp." *Jump Cut* 35 (1990): 66–72. http://www.
ejumpcut.org/archive/onlinessays/JC35folder/IBMtramp.html.

Park, David. "Critical Forum." *Critical Studies in Media Communication* 24,
no. 5 (2007): 466–48.

Patterson, Richard. "Introduction: Collective Identity, Television and
Europe." In *National Identity and Europe: The Television Revolution*. Phil-
lip Drummond, Richard Paterson, and Janet Willis, eds. London: BFI
Publishing, 1993.

Penley, Constance, and Andrew Ross, eds. *Technoculture*. Minneapolis: University of Minnesota Press, 1991.

Pew Research Center. *A Portrait of Generation Next*. http://pewresearch.org/
millennials/.

Poiger, Uta. *Jazz, Rock, and Rebels: Cold War Politics and American Culture in a Divided Germany.* Berkeley: University of California Press, 2000.

Poster, Mark. *Information Please: Culture and Politics in the Age of Digital Machines.* Durham: Duke University Press, 2006.

Powell, Michael, Michael Armstrong, and Marsha J. MacBride. *Communications Y2K Sector Report.* Washington, D.C.: Federal Communications Commission, March 30, 1999. http://www.fcc.gov/Bureaus/Miscellaneous/News_Releases/1999/nrmc9014.html.

Prestowitz, Clyde. *Trading Places: How We Are Giving Our Future to Japan and How to Reclaim It.* New York: Basic Books, 1993.

Putnam, Robert. *Bowling Alone.* New York: Simon & Schuster, 2000.

Rabinovitz, Lauren, and Abraham Geil. *Memory Bytes: History Technology and Digital Culture.* Durham: Duke University Press, 2004.

Reich, Robert. *The Work of Nations.* New York: Random House, 1992.

Reidenberg, Joel. "Governing Networks and Rule-Making in Cyberspace." In *Borders in Cyberspace: Information Policy and the Global Information Infrastructure.* Brian Kahin and Charles Nesson, eds. Cambridge: MIT Press, 1997.

Rheingold, Howard. *The Virtual Community: Homesteading on the Electronic Frontier.* New York: Perennial, 1994.

Richardson, Jeremy. *European Union: Power and Policy-Making.* New York: Routledge, 2001.

Robbins, B. *Feeling Global: Internationalism in Distress.* New York: New York University Press, 1999.

Roberts, Graham, and Heather Wallis. *Introducing Film.* London: Oxford University Press, 2001.

Roberts, Lawrence G. "The Evolution of Packet Switching." Paper for the Institute of Electrical and Electronics Engineers, November 1978. http://www.packet.cc/files/ev-packet-sw.html#20.

Robocop. Dir. Paul Verhoeven. 1987; Los Angeles: Orion Pictures Corporation.

Rodman, Gilbert. "The Net Effect." In *Virtual Publics: Policy and Community in an Electronic Age.* Beth Kolko, ed. New York: Columbia University Press, 2003.

Rogowski, Ralf, and Charles Turner. *The Shape of the New Europe.* Cambridge: Cambridge University Press, 2006.

Rosen, Jay. "The People Formerly Known as the Audience." *PressThink*, June 27, 2006. http://archive.pressthink.org/2006/06/27/ppl_frmr.html.

Ross, Andrew. "Hacking Away at the Counterculture." In *Electronic Media and Technoculture*. John Thorton, ed. New Brunswick: Rutgers University Press, 2000.

Ryan, Marie-Laure. "Introduction: From Possible Worlds to Virtual Reality." *Style* 29 (Summer 1995): 173–183.

S.4.1 103rd Cong. March 16, 1994. *National Competitiveness Act of 1993*.

Sassen, Saskia. *Losing Control? Sovereignty in an Age of Globalization*. New York: Columbia University Press, 1996.

Schaefer, Eric. "Gauging a Revolution: 16 mm Film and the Rise of the Pornographic Feature." In *Porn Studies*. Linda Williams, ed. Durham: Duke University Press, 2004.

Schaller, Michael. *Right Turn: American Life in the Reagan-Bush Era, 1980–1992*. New York: Oxford University Press, 2007.

Schlesinger, Philip. "Tension in the Construction of European Media Policies." In *Media and Globalization: Why the State Matters*. Nancy Morris and Silvio Waisbord, eds. New York: Rowman & Littlefield, 2001.

Schwartz, Paul M. "European Data Protection Law and the Restrictions on International Data Flows," *Iowa Law Review* 80 (1995): 471–472.

Sconce, Jeffrey. "Tulip Theory." In *New Media: Theories and Practices of Digitextuality*. Ana Everett and John Caldwell, eds. New York: Routledge, 2003.

Segal, Howard. *Technological Utopianism in American Culture*. Chicago: University of Chicago Press, 1985.

Senate Subcommittee on Communications, Committee on Commerce, Science, and Transportation, *Hearings on S. 261, International Telecommunications*, February 28, 1987.

Senate Subcommittee on Governmental Affairs, *Hearings on S. 401, Government's Role in Economic Competitiveness*, June 8–9, 1987.

Senate Subcommittee on International Trade, Committee on Finance, *Hearings on S. 361, Export of U.S. Telecommunications Products*, May 3, 1985.

Senate Subcommittee on International Trade, Committee on Finance, *Hearing on S. 361, Telecommunications Trade*, June 26, 1984.

Shirky, Clay. *Cognitive Surplus: Creativity and Generosity in a Connected Age*. New York: Penguin, 2010.

Sifry, Micah L. *WikiLeaks and the Age of Transparency*. Berkeley: Counterpoint, 2011.

Sigel, Lisa. "Filth in the Wrong People's Hands: Postcards and the Expansion of Pornography in Britain and the Atlantic World, 1880–1914." *Journal of Social History* 33 (Winter 2000): 859–85.

Silver, David, and Adrienne Massanari, eds. *Critical Cyberculture Studies.* New York: New York University Press, 2006.

Simon, Leslie. *NetPolicy.Com: Public Agenda for a Digital World.* Washington, DC: Woodrow Wilson Center Press, 2000.

Slotkin, Richard. *The Fatal Environment: The Myth of the Frontier in the Age of Industrialization, 1800–1890.* New York: Atheneum, 1985.

Smith, Aaron. "Government Online." Pew Internet and American Life Center, April 27, 2010. http://www.pewinternet.org/Reports/2010/Government-Online/Summary-of-Findings/Findings.aspx.

Sobchack, Vivian. "Reading *Mondo 2000*: New Age Mutant Ninja Hackers." In *Flame Wars: The Discourse of Cyberculture.* Mark Dery, ed. Durham: Duke University Press, 1994.

Spigel, Lynn. *Make Room for TV: Television and the Family Ideal in Postwar America.* Chicago: University of Chicago Press, 1992.

Stald, Gitte, and Thomas Tufte, eds. *Global Encounters: Media and Cultural Transformation.* United Kingdom: University of Luton Press, 2002.

Standage, Tom. *The Victorian Internet.* New York: Walker, 1998.

Stoll, Cliff. *Cuckoo Egg.* New York: Doubleday, 1989.

Stone, Allucquère Rosanne. *The War of Desire and Technology at the Close of the Mechanical Age.* Cambridge: MIT Press, 1995.

Stone, Deborah. *Policy Paradox and Political Reason.* New York: HarperCollins, 1988.

Strate, Lance. "The Varieties of Cyberspace: Problems in Definition and Delimitation." *Western Journal of Communication* 63 (Summer 1999): 382–412.

Streeter, Thomas. *The Net Effect: Romanticism, Capitalism, and the Internet.* New York: New York University Press, 2011.

Stross, Randall. *The Microsoft Way: The Real Story of How the Company Outsmarts Its Competition.* Reading, Mass: Addison-Wesley, 1996.

Sunstein, Cass. *Republic.com.* Princeton: Princeton University Press, 2001.

Sutter, Gavin. "Nothing New Under the Sun: Old Fears and New Media." *International Journal of Law and Information Technology* 8 (2002): 338–379.

Swisher, Kara. *Aol.com: How Steve Case Beat Bill Gates, Nailed the Netheads, and Made Millions in the War for the Web.* New York: Random House, 1990.

Tan, Shuschen. "An Interview with Marleen Stikker." Patrice Riemens, trans. *CTheory.net,* February 8, 1995. http://www.ctheory.net/articles. aspx?id=65.

Terminator. Dir. James Cameron. 1984; Los Angeles: Hemdale Films.

Thussu, D. K. *Electronic Empires: Global Media and Local Resistance.* London: Arnold, 1998.

Tomorrow Never Dies. Dir. Roger Spottiswoode. 1997; Los Angeles: Danjag.

Tron. Dir. Steven Lisberger. 1982, Lisberger/Kushner.

Turkle, Sherry. *Life on the Screen: Identity in the Age of the Internet.* New York: Simon & Schuster, 1995.

Turner, Fred. *From Counterculture to Cyberculture: Stewart Brand, the Whole Earth Network, and the Rise of Digital Utopianism.* Chicago: University of Chicago Press, 2006.

U.S. Census Bureau. "Computer Use in the United States: October 1984 (P23-155)," Table 1, 1988. http://www.census.gov/population/socdemo/ computer/p23-155/tab01.pdf.

U.S. Census Bureau, "Internet Activities of Adults by Type of Home Internet Connection: 2010." http://www.census.gov/compendia/statab/cats/information_communications/internet_publishing_and_broadcasting_and_ internet_usage.html.

U.S. Congress. House Committee on Energy and Commerce, *Cyber Security: Private-Sector Efforts Addressing Cyber Threats,* February 2002, H. 361.

U.S. Congress. House Committee on Energy and Commerce, *Establishing Kid-friendly Top-level Domain: Dot Kids Name Act of 2001,* February 2002, H. 361.

U.S. Congress. House Committee on Government Reform, *Turning the Tortoise into the Hare: How the Federal Government Can Transition from Old Economy Speed to Become a Model for Electronic Government,* May 2003, H. 401.

U.S. Congress. House Committee on the Judiciary, *Immigration and Naturalization Service's Implementation of the Foreign Student Tracking Program,* January 2003, H. 521.

U.S. Congress. House Committee on the Judiciary, *WHOIS Database: Privacy and Intellectual Property Issues,* September 2001, H. 521.

U.S. Congress. House Congressional-Executive Commission on China, *China's Cyber-Wall: Can Technology Break Through,* February 2003, H. 891.

U.S. Congress. House Congressional-Executive Commission on China, *Wired China: Who's Hand Is on the Switch,* August 2002, H. 891.

U.S. Congress. House Subcommittee on Transportation, Aviation, and Materials, Committee on Science and Technology, *Computer and Communication Security and Privacy Report*, April 1980, H. 702.

U.S. Congress. House. *Technology Education Act of 1986*. August 11, 1986. H 343.

U.S. Congress. House. *Telecommunications Trade Act of 1986*. February 6, 1986. H 363.

U.S. Congress. Senate Committee on Commerce, Science, and Transportation, *Holes in the Net: Security Risks and the E-Consumer*, July 2004, S. 107–674.

U.S. Congress. Senate Committee on Foreign Relations, *America's Global Dialog: Sharing American Values and the Way Ahead for Public Diplomacy*, January 2003, S. 381.

U.S. Congress. Senate. *Education for a Competitive America Act*. June 16, 1987. S 543.

U.S. Congress. Senate. *Promoting Expansion of International Trade in Telecommunications Equipment and Services*. November 26, 1985. S 363.

U.S. Congress. Senate. *Technology Competitiveness Act of 1987*. June 22, 1987. S 263.

U.S. Public Law 98-473. 98th Cong., October 12, 1984. *Counterfeit Access Device and Computer Fraud and Abuse Act of 1984*.

U.S. Public Law 100-418. August 23, 1988. *Omnibus Trade and Competitiveness Act of 1988*.

U.S. Public Law 102-194. 102nd Cong. December 9, 1991. *High Performance Computing and Communication Act of 1991*.

U.S. Public Law 106-578. 106th Cong., December 28, 2000. *Internet False Identification Prevention Act of 2000*.

U.S. Public Law 107-317. 107th Cong., December 4, 2002. *Dot Kids Implementation and Efficiency Act of 2002*.

U.S. Public Law 107-347. 107th Cong., December 17, 2002. *E-Government Act of 2002*.

U.S. Public Law 109-282. 109th Cong., September 26, 2006. *Federal Funding Accountability and Transparency Act of 2006*.

Vaidhyanathan, Siva. *Anarchist in the Library: How the Clash between Freedom and Control Is Hacking the Real World and Crashing the System*. New York: Basic Books, 2004.

———. *The Googlization of Everything: And Why We Should Worry*. Berkeley: University of California Press, 2011.

Van Os, Renée, Fred Wester, and Nicholas Jankowski. "Presentations of Europe on Political Party Websites during 2004 Election." *The Public* 14, no 2 (2007): 63–82.

Vegh, Sandor. "Hacking for Democracy: A Study of the Internet as a Political Force and Its Representations in Mainstream Media." Dissertation, University of Maryland, College Park, March 2003.

Volti, Rudi. *Society and Technological Change.* New York: St. Martin's Press, 1992.

Wagnleitner, Reinhold. *Coca-Colonization and the Cold War: The Cultural Mission of the United States in Austria after the Second World War.* Chapel Hill: University of North Carolina Press, 1994.

Waldman, Diane. "Critical Theory and Film: Adorno and 'The Culture Industry' Revisited." *New German Critique* 12 (1977): 39-60.

Wallace, James, and Jim Erickson. *Hard Drive: Bill Gates and the Making of the Microsoft Empire.* New York: Wiley, 1992.

Wang, G., J. Servaes, and A. Goonasekera. *The New Communications Landscape: Demystefying Media Globalization.* New York: Routledge, 2000.

WarGames. Dir. John Badham. 1983; Los Angeles: Metro-Goldwyn-Mayer.

WarGames Script. Dir. John Badham. 1983; Los Angeles: Metro-Goldwyn-Mayer.

Watson, Christopher, and Tom Wheatdon. *Telecommunications: The E.U. Law.* Isle of Wight: Simmons & Simmons, 1999.

Weber, Max. *The Protestant Ethic and the Spirit of Capitalism.* New York: Routledge Classics, 1930.

Weinberger, David. "Transparency Is the New Objectivity." *Joho,* July 19, 2009. http://www.hyperorg.com/blogger/2009/07/19/transparency-is-the-new-objectivity/.

Williams, Raymond. *Television, Technology and Cultural Form.* New York: Schocken, 1975.

Wilson, R., and W. Dissanayake. *Global/Local: Cultural Production and the Transnational Imaginary.* Durham: Duke University Press, 1996.

Wise, J. MacGregor. "Community, Affect, and the Virtual: The Politics of Cyberspace." In *Virtual Publics: Policy and Community in an Electronic Age.* Beth Kolko, ed. New York: Columbia University Press, 2003.

Wood, Brennon. "Stuart Hall's Cultural Studies and the Problem of Hegemony." *British Journal of Sociology* 49, no. 3 (1998): 399–414.

Wright, Robert. *Nonzero: The Logic of Human Destiny.* New York: Vintage, 2001.

Wu, Tim. *The Master Switch: The Rise and Fall of Information Empires.* New York: Alfred A. Knopf, 2010.

You've Got Mail. Dir. Nora Ephron. 1998; Los Angeles: Warner Brothers Pictures.

Zickgraf, Ralph. *William Gates: From Whiz Kid to Software King (Wizards of Business).* New York: Reed Business Information, 1992.

Policy: Computer Fraud and Abuse Act
of 1984, 16, 22, 47, 76, 182n7; as cul-
ture, 10–19, 172–73; decency laws,
118–19; Education and Training for a
Competitive America Act, 79; Federal
Computer Systems Protection Act of
1983, 79; "roads not taken," 18; Federal
Criminal Code Amendment, 181n4;
Federal Funding Accountability
and Transparency Act of 2006, 151;
High Performance Computing and
Communication Act of 1991, 102,
208n103; images, 23, 28, 56, 128, 152;
National Technology Transfer and
Advancement Act of 1995, 107; North
American Free Trade Agreement
(NAFTA), 111; Omnibus Trade and
Competitiveness Act of 1988, 79, 198n115;
paternalism and protectionism, 18, 117,
122, 126; privatization, 115; regulatory sys-
tems, 115–17; Strategic Defense Initiative
(Star Wars), 24, 27; Telecommunications
Act of 1996, 86, 107; Television Without
Frontiers, 128; window, 49. See also
European Union
Politics: body politic, 148, 153; Democrat/
Republican/liberal/conservative, 56,
106–8, 144–50; government participatory
class, 150; participation, 19, 41, 46, 65, 135,
141–63, 167; politico-communication,
127. See also Campaign; Citizen; Nation;
Subjectivity; presidents by name
Polly, Jean Armour, 99
Pornography, 45, 74, 92, 117–18, 125, 214n22
Postel, Jon, 104
Postmodernism/postmodernity, 66–67, 89,
105
Powell, Michael, 224n118
Power: corporate, 10, 17, 93–95, 112, 143–45,
156–63; discipline, 22, 35, 40, 46–47,
81–82; economic, 16, 76–79, 132–37; resistance, 9, 101, 126, 153, 162; state, 18, 85–94,
111–12, 117; structures of, 5–7, 37–42,
100, 180n57. See also Americanization;
Capital; Colonization; Discourse;
Imperialism

Privacy, 13, 48, 114, 119, 126, 132, 147, 168. See
also Policy; Security
Productivity, 16, 47, 53, 59–81, 130
Progress narrative, 68–82. See also
Internet
Protocol, 5, 13, 40, 67, 128
Public: good, 15, 26, 26, 122; health, 131,
145, 153; sphere, 13, 75, 100–105, 122–28,
145–69; utility 18–19, 114–15, 126, 131–36,
169. See also Internet
Putnam, Robert, 148

Rabinovitz, Lauren, 178n20
Reagan, Ronald, 17, 24–27, 56, 76–82
Rebel/rebellion, 16–24, 27–29, 38, 41–56,
143–44, 160, 166. See also Adolescent;
Hacker; Teenager; Youth
Reidenberg, Joel, 119
Religion, 32, 46
Revolution: technology as, 10, 13–14, 19, 26,
64, 103. See also Facebook; Rebel/rebel-
lion; Twitter
Rheingold, Howard, 100
Roberts, Lawrence, 220n88
Robot, 57, 59, 66, 142
Rogowski, Ralf, 219n77
Rosen, Jay, 150
Ross, Andrew, 6, 74
Russia 24, 93–94. See also Soviet Union

Saturday Night Live, 168
Science fiction, 3, 57–58, 66, 96–97. See also
Film
Sconce, Jeffrey, 7, 9, 13, 142, 165, 179nn37, 49,
227n14
Scott, Ridley, 66
Security, 16, 21–29, 38–63, 74–81, 90, 102,
131–32, 157, 168; encryption, 80–81; na-
tional 25–28, 38–39, 47–60, 80. See also
Policy; Privacy
Shelley, Mary, 57
Shirky, Clay, 124, 157
Sifry, Micah, 150, 160
Simon, Leslie, 92, 213n13
Singularity, 58
Slotkin, Richard, 102

Watergate, 63, 80
Watson, Christopher, 219n74, 221n93
Weber, Max, 179n38
Weinberger, David, 152
Weinstein, Michael, 209n105
Wheatdon, Tom, 219n74, 221n93
WikiLeaks, 165–68
Woods, Rosemary, 63–64, 193n41
World Wide Web (WWW), 3, 14, 17, 84–95,
    109, 150, 155. *See also* Internet
Wozniak, Steve, 37

Wu, Tim, 92, 109, 154, 159, 166, 187n77,
    208n89

Y2K, 86, 135, 201n21, 224n118
Yahoo, 109, 154, 225n124
Youth, 22–53, 136, 140, 147, 153, 160–61. *See
    also* Adolescent; Teenager
YouTube, 149, 158. *See also* Social network

Zuckerberg, Mark, 167–68. *See also*
    Facebook

ABOUT THE AUTHOR

Stephanie Ricker Schulte is Assistant Professor of Communication at the University of Arkansas.